The Philosophy of
Friedrich Nietzsche

The Philosophy of
Friedrich Nietzsche

by Henry Louis Mencken

Table of Contents

Introduction

The philosophy of Friedrich Nietzsche and the music (and quasi-music) of Richard Strauss: herein we have our modern substitutes for Shakespeare and the musical glasses. There is no escaping Nietzsche. You may hold him a hissing and a mocking and lift your virtuous skirts as you pass him by, but his roar is in your ears and his blasphemies sink into your mind. He has colored the thought and literature, the speculation and theorizing, the politics and superstition of the time. He reigns as king in the German universities — where, since Luther's day, all the world's most painful thinking has been done — and his echoes tinkle, harshly or faintly, from Chicago to Mesopotamia. His ideas appear in the writings of men as unlike as Roosevelt and Bernard Shaw; even the newspapers are aware of him. He is praised and berated, accepted and denounced, canonized and damned. Pythagoras had no more devout disciples and Spinoza had no more murderous and violent foes. Wherefore it may be a toil of some profit to examine his ideas a bit closely; to differentiate between what he said in his books and what his apostles and interpreters and enemies say or think he said; and in the end, perhaps, to find out what he meant.

Despite the notion of those who know him but by name or ill-fame, there is nothing cryptic or mysterious about Nietzsche. His ideas are ever clear. Curiously enough, the popular comprehension of his philosophy suffers by this very fact, for the world has come to regard the metaphysic as something properly and necessarily occult and to expect its expounders, if they would seem truly wise, to show the abysmal turgidity of a Kant and the wild, cabalistic imbecility of Revelations. When there arises a prophet like Nietzsche, who thinks his thoughts accurately and puts them into the vulgar tongue, he is commonly suspected to be some sort of fantastic and preposterous joker. Instead of accepting his prophecy in its surface sense, his audience sees, in its very obviousness, a new and extraordinarily confusing form of riddle. Such is the curse that rabbinism, in and out of the church, has laid upon the propagation of ideas.

Nietzsche's literalness is the hallmark of his entire philosophy. He is the high priest of the actual, and the divine mysteries seem to him to be but so many grotesque lunacies. Stripping an idea of its holiness and romance, its antiquity and authority, he burrows down into the heart of it and tries to estimate it in terms of its actual probability and reasonableness. That a thing is sacred or venerable or ancient or beautiful does not interest him. The question is asked invariably, Is it true? If he concludes that it is not, he says so, and if it happens to be something that is regarded with unusual reverence by the majority of men — which means something whose inviolability is accepted without inquiry or the shadow of doubt — he says so with unusual heat and clamor. He is, indeed, the king of all axiom smashers and the arch dissenter of the age. To him such words as good and godly have no meaning whatever. He regards them as mere scarecrows and bugaboos, invented and employed by sophists and doctrinaires to ward off that free inquiry which would put their fallacies to rout.

Reduced to elementals, Nietzsche's philosophy consists of the following propositions:

1. That the ever-dominant and only inherent impulse in all living beings, including man, is the will to remain alive — the will, that is, to attain power over those forces which make life difficult or impossible.

2. That all schemes of morality are nothing more than efforts to put into permanent codes the expedients found useful by some given race in the course of its successful endeavors to remain alive.

3. That, despite the universal tendency to give these codes authority by crediting them to some god, they are essentially man-made and mutable, and so change, or should change, as the conditions of human existence in the world are modified.

4. That the human race should endeavor to make its mastery over its environment more and more certain, and that it is its destiny, therefore, to widen more and more the gap which now separates it from the lower races of animals.

5. That any code of morality which retains its permanence and authority after the conditions of existence which gave rise to it have changed, works against this upward progress of mankind toward greater and greater efficiency.

6. That all gods and religions, because they have for their main object the protection of moral codes against change, are inimitable to the life and well-being of healthy and efficient men.

7. That all the ideas which grow out of such gods and religions — such, for example, as the Christian ideas of humility, of self-sacrifice and of brotherhood — are enemies of life, too.

8. That human beings of the ruling, efficient class should reject all gods and religions, and with them the morality at the bottom of them and the ideas which grow out of them, and restore to its ancient kingship that primal instinct which enables every efficient individual to differentiate between the things which are beneficial to him and the things which are harmful.

Here we have the bare framework or skeleton of Nietzsche's system. How it leads to a rejection of Christianity and democracy; how it points out a possible evolution of the human race through the immoralist to the superman; how it combats the majority of the ideas held holy and impeccable by mankind today — all of this is set forth in the pages that follow. The aim of this book is to translate Nietzsche into terms familiar to everyone — to show the exact bearing of his philosophy upon matters which every man must consider every day. Nietzsche dealt chiefly with generalizations and abstractions, and when he descended to imminent concerns he naturally selected those things which most interested his countrymen. In this book his conclusions are applied to the things which most interest the two great races whose tongue is English. To this extent paraphrase has been admitted, but in all statements of fundamental doctrines there has been a faithful and literal rendering of the original text — a rendering interrupted, of course, whenever it has seemed necessary to explain or elucidate, by foot-note, parable or digression.

In the biographical portion of this book an effort has been made to show the growth of Nietzsche's system, from its beginning in mute consciousness to its maturity in clear and unmistakable propositions. In the last part an attempt has been made to trace out the origin of this system in the ideas of other men; to show how it agrees or disagrees with human experience; and finally, to estimate its influence upon the great and little men of the world today and its probable influence tomorrow. It is high time for the race of Darwin and Huxley to know Nietzsche better. When his ideas are calmly weighed, they may be rejected, but it will be infinitely better to weigh and reject them thus than to condemn them out of hand and without knowing what they are.

Nietzsche himself believed that he was but a link in an endless chain and that, in the course of time, his doctrines would be overthrown by the philosophy of better men. Be this as it may, the fact is apparent that he fought a good fight and made his fellow men his debtors. Error was his enemy and he was ever merciless in combating it, even when the combat meant a war upon himself. He attacked men, gods and devils, but his purpose was ever the lofty one of discovering the truth. It is the fashion among the adherents of the old order to berate him for his ferocity, and to urge the sorrows of his darkened life against him, but some day, perhaps, the world will learn to give men of his kind the honor that is their due. It is a fine thing to face machine guns for immortality and a medal, but isn't it fine, too, to face calumny, injustice and loneliness for the truth which makes men free?

Boyhood and Youth

Friedrich Nietzsche was a preacher's son, brought up in the fear of the Lord. It is the ideal training for sham-smashers and freethinkers. Let a boy of alert, restless intelligence come to early manhood in an atmosphere of strong faith, wherein doubts are blasphemies and inquiry is a crime, and rebellion is certain to appear with his beard. So long as his mind feels itself puny beside the overwhelming pomp and circumstance of parental authority, he will remain docile and even pious. But so soon as he begins to see authority as something ever finite, variable and all-too-human — when he begins to realize that his father and his mother, in the last analysis, are mere human beings, and fallible like himself — then he will fly precipitately toward the intellectual wailing places, to think his own thoughts in his own way and to worship his own gods beneath the open sky.

As a child Nietzsche was holy; as a man he was the symbol and embodiment of all unholiness. At nine he was already versed in the lore of the reverend doctors, and the pulpit, to his happy mother — a preacher's daughter as well as a preacher's wife — seemed his logical and lofty goal; at thirty he was chief among those who held that all pulpits should be torn down and fashioned into bludgeons, to beat out the silly brains of theologians.

The awakening came to him when he made his first venture away from the maternal apron-string and fireside: when, as a boy of ten, he learned that there were many, many men in the world and that these men were of many minds. With the clash of authority came the end of authority. If A was right, B was wrong — and B had a disquieting habit of standing for one's mother, one's grandmother or the holy prophets. Here was the beginning of intelligence in the boy — the beginning of that weighing and choosing faculty which seems to give man at once his sense of mastery and his feeling of helplessness. The old notion that doubt was a crime crept away. There remained in its place the new notion that the only real crime in the world — the only unmanly, unspeakable and unforgivable offense against the race — was unreasoning belief. Thus the orthodoxy of the Nietzsche home turned upon and devoured itself.

The philosopher of the superman was born on October 15th, 1844, at Röcken, a small town in the Prussian province of Saxony. His father, Karl Ludwig Nietzsche, was a country pastor of the Lutheran Church and a man of eminence in the countryside. But he was more than a mere rural worthy, with an outlook limited by the fringe of trees on the horizon, for in his time he had seen something of the great world and had even played his humble part in it. Years before his son Friedrich was born he had been tutor to the children of the Duke of Altenburg. The duke was fond of him and took him, now and then, on memorable and eventful journeys to Berlin, where that turbulent monarch, King Friedrich Wilhelm IV, kept a tinsel court and made fast progress from imbecility to acute dementia. The king met the young tutor and found him a clever and agreeable person, with excellent opinions regarding all those things whereon monarchs are wont to differ with mobs. When the children of the duke became sufficiently saturated with learning, the work of Pastor Nietzsche at Altenburg was done and he journeyed to Berlin to face weary days in the anterooms of ecclesiastical magnates and jobbers of places. The king, hearing by chance of his presence and remembering him pleasantly, ordered that he be given without delay a vicarage worthy of his talents. So be was sent to Röcken, and there, when a son was born to him, he called the boy Friedrich Wilhelm, as a graceful compliment to his royal patron and admirer.

There were two other children in the house. One was a boy, Josef, who was named after the Duke of Altenburg, and died in infancy in 1850. The other was a girl, Therese Elisabeth Alexandra, who became in after years her brother's housekeeper, guardian angel and biographer. Her three names were those of the three noble children her father had grounded in the humanities. Elisabeth — who married toward middle age and is best known as Frau Förster-Nietzsche — tells us practically all that we know about the Nietzsche family and the private life of its distinguished son. The clan came out of Poland, like so many other families of Eastern Germany, at the time of the sad, vain wars. Legend maintains that it was noble in its day and Nietzsche himself liked to think so. The name, says Elisabeth, was originally Nietzschy. "Germany is a great nation," Nietzsche would say, "only because its people have so much Polish blood in their veins.... I am proud of my Polish descent. I remember that in former times a Polish noble, by his simple veto, could overturn the resolution of a popular assembly. There were giants in Poland in the time of my forefathers." He wrote a tract with the French title *L'Origine de la famille de Nietzsche* and presented the manuscript to his sister, as a document to be treasured and held sacred. She tells us that he was fond of maintaining that the Nietzsches had suffered greatly and fallen from vast grandeur for their opinions, religious and political. He had no proof of this, but it pleased him to think so.

Pastor Nietzsche was thrown from his horse in 1848 and died, after a lingering illness, on July 28th, 1849, when Friedrich was barely five years old. Frau Nietzsche then moved her little family to Naumburg-on-the-Saale — "a Christian, conservative, loyal city." The household consisted of the mother, the two children, their paternal grandmother and two maiden aunts — the sisters of the dead pastor. The grandmother was something of a bluestocking and had been, in her day, a member of that queer circle of intellectuals and amateurs which raged and roared around Goethe at Weimar. But that was in the long ago, before she dreamed of becoming the wife of one preacher and the mother of another. In the year 1850 she was well of all such youthful fancies and there was no doubt of the divine revelations beneath her pious roof. Prayers began the day and ended the day. It was a house of holy women, with something of a convent's placidity and quiet exaltation. Little Friedrich was the idol in the shrine. It was the hope of all that he would grow up into a man illimitably noble and impossibly good.

Pampered thus, the boy shrank from the touch of the world's rough hand. His sister tells us that he disliked the bad little boys of the neighborhood, who robbed bird's nests, raided orchards and played at soldiers. There appeared in him a quaint fastidiousness which went counter to the dearest ideals of the healthy young male. His school fellows, in derision, called him "the little pastor" and took delight in waylaying him and venting upon him their grotesque and barbarous humor. He liked flowers and books and music and when he went abroad it was for solitary walks. He could recite and sing and he knew the Bible so well that he was able to dispute about its mysteries. "As I think of him," said an old school-mate years afterward, "I am forced irresistibly into a thought of the 12-year-old Jesus in the Temple." "The serious introspective child, with his dignified politeness," says his sister, "seemed so strange to other boys that friendly advances from either side were out of the question."

There is a picture of the boy in all the glory of his first long-tailed coat. His trousers stop above his shoetops, his hair is long and his legs seem mere airy filaments. As one gazes upon the likeness one can almost smell the soap that scoured that high, shiny brow and those thin, white cheeks. The race of such seraphic boys has died out in the world. Gone are their slick, plastered locks and their translucent ears! Gone are their ruffled cuffs and their spouting of the golden text!

Nietzsche wrote verses before he was ten: pious, plaintive verses that scanned well and showed rhymes and metaphors made respectable by ages of honorable employment. His maiden effort, so far as we know, was an elegy entitled "The Grave of My Father." Later on he became aware of material things and sang the praises of rose and sunset. He played the piano, too, and knew his Beethoven well, from the snares for the left hand in "*Für Elise*" to the raging tumults of the C minor symphony.

One Sunday — it was Ascension day — he went to the village church and heard the choir sing the Hallelujah Chorus from "*The Messiah*." Here was music that benumbed the senses and soothed the soul and, boy as he was, he felt its supreme beauty. That night he covered pages of ruled paper with impossible pot-hooks. He, too, would write music!

Later on the difficulties of thorough-bass, as it was taught in the abyssmal German text-books of the time, somewhat dampened his ardor, but more than once during his youth he thought seriously of becoming a musician. His first really ambitious composition was a piano piece called "*Mondschein auf der Pussta*" — "*Moonlight on the Pussta*." Whether the Pussta was a river, a mountain or a mere creature of the imagination does not appear. All the same we may conjure up a picture of little Friedrich playing this maiden opus of a quiet evening in Naumburg, while mother, grandmother, sister and aunts gathered round and marvelled at his genius. In later life he wrote songs and sonatas, and — if an enemy is to be believed — an opera in the grand manner. His sister, in her biography, prints some samples of his music. Candor compels the admission that it is even worse than it sounds.

Nietzsche, at this time, still seemed like piety on a monument, but as much as he revered his elders and as much as he relied upon their infallibility, there were yet problems which assailed him and gave him disquiet. When he did not walk and think alone, his sister was his companion, and to her he opened his heart, as one might to a sexless, impersonal confessor. In her presence, indeed, he really thought aloud, and this remained his habit until the end of his life. His mind, awakening, wandered beyond the little world hedged about by doting and complacent women. Until he entered the gymnasium — that great weighing place of German brains — he shrank from open revolt, and even from the thought of it, but he could not help dwelling upon the mysteries that rose before him. There were things upon which the scriptures, search them as he might, seemed to throw no light, and of which mothers and grandmothers and maiden aunts did not discourse. "One day," says Elisabeth, "when he was yet very young, he said to me: 'You mustn't expect me to believe those silly stories about storks bringing babies. Man is a mammal and a mammal must get his own children for himself.'" Every child, perhaps, ponders such problems, but in the vast majority knowledge must wait until it may enter fortuitously and from without. Nietzsche did not belong to the majority. To him ideas were ever things to be sought out eagerly, to be weighed calmly, to be tried in the fire. For weal or for woe, the cornerstones of his faith were brought forth, with sweat and pain, from the quarry of his own mind.

Nietzsche went to various village schools — public and private — until he was ten, dutifully trudging away each morning with knapsack and lunch-basket. He kissed his mother at the gate when he departed and she was waiting for him, with another kiss, when he returned. As happiness goes, his was probably a happy childhood. The fierce joy of boyish combat — of fighting, of robbing, of slaying — was never his, but to a child so athirst for knowledge, each fresh discovery — about the sayings of Luther, the lions of Africa, the properties of an inverted fraction — must have brought its thrill. But as he came to the last year of his first decade, unanswerable questions brought their discontent and disquiet — as they do to all of us. There is a feeling of oppression and poignant pain in facing problems that defy solution and facts that refuse to fit into ordered chains. It is only when mastery follows that the fine stimulation of conscious efficiency drowns out all moody vapors.

When Nietzsche went to the gymnasium his whole world was overturned. Here boys were no longer mute and hollow vessels, to be stuffed with predigested learning, but human beings whose approach to separate entity was recognized. It was possible to ask questions and to argue moot points, and teaching became less the administration of a necessary medicine and more the sharing of a delightful meal. Your German school-master is commonly a martinet, and his birch is never idle, but he has the saving grace of loving his trade and of readily recognizing true diligence in his pupils. History does not record the name of the pedagogue who taught Nietzsche at the Naumburg gymnasium, but he must have been one who ill deserved his oblivion. He fed the eager, inquiring mind of his little student and made a new boy of him. The old unhealthy, uncanny embodiment of a fond household's impossible dreams became more likeable and more human. His exclusiveness and fastidiousness were native and ineradicable, perhaps, for they remained with him, in some degree, his whole life long, but his thirst for knowledge and yearning for disputation soon led him to the discovery that there were other boys worth cultivating: other boys whose thoughts, like his own, rose above misdemeanor and horse-play. With two such he formed a quick friendship, and they were destined to influence him greatly to the end of his youth. They organized a club for mutual culture, gave it the sonorous name of *"Der litterarischen Vereinigung Germania"* ("The German Literary Association") and drew up an elaborate scheme of study. Once a week there was a meeting, at which each of the three submitted an essay or a musical composition to the critical scrutiny of the others. They waded out into the deep water. One week they discussed "The Infancy of Nations," and after that, "The Demonic Element in Music," "Napoleon III" and "Fatalism in History." Despite its praiseworthy earnestness, this program causes a smile — and so does the transformation of the retiring and well-scrubbed little Nietzsche we have been observing into the long, gaunt Nietzsche of 14, with a yearning for the companionship of his fellows, and a voice beginning to grow comically harsh and deep, and a mind awhirl with unutterable things.

Nietzsche was a brilliant and spectacular pupil and soon won a scholarship at Pforta, a famous and ancient preparatory academy not far away. Pforta, in those days, was of a dignity comparable to Eton's or Harrow's. It was a great school, but tradition overpowered it. Violent combats between amateur sages were not encouraged: it was a place for gentlemen to acquire Euclid and the languages in a decent, gentlemanly way, and not an arena for gawky country philosophers to prance about in. But Nietzsche, by this time, had already become a frank rebel and delighted in elaborating and controverting the doctrines of the learned doctors. He drew up a series of epigrams under the head of "Ideen" and thought so well of them that he sent them home, to astonish and alarm his mother. Some of them exhibited a quite remarkable faculty for pithy utterance — as, for example, "War begets poverty and poverty begets peace" — while others were merely opaque renderings of thoughts half formed. He began to believe in his own mental cunning, with a sincerity which never left him, and, as a triumphant proof of it, he drew up a series of syllogisms designed to make homesickness wither and die. Thus he wrestled with life's problems as his boy's eyes saw them.

All this was good training for the philosopher, but to the Pforta professors it gave disquiet. Nietzsche became a bit too sure of himself and a bit too arrogant for discipline. It seemed to him a waste of time to wrestle with the studies that every oafish baron's son and future guardsman sought to master. He neglected mathematics and gave himself up to the hair-splitting of the Eleatics and the Pythagoreans, the Sophists and the Skeptics. He pronounced his high curse and anathema upon geography and would have none of it. The result was that when he went up for final examination he writhed and floundered miserably and came within an ace of being set down for further and more diligent labor with his books. Only his remarkable mastery of the

German language and his vast knowledge of Christian doctrine — a legacy from his pious childhood — saved him. The old Nietzsche — the shrinking mother's darling of Naumburg — was now but a memory. The Nietzsche that went up to Bonn was a young man with a touch of cynicism and one not a little disposed to pit his sneer against the jurisprudence of the world: a young man with a swagger, a budding moustache and a head full of violently novel ideas about everything under the sun.

Nietzsche entered Bonn in October, 1864, when he was just 20 years old. He was enrolled as a student of philology and theology, but the latter was a mere concession to family faith and tradition, made grudgingly, and after the first semester, the reverend doctors of exegetics knew him no more. At the start he thought the university a delightful place and its people charming. The classrooms and beer gardens were full of young Germans like himself, who debated the doings of Bismarck, composed eulogies of Darwin, sang Rabelaisian songs in bad Latin, kept dogs, wore ribbons on their walking sticks, fought duels, and drank unlimited steins of pale beer. In the youth of every man there comes over him a sudden yearning to be a good fellow: to be "Bill" or "Jim" to multitudes, and to go down into legend with Sir John Falstaff and Tom Jones. This melancholy madness seized upon Nietzsche during his first year at Bonn. He frequented the theatres and posed as a connoisseur of opera bouffe, malt liquor and the female form divine. He went upon students' walking tours and carved his name upon the mutilated tables of country inns. He joined a student corps, bought him a little cap and set up shop as a devil of a fellow. His mother was not poor, but she could not afford the outlays that these ambitious enterprises required. Friedrich overdrew his allowance and the good woman, no doubt, wept about it, as mothers will, and wondered that learning came so dear.

But the inevitable reaction followed. Nietzsche was not designed by nature for a hero of pot-houses and duelling sheds. The old fastidiousness asserted itself — that queer, unhealthy fastidiousness which, in his childhood, had set him apart from other boys, and was destined, all his life long, to make him shrink from too intimate contact with his fellow-men. The touch of the crowd disgusted him: he had an almost insane fear of demeaning himself. All of this feeling had been obscured for awhile, by the strange charm of new delights and new companions, but in the end, the gloomy spinner of fancies triumphed over the university buck. Nietzsche resigned from his student corps, burned his walking sticks, foreswore smoking and roistering, and bade farewell to Johann Strauss and Offenbach forever. The days of his youth —

of his carefree, merry gamboling — were over. Hereafter he was all solemnity and all seriousness.

"From these early experiences," says his sister, "there remained with him a life-long aversion to smoking, beer-drinking and the whole *biergemüthlichkeit*. He maintained that people who drank beer and smoked pipes were absolutely incapable of understanding him. Such people, he thought, lacked the delicacy and clearness of perception necessary to grasp profound and subtle problems."

The Beginnings of the Philosopher

At Bonn Nietzsche became a student of Ritschl, the famous philologist, and when Ritschl left Bonn for Leipsic, Nietzsche followed him. All traces of the good fellow had disappeared and the student that remained was not unlike those sophomores of medieval Toulouse who "rose from bed at 4 o'clock, and having prayed to God, went at 5 o'clock to their studies, their big books under their arms, their inkhorns and candles in their hands." Between teacher and pupil there grew up a bond of strong friendship. Nietzsche was taken, too, under the wing of motherly old Frau Ritschl, who invited him to her afternoons of coffee and cinnamon cake and to her evening soirées, where he met the great men of the university world and the eminent strangers who came and went. To Ritschl the future philosopher owed many things, indeed, including his sound knowledge of the ancients, his first (and last) university appointment and his meeting with Richard Wagner. Nietzsche always looked back upon these days with pleasure and there was ever a warm spot in his heart for the kindly old professor who led him up to grace.

Two years or more were thus spent, and then, in the latter part of 1867, Nietzsche began his term of compulsory military service in the fourth regiment of Prussian field artillery. He had hoped to escape because he was near-sighted and the only son of a widow, but a watchful oberst-lieutenant found loopholes in the law and so ensnared him. He seems to have been some sort of officer, for a photograph of the period shows him with epaulets and a sword. But lieutenant or sergeant, soldiering was scarcely his forte, and he cut a sorry figure on a horse. After a few months of unwilling service, in fact, he had a riding accident and came near dying as his father had died before him. As it was he wrenched his breast muscles so badly that he was condemned by a medical survey and discharged from the army.

During his long convalescence he busied himself with philological studies and began his first serious professional work — essays on the Theogony of Hesiod, the sources of Diogenes Laërtius and the eternal strife between Hesiod and Homer. He also made an index to an elaborate collection of

German historical fragments and performed odd tasks of like sort for various professors. In October, 1868, he returned to Leipsic — not as an undergraduate, but as a special student. This change was advantageous, for it gave him greater freedom of action and protected him from that student bonhomie he had learned to despise. Again old Ritschl was his teacher and friend and again Frau Ritschl welcomed him to her salon and gave him of her good counsel and her excellent coffee.

Meanwhile there had occurred something that was destined to direct and color the whole stream of his life. This was his discovery of Arthur Schopenhauer. In the 1860s, it would appear, the great pessimist was still scarcely more than a name in the German universities, which, for all their later heterodoxy, clung long to their ancient first causes. Nietzsche knew nothing of him, and in the seminaries of Leipsic not a soul maintained him. Of Kant and of Hegel there was talk unlimited, and of Lotze and Fichte there were riotous disputations that roared and raged about the classroom of Fechner, then the university professor of philosophy. But of Schopenhauer nothing was heard, and so, when Nietzsche, rambling through an old Leipsic bookshop, happened upon a second-hand copy of *Die Welt als Wille and Voystellung* [*The World As Will And Idea*], a new world came floating into his view. This was in 1865.

"I took the book to my lodgings," he said years afterward, "and flung myself on a sofa and read and read and read. It seemed as if Schopenhauer were addressing me personally. I felt his enthusiasm and seemed to see him before me. Every line cried aloud for renunciation, denial, resignation!"

So much for the first flush of the ecstasy of discovery. That Nietzsche entirely agreed with everything in the book, even in his wildest transports of admiration, is rather doubtful. He was but 21 — the age of great passions and great romance — and he was athirst for some writing that would solve the problems left unanswered by the accepted sages, but it is probable that when he shouted the Schopenhauer manifesto loudest he read into the text wild variations of his own. The premises of the pessimist gave credit and order to thoughts that had been rising up in his own mind; but the conclusions, if he subscribed to them at all, led him far afield. No doubt he was like one of those fantastic messiahs of new cults who search the scriptures for testimony — and find it. Late in life, when he was accused of inconsistency in first deifying Schopenhauer and then damning him, he made this defense, and despite the derisive sneers of his enemies, it seemed a fairly good one.

Schopenhauer's argument, to put it briefly, was that the will to exist — the primary instinct of life — was the eternal first cause of all human actions, motives and ideas. The old philosophers of Christendom had regarded intelligence as the superior of instinct. Some of them thought that an intelligent god ruled the universe and that nothing happened without his knowledge and desire. Others believed that man was a free agent, that whatever he did was the result of his own thought and choice, and that it was right, in consequence, to condemn him to hell for his sins and to exalt him to heaven for any goodness he might chance to show. Schopenhauer turned all this completely about. Intelligence, he said, was not the source of will, but its effect. When life first appeared upon earth, it but one aim and object: that of perpetuating itself. This instinct, he said, was still at the bottom of every function of all living beings. Intelligence grew out of the fact that mankind, in the course of ages, began to notice that certain manifestations of the will to live were followed by certain invariable results. This capacity of perceiving was followed by a capacity for remembering, which in turn produced a capacity for anticipating. An intelligent man, said Schopenhauer, was merely one who remembered so many facts (the result either of personal experience or of the transmitted experience of others) that he could separate them into groups and observe their relationship, one to the other, and hazard a close guess as to their future effects; i. e. could reason about them.

Going further, Schopenhauer pointed out that this will to exist, this instinct to preserve and protect life, this old Adam, was to blame for the unpleasant things of life as well as for the good things — that it produced avarice, hatred and murder just as well as industry, resourcefulness and courage — that it led men to seek means of killing one another as well as means of tilling the earth and procuring food and raiment. He showed, yet further, that its bad effects were a great deal more numerous than its good effects and so accounted for the fact — which many men before him had observed — that life, at best, held more of sorrow than of joy.

The will-to-live, argued Schopenhauer, was responsible for all this. Pain, he believed, would always outweigh pleasure in this sad old world until men ceased to want to live — until no one desired food or drink or house or wife or money. To put it more briefly, he held that true happiness would be impossible until mankind had killed will with will, which is to say, until the will-to-live was willed out of existence. Therefore the happiest man was the one who had come nearest this end — the man who had killed all the more obvious human desires, hopes and aspirations — the solitary ascetic — the monk in his cell — the soaring, starving poet — the cloud-enshrouded philosopher.

Nietzsche very soon diverged from this conclusion. He believed, with Schopenhauer, that human life, at best, was often an infliction and a torture, but in his very first book he showed that he admired, not the ascetic who tried to escape from the wear and tear of life altogether, but the proud, stiff-necked hero who held his balance in the face of both seductive pleasure and staggering pain; who cultivated within himself a sublime indifference, so that happiness and misery, to him, became mere words, and no catastrophe, human or superhuman, could affright or daunt him.

It is obvious that there is a considerable difference between these ideas, for all their similarity in origin and for all Nietzsche's youthful worship of Schopenhauer. Nietzsche, in fact, was so enamoured by the honesty and originality of what may be called the data of Schopenhauer's philosophy that he took the philosophy itself rather on trust and did not begin to inquire into it closely or to compare it carefully with his own ideas until after he had committed himself in a most embarrassing fashion. The same phenomena is no curiosity in religion, science or politics.

Before a realization of these differences quite dawned upon Nietzsche he was busied with other affairs. In 1869, when he was barely 25, he was appointed, upon Ritschl's recommendation, to the chair of classical philology at the University of Basel, in Switzerland, an ancient stronghold of Lutheran theology. He had no degree, but the University of Leipsic promptly made him a doctor of philosophy, without thesis or examination, and on April 13th he left the old home at Naumburg to assume his duties. Thus passed that pious household. The grandmother had died long before — in 1856 — and one of the maiden aunts had preceded her to the grave by a year. Nietzsche's mother lived until 1897, and his sister, as we know, survived him. The other maiden aunt vanishes from the scene in a cloud of uncertainty.

Nietzsche was officially professor of philology, but he also became teacher of Greek in the pedagogium attached to the University. He worked like a Trojan and mixed Schopenhauer and Hesiod in his classroom discourses upon the origin of Greek verbs and other such dull subjects. But it is not recorded that he made a very profound impression, except upon a relatively small circle. His learning was abyssmal, but he was far too impatient and unsympathetic to be a good teacher. His classes, in fact, were never large, except in the pedagogium. This, however, may have been partly due to the fact that in 1869, as in later years, there were comparatively few persons impractical enough to spend their days and nights in the study of philology.

In 1870 came the Franco-Prussian war and Nietzsche decided to go to the front. Despite his hatred of all the cant of cheap patriotism and his pious thankfulness that he was a Pole and not a German, he was at bottom a good citizen and perfectly willing to suffer and bleed for his country. But unluckily he had taken out Swiss naturalization papers in order to be able to accept his appointment at Basel, and so, as the subject of a neutral state, he had to go to the war, not as a warrior, but as a hospital steward.

Even as it was, Nietzsche came near giving his life to Germany. He was not strong physically — he had suffered from severe headaches as far back as 1862 — and his hard work at Basel had further weakened him. On the battlefields of France he grew ill. Diphtheria and what seems to have been cholera morbus attacked him and when he finally reached home again he was a neurasthenic wreck. Ever thereafter his life was one long struggle against disease. He suffered from migraine, that most terrible disease of the nerves, and chronic catarrh of the stomach made him a dyspeptic. Unable to eat or sleep, he resorted to narcotics, and according to his sister, he continued their use throughout his life. "He wanted to get well quickly," she says, "and so took double doses." Nietzsche, indeed, was a slave to drugs, and more than once in after life, long before insanity finally ended his career, he gave evidence of it.

Despite his illness he insisted upon resuming work, but during the following winter he was obliged to take a vacation in Italy. Meanwhile he had delivered lectures to his classes on the Greek drama and two of these he revised and published, in 1872, as his first book, *Die Geburt der Tragödie* (*The Birth of Tragedy*). Engelmann, the great Leipsic publisher, declined it, but Fritsch, of the same city, put it into type. This book greatly pleased his friends, but the old-line philologists of the time thought it wild and extravagant, and it almost cost Nietzsche his professorship. Students were advised to keep away from him, and during the winter of 1872-3, it is said, he had no pupils at all.

Nevertheless the book, for all its iconoclasm, was an event. It sounded Nietzsche's first, faint battle-cry and put the question mark behind many things that seemed honorable and holy in philology. Most of the philologists of that time were German savants of the comic-paper sort, and their lives were spent in wondering why one Greek poet made the name of a certain plant masculine while another made it feminine. Nietzsche, passing over such scholastic futilities, burrowed down into the heart of Greek literature. Why, he asked himself, did the Greeks take pleasure in witnessing representations of bitter, hopeless conflicts, and how did this form of entertainment arise among them? Later on, his conclusions will be given at length, but in this place it may be well to sketch them in outline, because of the bearing they have upon his later work, and even upon the trend of his life.

In ancient Greece, he pointed out at the start, Apollo was the god of art —
of life as it was recorded and interpreted — and Bacchus Dionysus was the
god of life itself — of eating, drinking and making merry, of dancing and
roistering, of everything that made men acutely conscious of the vitality and
will within them. The difference between the things they represented has
been well set forth in certain homely verses addressed by Rudyard Kipling to
Admiral Robley D. Evans, U. S. N.:

Zogbaum draws with a pencil
And I do things with a pen,
But you sit up in a conning tower,
Bossing eight hundred men.
To him that hath shall be given
And that's why these books are sent
To the man who has lived more stories
Than Zogbaum or I could invent.

Here we have the plain distinction: Zogbaum and Kipling are apollonic,
while Evans is dionysian. Epic poetry, sculpture, painting and story-telling are
apollonic: they represent, not life itself, but some one man's visualized idea
of life. But dancing, great deeds and, in some cases, music, are dionysian: they
are part and parcel of life as some actual human being, or collection of human
beings, is living it.

Nietzsche maintained that Greek art was at first apollonic, but that
eventually there appeared a dionysian influence — the fruit, perhaps, of
contact with primitive, barbarous peoples. Ever afterward there was constant
conflict between them and this conflict was the essence of Greek tragedy. As
Sarcey tells us, a play, to hold our attention, must depict some sort of battle,
between man and man or idea and idea. In the melodrama of today the battle
is between hero and villain; in the ancient Greek tragedy it was between
Apollo and Dionysus, between the life contemplative and the life strenuous,
between law and outlaw, between the devil and the seraphim.

Nietzsche, as we shall see, afterward applied this distinction in morals and
life as well as in art. He called himself a dionysian and the crowning volume
of his system of philosophy, which he had barely started when insanity
overtook him, was to have been called "Dionysus."

1. Friedrich Wilhelm Ritschl (1806-1876), the foremost philologist of
modern times. He became a professor of classical literature and rhetoric in

1839 and founded the science of historical literary criticism, as we know it to-day.

2. Arthur Schopenhauer (1788-1860) published this book, his magnum opus, at Leipsic in 1819. It has been translated into English and has appeared in many editions.

3. Schopenhauer (*Nächtträge zur Lehre vom Leiden der Welt*) puts the argument thus: " Pleasure is never as pleasant as we expect it to be and pain is always more painful. The pain in the world always outweighs the pleasure. If you don't believe it, compare the respective feelings of two animals, one of which is eating the other."

4. Later on, in "*Menschliches allzu Menschliches* [*Human, All Too Human*], II, Nietzsche argued that the ascetic was either a coward, who feared the temptations of pleasure and the agonies of pain, or an exhausted worldling who had become satiated with life.

5. Begun in 1869, this maiden work was dedicated to Richard Wagner. At Wagner's suggestion Nietzsche eliminated a great deal of matter in the original draft. The full title was *The Birth of Tragedy* from the Spirit of Music, but this was changed, in 1886, when a third edition was printed, to *The Birth of Tragedy, or Hellenism and Pessimism*. Nietzsche then also added a long preface, entitled "An Attempt at Self-Criticism." The material originally excluded was published in 1896.

Blazing A New Path

Having given birth, in this theory of Greek tragedy, to an idea which, whatever its defects otherwise, was at least original, understandable and workable, Nietzsche began to be conscious, as it were, of his own intellect or, in his sister's phrase, "to understand what a great man he was." He led a lonely and morose life at Basel, with an occasional visit to Richard Wagner — who lived then in Switzerland and not far away — as his only recreation. In the prim, scholastic society of the university town he played no part whatever. To one of his turn of mind, indeed, the whole atmosphere of the place must have been oppressive. He was not a man to bear with equanimity the unctuous complacency of college dons and dignitaries, and he was devoid entirely of those graces which make a young professor a welcome guest at university dinner parties and a favorite of each frau professorin. His headaches, his sacrileges and his callous savagery made him more enemies than friends. To dispute with him, to controvert him, or even to agree with him, was a decidedly hazardous business.

There are critics who see in all this proof that Nietzsche showed signs of insanity from early manhood, but as a matter of fact it was his abnormally accurate vision and not a vision gone awry, that made him stand so aloof from his fellows. In the vast majority of those about him he saw the coarse metal of sham and pretense beneath the showy gilding of learning. He had before him, at close range, a good many of the great men of his time — the intellectuals whose word was law in the schools. He saw them on parade and he saw them in their shirtsleeves. What wonder that he lost all false reverence for them and began to estimate them in terms, not of their dignity and reputation, but of their actual credibility and worth? It was inevitable that he should compare his own ideas to theirs, and it was inevitable that he should perceive the difference between his own fanatical striving for the truth and the easy dependence upon precedent and formula which lay beneath their blooming bombast. Thus there arose in him a fiery loathing for all authority, and a firm belief that his own opinion regarding any matter to which he had given thought was as sound, at the least, as any other man's.

Thenceforth the assertive "ich" began to besprinkle his discourse and his pages. "I condemn Christianity. I have given to mankind.... I was never yet modest.... I think.... I say.... I do...." Thus he hurled his javelin at authority until the end.

To those about him, perhaps, Nietzsche seemed wild and impossible, but it is not recorded that any one ever looked upon him as ridiculous. His high brow, bared by the way in which he brushed his hair; his keen eyes, with their monstrous overhanging brows, and his immense, untrimmed moustache gave him an air of alarming earnestness. Beside the pedagogues about him — with their well-barbered, professorial beards, their bald heads and their learned spectacles — he seemed like some incomprehensible foreigner. The exotic air he bore delighted him and he cultivated it assiduously. He regarded himself as a Polish grandee set down by an unkind fate among German shopkeepers, and it gave him vast pleasure when the hotel porters and street beggars, deceived by his disorderly facade, called him "The Polack."

Thus he lived and had his being. The inquisitive boy of old Naumburg, the impudent youth of Pforta and the academic free lance of Bonn and Leipsic had become merged into a man sure of himself and contemptuous of all whose search for the truth was hampered or hedged about by any respect for statute or precedent. He saw that the philosophers and sages of the day, in many of their most gorgeous flights of logic, started from false premises, and he observed the fact that certain of the dominant moral, political and social maxims of the time were mere foolishness. It struck him, too, that all of this faulty ratiocination — all of this assumption of outworn doctrines and dependence upon exploded creeds — was not confined to the confessedly orthodox. There was fallacy no less disgusting in the other camp. The professed apostles of revolt were becoming as bad as the old crusaders and apologists.

Nietzsche harbored a fevered yearning to call all of these false prophets to book and to reduce their fine axioms to absurdity. Accordingly, he planned a series of twenty-four pamphlets and decided to call them *Unzeitgemässe Betrachtungen* [*Untimely Meditations*], which may be translated as "Inopportune Speculations," or more clearly, "Essays in Sham-Smashing." In looking about for a head to smash in essay number one, his eye, naturally enough, alighted upon that of David Strauss, the favorite philosopher and fashionable iconoclast of the day. Strauss had been a preacher but had renounced the cloth and set up shop as a critic of Christianity. He had labored with good intentions, no doubt, but the net result of all his smug agnosticism was that his disciples were as self-satisfied, bigoted and prejudiced in the garb of agnostics, as they had been before as Christians. Nietzsche's clear eye saw this and in the first of his little pamphlets, *"David Strauss, der Bekenner and der Schriftsteller"* ("David Strauss, the Confessor and the Writer"), he bore down upon Strauss' bourgeoise pseudo-skepticism most savagely. This was in 1873.

"Strauss," he said, "utterly evades the question, What is the meaning of life? He had an opportunity to show courage, to turn his back upon the Philistines, and to boldly deduce a new morality from that constant warfare which destroys all but the fittest, but to do this would have required a love of truth infinitely higher than that which spends itself in violent invectives against parsons, miracles and the historical humbug of the resurrection. Strauss had no such courage. Had he worked out the Darwinian doctrine to its last decimal he would have had the Philistines against him to a man. As it is, they are with him. He has wasted his time in combatting Christianity's nonessentials. For the idea at the bottom of it he has proposed no substitute. In consequence, his philosophy is stale."

As a distinguished critic has pointed out, Nietzsche's attack was notable, not only for its keen analysis and ruthless honesty, but also for its courage. It required no little bravery, three years after Sedan, to tell the Germans that the new culture which constituted their pride was rotten, and that, unless it were purified in the fire of absolute truth, it might one day wreck their civilization.

In the year following Nietzsche returned to the attack with a criticism of history, which was then the fashionable science of the German universities, on account, chiefly, of its usefulness in exploding the myths of Christianity. He called his essay *"Vom Nutzen and Nachtheil der Historie für das Leben"* ["The Use and Abuse of History"] and in it he took issue with the reigning pedagogues and professors of the day. There was much hard thinking and no little good writing in this essay and it made its mark. The mere study of history, argued Nietzsche, unless some definite notion regarding the destiny of man were kept ever in mind, was misleading and confusing. There was great danger in assuming that everything which happened was part of some divine and mysterious plan for the ultimate attainment of perfection. As a matter of fact, many historical events were meaningless, and this was particularly true of those expressions of "governments, public opinion and majorities" which historians were prone to accentuate. To Nietzsche the ideas and doings of peoples seemed infinitely less important than the ideas and doings of exceptional individuals. To put it more simply, he believed that one man, Hannibal, was of vastly more importance to the world than all the other

Carthaginians of his time taken together. Herein we have a reappearance of Dionysus and a foreshadowing of the *herrenmoral* [*master morality*] and superman of later days.

Nietzsche's next essay was devoted to Schopenhauer and was printed in 1874. He called it *"Schopenhauer als Erzieher"* ["Schopenhauer as Educator"] and in it he laid his burnt offering upon the altar of the great pessimist, who was destined to remain his hero, if no longer his god, until the end. Nietzsche was already beginning to read rebellious ideas of his own into The World as Will and Idea, but in two things — the theory of will and the impulse toward truth — he and Schopenhauer were ever as one. He preached a holy war upon all those influences which had made the apostle of pessimism, in his lifetime, an unheard outcast. He raged against the narrowness of university schools of philosophy and denounced all governmental interference in speculation whether it were expressed crudely, by inquisitorial laws and the Index, or softly and insidiously, by the bribery of comfortable berths and public honors.

"Experience teaches us," he said, "that nothing stands so much in the way of developing great philosophers as the custom of supporting bad ones in state universities.... It is the popular theory that the posts given to the latter make them 'free' to do original work; as a matter of fact, the effect is quite the contrary.... No state would ever dare to patronize such men as Plato and Schopenhauer. And why? Because the state is always afraid of them.... It seems to me that there is need for a higher tribunal outside the universities to critically examine the doctrines they teach. As soon as philosophers are willing to resign their salaries, they will constitute such a tribunal. Without pay and without honors, it will be able to free itself from the prejudices of the age. Like Schopenhauer, it will be the judge of the so-called culture around it."

Years later Nietzsche denied that, in this essay, he committed himself irretrievably to the whole philosophy of Schopenhauer and a fair reading bears him out. He was not defending Schopenhauer's doctrine of renunciation, but merely asking that he be given a hearing. He was pleading the case of foes as well as of friends: all he asked was that the forum be opened to every man who had something new to say.

Nietzsche regarded Schopenhauer as a king among philosophers because he shook himself entirely free of the dominant thought of his time. In an age marked, beyond everything, by humanity's rising reliance upon human reason, he sought to show that reason was a puny offshoot of an irresistible natural law — the law of self-preservation. Nietzsche admired the man's courage and agreed with him in his insistence that this law was at the bottom of all sentient activity, but he was never a subscriber to Schopenhauer's surrender and despair. From the very start, indeed, he was a prophet of defiance, and herein his divergence from Schopenhauer was infinite. As his knowledge broadened and his scope widened, he expanded and developed his philosophy, and often he found it necessary to modify it in detail. But that he ever turned upon himself in fundamentals is untrue. Nietzsche at 40 and Nietzsche at 25 were essentially the same. The germ of practically all his writings lies in his first book — nay, it is to be found further back: in the wild speculations of his youth.

The fourth of the *Unzeitgemässe Betrachtungen* (and the last, for the original design of the series was not carried out) was "Richard Wagner in Bayreuth." This was published in 1876 and neither it nor the general subject of Nietzsche's relations with Wagner need be considered here. In a subsequent chapter the whole matter will be discussed. For the present, it is sufficient to say that Nietzsche met Wagner through the medium of Ritschl's wife; that they became fast friends; that Nietzsche hailed the composer as a hero sent to make the drama an epitome of the life unfettered and unbounded, of life defiant and joyful; that Wagner, after starting from the Schopenhauer base, travelled toward St. Francis rather than toward Dionysus, and that Nietzsche, after vain expostulations, read the author of "*Parsifal*" out of meeting and pronounced him anathema. It was all a case of misunderstanding. Wagner was an artist, and not a philosopher. Right or wrong, Christianity was beautiful, and as a thing of beauty it called aloud to him. To Nietzsche beauty seemed a mere phase of truth.

It was during this period of preliminary skirmishing that Nietzsche's ultimate philosophy began to formulate itself. He saw clearly that there was something radically wrong with the German culture of the day — that many things esteemed right and holy were, in reality, unspeakable, and that many things under the ban of church and state were far from wrong in themselves. He saw, too, that there had grown up a false logic and that its taint was upon the whole of contemporary thought. Men maintained propositions plainly erroneous and excused themselves by the plea that ideals were greater than actualities. The race was subscribing to one thing and practicing another. Christianity was official, but not a single real Christian was to be found in all Christendom. Thousands bowed down to men and ideas that they despised and denounced things that every sane man knew were necessary and inevitable. The result was a flavor of dishonesty and hypocrisy in all human affairs. In the abstract the laws — of the church, the state and society —

were looked upon as impeccable, but every man, in so far as they bore upon him personally, tried his best to evade them.

Other philosophers, in Germany and elsewhere, had made the same observation and there was in progress a grand assault-at-arms upon old ideas. Huxley and Spencer, in England, were laboring hard in the vineyard planted by Darwin; Ibsen, in Norway, was preparing for his epoch-making life-work, and in far America Andrew D. White and others were battling to free education from the bonds of theology. Thus it will be seen that, at the start, Nietzsche was no more a pioneer than any one of a dozen other men. Some of these other men, indeed, were far better equipped for the fray than he, and their services, for a long while, seemed a great deal more important. But it was his good fortune, before his working days were over, to press the conflict much further afield than the others. Beginning where they ended, he fought his way into the very citadel of the enemy.

His attack upon Christianity, which is described at length later on, well exemplifies this uncompromising thoroughness. Nietzsche saw that the same plan would have to be pursued in examining all other concepts — religious, political or social. It would be necessary to pass over surface symptoms and go to the heart of things: to tunnel down deep into ideas; to trace out their history and seek out their origins. There were no willing hands to help him in this: it was, in a sense, a work new to the world. In consequence Nietzsche perceived that he would have to go slowly and that it would be needful to make every step plain. It was out of the question to expect encouragement: if the task attracted notice at all, this notice would probably take the form of blundering opposition. But Nietzsche began his clearing and his road cutting with a light heart. The men of his day might call him accursed, but in time his honesty would shame all denial. This was his attitude always: he felt that neglect and opprobrium were all in his day's work and he used to say that if ever the generality of men endorsed any idea that he had advanced he would be convinced at once that he had made an error.

In his preliminary path-finding Nietzsche concerned himself much with the history of specific ideas. He showed how the thing which was a sin in one age became the virtue of the next. He attacked hope, faith and charity in this way, and he made excursions into nearly every field of human thought — from art to primary education. All of this occupied the first half of the 1870s. Nietzsche was in indifferent health and his labors tired him so greatly that he thought more than once of giving up his post at Basel, with its dull round of lecturing and quizzing. But his private means at this time were not great enough to enable him to surrender his salary and so he had to hold on. He thought, too, of going to Vienna to study the natural sciences so that he might attain the wide and certain knowledge possessed by Spencer, but the same considerations forced him to abandon the plan. He spent his winters teaching and investigating and his summers at various watering-places — from Tribschen, in Switzerland, where the Wagners were his hosts, to Sorrento, in Italy.

At Sorrento he happened to take lodgings in a house which also sheltered Dr. Paul Rée, the author of "Psychological Observations," "The Origin of Moral Feelings," and other metaphysical works. That Rée gave him great assistance he acknowledged himself in later years, but that his ideas were, in any sense, due to this chance meeting (as Max Nordau would have us believe) is out of the question, for, as we have seen, they were already pretty clear in his mind a long while before. But Rée widened his outlook a great deal, it is evident, and undoubtedly made him acquainted with the English naturalists who had sprung up as spores of Darwin, and with a number of great Frenchmen — Montaigne, La Rochefoucauld, La Bruyère, Fontenelle, Vauvenargues and Chamfort.

Nietzsche had been setting down his thoughts and conclusions in the form of brief memoranda and as he grew better acquainted with the French philosophers, many of whom published their works as collections of aphorisms, he decided to employ that form himself. Thus he began to arrange the notes which were to be given to the world as *Menschliches allzu Menschliches* [*Human, All-Too-Human*]. In 1876 he got leave from Basel and gave his whole time to the work. During the winter of 1876-7, with the aid of a disciple named Bernhard Cron (better known as Peter Gast) he prepared the first volume for the press. Nietzsche was well aware that it would make a sensation and while it was being set up his courage apparently forsook him and he suggested to his publisher that it be sent forth anonymously. But the latter would not hear of it and so the first part left the press in 1878.

As the author had expected, the book provoked a fine frenzy of horror among the pious. The first title chosen for it, *"Die Pflugschar"* ("The Plowshare"), and the one finally selected, indicate that it was an attempt to examine the underside of human ideas. In it Nietzsche challenged the whole of current morality. He showed that moral ideas were not divine, but human, and that, like all things human, they were subject to change. He showed that good and evil were but relative terms, and that it was impossible to say, finally and absolutely, that a certain action was right and another wrong. He applied the acid of critical analysis to a hundred and one specific ideas, and his general conclusion, to put it briefly, was that no human being had a right, in any way or form, to judge or direct the actions of any other being. Herein we have, in a few words, that gospel of individualism which all our sages preach today.

Nietzsche sent a copy of the book to Wagner and the great composer was so appalled that he was speechless. Even the author's devoted sister, who worshipped him as an intellectual god, was unable to follow him. Germany, in general, pronounced the work a conglomeration of crazy fantasies and wild absurdities — and Nietzsche smiled with satisfaction. In 1879 he published the second volume, to which he gave the sub-title of *"Vermischte Meinungen and Sprüche"* ["Assorted Opinions and Maxims"] and shortly thereafter he finally resigned his chair at Basel. The third part of the book appeared in 1880 as *"Der Wanderer and sein Schatten"* ("The Wanderer and His Shadow"). The three volumes were published as two in 1886 as *Menschliches allzu Menschliches*, with the explanatory sub-title, *"Ein Buch fur Freie Geister"* ("A Book for Free Spirits").

The Prophet of the Superman

Nietzsche spent the winter of 1879-80 at Naumburg, his old home. During the ensuing year he was very ill, indeed, and for awhile he believed that he had but a short while to live. Like all such invalids he devoted a great deal of time to observing and discussing his condition. He became, indeed, a hypochondriac of the first water and began to take a sort of melancholy pleasure in his infirmities. He sought relief at all the baths and cures of Europe: he took hot baths, cold baths, salt-water baths and mud baths. Every new form of pseudo-therapy found him in its freshman class. To owners of sanitoria and to inventors of novel styles of massage, irrigation, sweating and feeding he was a joy unlimited. But he grew worse instead of better.

After 1880, his life was a wandering one. His sister, after her marriage, went to Paraguay for a while, and during her absence Nietzsche made his progress from the mountains to the sea, and then back to the mountains again. He gave up his professorship that he might spend his winters in Italy and his summers in the Engadine. In the face of all this suffering and travelling about, close application, of course, was out of the question. So he contented himself with working whenever and however his headaches, his doctors and the railway timetables would permit — on hotel verandas, in cure-houses and in the woods. He would take long, solitary walks and struggle with his problems by the way. He swallowed more and more pills; he imbibed mineral waters by the gallon; he grew more and more moody and ungenial. One of his favorite haunts, in the wintertime, was a verdant little neck of land that jutted out into Lake Maggiore. There he could think and dream undisturbed. One day, when he found that some one had placed a rustic bench on the diminutive peninsula, that passersby might rest, he was greatly incensed.

Nietzsche would make brief notes of his thoughts during his daylight rambles, and in the evenings would polish and expand them. As we have seen, his early books were sent to the printer as mere collections of aphorisms, without effort at continuity. Sometimes a dozen subjects are considered in two pages, and then again, there is occasionally a little essay of three or four pages. Nietzsche chose this form because it had been used by the French philosophers he admired, and because it well suited the methods of work that a pain-racked frame imposed upon him.

He was ever in great fear that some of his precious ideas would be lost to posterity — that death, the ever-threatening, would rob him of his rightful immortality and the world of his stupendous wisdom — and so he made efforts, several times, to engage an amanuensis capable of jotting down, after the fashion of Johnson's Boswell, the chance phrases that fell from his lips. His sister was too busy to undertake the task: whenever she was with him her whole time was employed in guarding him from lion-hunters, scrutinizing his daily fare and deftly inveigling him into answering his letters, brushing his clothes and getting his hair cut. A number of young men, it would appear, essayed the impossible service, but all departed quickly. Finally, the philosopher's old friend, Rée, discovered a likely candidate in the person of Fraulein Lou Salomé, a young German woman. Fraulein Salomé (who afterward became Frau Andreas-Salomé) was an intellectual, but attractive person and her enthusiastic admiration flattered Nietzsche into engaging her. No more grotesque contrast than that which existed between the ponderous and humorless prophet of the superman and this superficial and flighty dilletante could be imagined. From the start they clashed and after five months Nietzsche sent her away. Later on, she printed a sort of fanciful biography of the philosopher, full of extravagant eulogy and truly feminine blunders. Nietzsche's sister dismisses it as a fabric of well-meant, but ridiculous errors and misrepresentations.

Early in 1881 Nietzsche published *Morgenröte* [*The Dawn of Day*]. It was begun at Venice in 1880 and continued at Marienbad, Lago Maggiore and Genoa. It was, in a broad way, a continuation of *Menschliches allzu Menschliches*. It dealt with an infinite variety of subjects, from matrimony to Christianity, and from education to German patriotism. To all the test of fundamental truth was applied: of everything Nietzsche asked, not, Is it respectable or lawful? but, Is it essentially true? These early works, at best, were mere notebooks. Nietzsche saw that the ground would have to be plowed, that people would have to grow accustomed to the idea of questioning high and holy things, before a new system of philosophy would be understandable or possible. In *Menschliches allzu Menschliches* and in *Morgenröte* he undertook this preparatory cultivation.

The book which followed, *Die fröhliche Wissenschaft* [*The Joyful Science*] continued the same task. The first edition contained four parts and was published in 1882. In 1887 a fifth part was added. Nietzsche had now completed his plowing and was ready to sow his crop. He had demonstrated, by practical examples, that moral ideas were vulnerable, and that the Ten Commandments might be debated. Going further, he had adduced excellent historical evidence against the absolute truth of various current conceptions of right and wrong, and had traced a number of moral ideas back to decidedly lowly sources. His work so far had been entirely destructive and he had scarcely ventured to hint at his plans for a reconstruction of the scheme of things. As he himself says, he spent the four years between 1878 and 1882 in preparing the way for his later work.

"I descended," he says, "into the lowest depths, I searched to the bottom, I examined and pried into an old faith on which, for thousands of years, philosophers had built as upon a secure foundation. The old structures came tumbling down about me. I undermined our old faith in morals."

This labor accomplished, Nietzsche was ready to set forth his own notion of the end and aim of existence. He had shown that the old morality was like an apple rotten at the core — that the Christian ideal of humility made mankind weak and miserable; that many institutions regarded with superstitious reverence, as the direct result of commands from the creator (such, for instance, as the family, the church and the state), were mere products of man's "all-too-human" cupidity, cowardice, stupidity and yearning for ease. He had turned the searchlight of truth upon patriotism, charity and self-sacrifice. He had shown that many things held to be utterly and unquestionably good or bad by modern civilization were once given quite different values — that the ancient Greeks considered hope a sign of weakness, and mercy the attribute of a fool, and that the Jews, in their royal days, looked upon wrath, not as a sin, but as a virtue — and in general he had demonstrated, by countless instances and arguments, that all notions of good and evil were mutable and that no man could ever say, with utter certainty, that one thing was right and another wrong.

The ground was now cleared for the work of reconstruction and the first structure that Nietzsche reared was *Also sprach Zarathustra* [*Thus Spake Zarathustra*]. This book, to which he gave the sub-title of "Ein Buch für Alle and Keinen" ("A Book for All and None"), took the form of a fantastic, half-poetical half-philosophical rhapsody. Nietzsche had been delving into oriental mysticism and from the law-giver of the ancient Persians he borrowed the name of his hero — Zarathustra. But there was no further resemblance between the two, and no likeness whatever between Nietzsche's philosophy and that of the Persians.

The Zarathustra of the book is a sage who lives remote from mankind, and with no attendants but a snake and an eagle. The book is in four parts and all are made up of discourses by Zarathustra. These discourses are delivered to various audiences during the prophet's occasional wanderings and at the conferences he holds with various disciples in the cave that he calls home. They are decidedly oriental in form and recall the manner and phraseology of the biblical rhapsodists. Toward the end Nietzsche throws all restraint to the winds and indulges to his heart's content in the rare and exhilarating sport of blasphemy. There is a sort of parody of the last supper and Zarathustra's backsliding disciples engage in the grotesque and indecent worship of a jackass. Wagner and other enemies of the author appear, thinly veiled, as ridiculous buffoons.

In his discourses Zarathustra voices the Nietzschean idea of the superman — the idea that has come to be associated with Nietzsche more than any other. Later on, it will be set forth in detail. For the present, suffice it to say that it is the natural child of the notions put forward in Nietzsche's first book, *The Birth of Tragedy*, and that it binds his entire life work together into one consistent, harmonious whole. The first part of *Also sprach Zarathustra* was published in 1883, the second part following in the same year, and the third part was printed in 1884. The last part was privately circulated among the author's friends in 1885, but was not given to the public until 1892, when the entire work was printed in one volume. As showing Nietzsche's wandering life, it may be recorded that the book was conceived in the Engadine and written in Genoa, Sils Maria, Nice and Mentone.

Jenseits von Gut and Böse (Beyond Good and Evil) appeared in 1886. In this book Nietzsche elaborated and systematized his criticism of morals, and undertook to show why he considered modern civilization degrading. Here he finally formulated his definitions of master-morality and slave-morality, and showed how Christianity was necessarily the idea of a race oppressed and helpless, and eager to escape the lash of its masters.

Zur Genealogie der Moral (The Genealogy of Morals), which appeared in 1887, developed these propositions still further. In it there was also a partial return to Nietzsche's earlier manner, with its merciless analysis of moral concepts. In 1888 Nietzsche published a most vitriolic attack upon Wagner, under the title of "Der Fall Wagner" ("The Case of Wagner"), the burden of which was the author's discovery that the composer, starting, with him, from Schopenhauer's premises, had ended, not with the superman, but with the Man on the cross. *Götzendämmerung* ("The Twilight of the Idols") a sort of parody of Wagner's

Götterdämmerung (The Twilight of the Gods) followed in 1889. Nietzsche contra Wagner (Nietzsche versus Wagner) was printed the same year. It was made up of extracts from the philosopher's early works, and was designed to prove that, contrary to the allegations of his enemies, he had not veered completely about in his attitude toward Wagner.

Meanwhile, despite the fact that his health was fast declining and he was approaching the verge of insanity, Nietzsche made plans for a great four volume work that was to sum up his philosophy and stand forever as his magnum opus. The four volumes, as he planned them, were to bear the following titles: *"Der Antichrist: Versuch einer Kritik des Christenthums"* ("The Anti-Christ: an Attempt at a Criticism of Christianity").

"Der freie Geist: Kritik der Philosophie als einer nihilistichen Bewegung" ("The Free Spirit: a Criticism of Philosophy as a Nihilistic Movement").

"Der Immoralist: Kritik der verhängnissvollsten Art von Unwissenheit der Moral" ("The Immoralist : a Criticism of That Fatal Species of Ignorance, Morality").

"Dionysus, Philosophie der ewigen Wiederkunft" ("Dionysus, the Philosophy of Eternal Recurrence").

This work was to be published under the general title of *Der Wille zur Macht: Versuch einer Umwerthung aller Werthe* (The Will to Power: an Attempt at a Transvaluation of all Values), but Nietzsche got no further than the first book, *Der Antichrist*. This he wrote at great speed, between September 3rd and September 30th, 1888, but it was not published until 1895 — six years after the author had laid down his work forever.

In this same year C. G. Naumann, the great Leipsic publisher, began the issue of a definitive eight-volume edition of the philosopher's works, under the editorship of Frau Forster-Nietzsche, Peter Gast, Dr. Fritz Koegel and other friends and disciples. Later on his notes for various books, both completed and projected, were published in six additional volumes. His early essays upon philological themes and a great variety of memoranda were included. This collection is of interest to the student who desires to make an exhaustive study of the origin and development of Nietzsche's ideas, but it is unfortunate that the editors chose to print so much inconsequential matter. More of his early notes are in his sister's biography. The philosopher, back in the 1880s wrote a sort of introspective autobiography under the title of *Ecce Homo!*

In January, 1889, at Turin, after a severe attack of migraine, Nietzsche became hopelessly insane and was confined in a private asylum. In the summer of 1890 he recovered sufficiently to be taken to his old home at

Naumburg, and when his mother died, in 1897, his sister removed him to Weimar, where she bought a villa called "Silberblick" ("Silver View"), in the suburbs. This villa had a garden overlooking the hills and the lazy river Ilm and a wide, sheltered veranda for the invalid's couch. But his mind never became clear enough for him to resume work. He had to grope for words, slowly and painfully, and his physical strength left him.

This is something poignantly pathetic in the picture of this valiant fighter — this arrogant Ja-sager — this foe of men, gods and devils — being nursed and coddled like a little child. His old fierce pride and courage disappeared and he became docile and gentle. "You and I, my sister — we are happy!" he would say and then his hand would slip out from his bed-clothes and grasp that of the tender and loving Lisbeth. Once she mentioned Wagner to him. "*Den habe ich sehy geliebt!*" he said. ["That man I loved well."] All his old fighting spirit was gone: he remembered only the glad days and the dreams of his youth.

Nietzsche died on August 25th, 1900, in the gray of the early morning.

The Philosopher And The Man

"My brother," says Frau Forster-Nietzsche, in her biography, "was stockily and broadly built and was anything but thin. He had a rather dark, healthy, ruddy complexion. In all things he was tidy and orderly, in speech he was soft-spoken, and in general, he was inclined to be serene under all circumstances. All in all, he was the very antithesis of a nervous man.

"In the fall of 1888, he said of himself, in a reminiscent memorandum: 'My blood moves slowly. A doctor who treated me a long while for what was at first diagnosed as a nervous affection said: "No, your trouble cannot be in your nerves. I myself am much more nervous than you.""...

"My brother, both before and after his long illness seized him, was a believer in natural methods of healing. He took cold baths, rubbed down every morning and was quite faithful in continuing light, bed-room gymnastics."

At one time, she says, Nietzsche became a violent vegetarian and afflicted his friends with the ancient vegetarian horror of making a sarcophagus of one's stomach. It seems surprising that a man so quick to perceive errors, saw none in the silly argument that, because an ape's organs are designed for a vegetarian diet, a man's are so planned also. An acquaintance with elementary anatomy and physiology would have shown him the absurdity of this, but apparently he knew little about the human body, despite his uncanny skill at unearthing the secrets of the human mind. Nietzsche had read Emerson in his youth, and those Emersonian seeds which have come to full flower in the United States as the so-called New Thought movement — with Christian Science, osteopathy, mental telepathy, occultism, pseudo-psychology and that grand lodge of credulous comiques, the Society for Psychical Research, as its final blossoms — all of this probably made its mark on the philosopher of the superman, too.

Frau Forster-Nietzsche, in her biography, seeks to prove the impossible thesis that her brother, despite his constant illness, was ever well-balanced in mind. It is but fair to charge that her own evidence is against her. From his youth onward, Nietzsche was undoubtedly a neurasthenic, and after the

Franco-Prussian war he was a constant sufferer from all sorts of terrible ills —
some imaginary, no doubt, but others real enough. In many ways, his own
account of his symptoms recalls vividly the long catalogue of aches and pains
given by Herbert Spencer in his autobiography. Spencer had queer pains in
his head and so did Nietzsche. Spencer roved about all his life in search of
health and so did Nietzsche. Spencer's working hours were limited and so
were Nietzsche's. The latter tells us himself that, in a single year, 1878, he
was disabled 118 days by headaches and pains in the eyes.

Dr. Gould, the prophet of eye-strain, would have us believe that both of
these great philosophers suffered because they read too much in their early
days. It is more likely, however, that each was the victim of specific organic
diseases. Twenty years ago, the word neurasthenia was appalling and bore
upon its face something of the loathsomeness of scrofula or leprosy, but now
we know that neurasthenics are quite numerous, and that most of them, for
all their chronic sufferings, are good citizens. In Nietzsche's case hard work
and constant turmoil aggravated the malady and it progressed, in a manner
almost classical, into hysteria, and then into melancholia and insanity.

Nietzsche was a hysteric in 1875, and by 1880, as his letters show, he was
already exhibiting symptoms of melancholia — a sense of isolation and
friendlessness, acute suspiciousness and a foreboding of approaching death.
The hostility with which his philosophy was received increased the depression
caused by his physical ills, but ever and anon the gorgeous egotism of the man
would flash forth and give him comfort.

"An animal, when it is sick," he wrote to Baron von Seydlitz, in 1888,
"slinks away to some dark cavern, and so, too, does the *bête philosophe*. I am
alone — absurdly alone — and in my unflinching and toilsome struggle
against all that men have hitherto held sacred and venerable, I have become
a sort of dark cavern myself something hidden and mysterious, which is not
to be explored...." But the mood vanished as the words were penned, and the
defiant dionysian roared his challenge at his foes. "It is not impossible," he
said, "that I am the greatest philosopher of the century — perhaps even more
than that! I may be the decisive and fateful link between two thousand
centuries!"

Max Nordau says that Nietzsche was crazy from birth, but the facts do not
bear him out. It is much more reasonable to hold that the philosopher came
into the world a sound and healthy animal, and that it remained for overstudy
in his youth, over-work and over drugging later on, exposure on the battle
field, functional disorders and constant and violent strife to undermine and
eventually overthrow his intellect.

But if we admit the indisputable fact that Nietzsche died a madman and the equally indisputable fact that his insanity was not sudden, but progressive, we by no means read him out of court as a thinker. A man's reasoning is to be judged, not by his physical condition, but by its own ingenuity and accuracy. If a raving maniac says that twice two make four, it is just as true as it would be if the Pope or any other undoubtedly sane man were to maintain it. Judged in this way Nietzsche's philosophy is very far from insane. Later on we shall consider it as a workable system, and point out its apparent truths and apparent errors, but in no place (saving, perhaps, one) is his argument to be dismissed as the phantasm of a lunatic.

Nietzsche's sister says that, in the practical affairs of life, the philosopher was absurdly impractical. He cared nothing for money and during the better part of his life had little need to do so. His mother, for a country pastor's widow, was well-to-do, and when he was twenty-five his professorship at Basel brought him 3,000 francs a year. At Basel, in the late 1860s, 3,000 francs was the income of an independent, not to say opulent man. Nietzsche was a bachelor and lived very simply. It was only upon books and music and travel that he was extravagant.

After two years' service at Basel, the university authorities raised his wage to 4,000 francs, and in 1879, when ill health forced him to resign, they gave him a pension of 3,000 francs a year. Besides that, he inherited 30,000 marks from one of his aunts, and so, altogether, he had an income of $900 or $1,000 a year — the sum which Herbert Spencer regarded, all his life, as an insurance of perfect tranquillity and happiness.

Nietzsche's passion and dissipation, throughout his life, was music. In all his books musical terms and figures of speech are constantly encountered. He played the piano very well, indeed, and was especially fond of performing transcriptions of the Wagner opera scores. "My three solaces," he wrote home from Leipsic, "are Schopenhauer's philosophy, Schumann's music and solitary walks." In his late youth, Wagner engrossed him, but his sympathies were broad enough to include Bach, Schubert and Mendelssohn. His admiration for the last named, in fact, helped to alienate him from Wagner, who regarded the Mendelssohn scheme of things as unspeakable.

Nietzsche's own compositions were decidedly heavy and scholastic. He was a skillful harmonist and contrapuntalist, but his musical ideas lacked life. Into the simplest songs he introduced harsh and far-fetched modulations. The music of Richard Strauss, who professes to be his disciple and has found inspiration in his *Also sprach Zarathustra* would have delighted him. According to W. J. Henderson, Strauss has achieved the uncanny feat of writing in two keys at once. Such an effort would have enlisted Nietzsche's keen interest.

All the same, his music was not a mere creature of the study and of rules, and we have evidence that he was frequently inspired to composition by bursts of strong emotion. On his way to the Franco-Prussian war, he wrote a patriotic song, words and music, on the train. He called it "Adieu! I Must Go!" and arranged it for men's chorus, a capella. It would be worth while to hear a German männerchor, with its high, beery tenors, and ponderous basses, sing this curious composition. Certainly no more grotesque music was ever put on paper by mortal man.

Much has been written by various commentators about the strange charm of Nietzsche's prose style. He was, indeed, a master of the German language, but this mastery was not inborn. Like Spencer he made a deliberate effort, early in life, to acquire ease and force in writing. His success was far greater than Spencer's. Toward the end — in *Der Antichrist*, for instance — he attained a degree of powerful and convincing utterance almost comparable to Huxley's. But his style never exhibited quite that wonderful air of clearness, of utter certainty, of inevitableness which makes the "Lay Sermons" so tremendously impressive. Nietzsche was ever nearer to Carlyle than to Addison. "His style," says a writer in the Athenaeum, "is a shower of sparks, which scatter, like fireworks, all over the sky."

"My sense for form," says Nietzsche himself, "awakened on my coming in contact with Sallust." Later on he studied the great French stylists, particularly La Rochefaucauld, and learned much from them. He became a master of the aphorism and the epigram, and this skill, very naturally, led him to descend, now and then, to mere violence and invective. He called his opponents all sorts of harsh names — liar, swindler, counterfeiter, ox, ass, snake and thief. Whatever he had to say, he hammered in with gigantic blows, and to the accompaniment of fearsome bellowing and grimacing. "Nervous, vivid and picturesques, full of fire and a splendid vitality," says one critic, "his style flashed and coruscated like a glowing flame, and had a sort of dithyrambic movement that at times recalls the swing of the Pindaric odes." Naturally, this very abandon made his poetry formless and grotesque. He scorned metres and rhymes and raged on in sheer savagery. Reading his verses one is forced irresistibly into the thought that they should be printed in varied fonts of type and in a dozen brilliant inks.

Nietzsche never married, and so far as it is recorded though he often talked of facing the sacrificial altar he never fell in love. His sister tells us that, in his early manhood, Schopenhauer's famous — not to say notorious essay "On

Women" — greatly influenced him, and that he was too good a European to have much admiration of the German hausfrau, but she denies, with great vigor, that he was the frauenfeind (woman-hater) his acquaintances thought him to be. She proves, by citing chapter and verse, that he frequently considered the advisability of marriage, but her own evidence shows that he invariably decided against it, and that his scarcely-phosphorescent passion, whenever it broke forth, commonly illumined some impossible charmer. Nietzsche, during his wanderings, was much petted by women, and because his philosophy bore the reputation of being blasphemous and indecent he was quite a hero in the pump-rooms and on the piazzas of many watering places, but nearly all of the fair worshippers he singled out of the passing throng were either safely married or infinitely antique. "For me to marry," he soliloquized with grim humor in 1887, "would probably be sheer asininity."

There are sentimental critics who hold that Nietzsche's utter lack of geniality was due to his lack of a wife. A good woman — alike beautiful and sensible — would have rescued him, they say, from his gloomy fancies. He would have expanded and mellowed in the sunshine of her smiles, and children would have civilized him. The defect in this theory lies in the fact that philosophers do not seem to flourish amid scenes of connubial joy. High thinking, it would appear, presupposes boarding house fare and hall bedrooms. Spinoza, munching his solitary herring up his desolate backstairs, makes a picture — that pains us, perhaps, but it must be admitted that it also satisfies our sense of eternal fitness. A married Spinoza, with two sons at college, another managing the family lens business, a daughter busy with her trousseau and a wife growing querulous and fat — the vision, alas, is preposterous, outrageous and impossible! We must think of philosophers as beings alone but not lonesome. A married Schopenhauer or Kant or Nietzsche would be unthinkable.

That a venture into matrimony might have somewhat modified Nietzsche's view of womankind is not at all improbable, but that this change would have been in the direction of greater accuracy does not follow. He would have been either a ridiculously henpecked slave or a violent domestic tyrant. As a bachelor he was comparatively well-to-do, but with a wife and children his thousand a year would have meant genteel beggary. His sister had her own income and her own affairs. When he needed her, she was ever at his side, but when his working fits were upon him — when he felt efficient and self-sufficient — she discreetly disappeared. A wife's constant presence, day in and day out, would have irritated him beyond measure or reduced him to a state of compliance and sloth. Nietzsche himself sought to show, in more than one place, that a man whose whole existence was colored by one woman would inevitably acquire some trace of her feminine outlook, and so lose his own sure vision. The ideal state for a philosopher, indeed, is celibacy tempered by polygamy. He must study women, but he must be free, when he pleases, to close his notebook and go away and digest its contents with an open mind.

Toward the end of his life, when increasing illness made him helpless, Nietzsche's faithful sister took the place of wife and mother in his clouding world. She made a home for him and she sat by and watched him. They talked for hours — Nietzsche propped up with pillows, his old ruddiness faded into a deathly white, and his Niagara of a moustache showing dark against his pallid skin. They talked of Naumburg and the days of long ago and the fiery prophet of the superman became simple Brother Fritz. We are apt to forget that a great man is thus not only great, but also a man: that a philosopher, in a lifetime, spends less hours pondering the destiny of the race than he gives over to wondering if it will rain tomorrow and to meditating upon the toughness of steaks, the dustiness of roads, the stuffiness of railway coaches and the brigandage of gas companies.

Nietzsche's sister was the only human being that ever saw him intimately, as a wife might have seen him. Her affection for him was perfect and her influence over him perfect, too. Love and understanding, faith and gentleness — these are the things which make women the angels of joyous illusion. Lisbeth, the calm and trusting, had all in boundless richness. There was, indeed, something noble, and almost holy in the eagerness with which she sought her brother's comfort and peace of mind during his days of stress and storm, and magnified his virtues after he was gone.

Dionysius vs. Apollo

In one of the preceding chapters Nietzsche's theory of Greek tragedy was given in outline and its dependence upon the data of Schopenhauer's philosophy was indicated. It is now in order to examine this theory a bit more closely and to trace out its origin and development with greater dwelling upon detail. In itself it is of interest only as a step forward in the art of literary criticism, but in its influence upon Nietzsche's ultimate inquiries it has colored, to a measurable extent, the whole stream of modern thought.

Schopenhauer laid down, as his cardinal principle, it will be recalled, the idea that, in all the complex whirlpool of phenomena we call human life, the mere will to survive is at the bottom of everything, and that intelligence, despite its seeming kingship in civilization, is nothing more, after all, than a secondary manifestation of this primary will. In certain purely artificial situations, it may seem to us that reason stands alone (as when, for example, we essay to solve an abstract problem in mathematics), but in everything growing out of our relations as human beings, one to the other, the old instinct of race- and self-preservation is plainly discernible. All of our acts, when they are not based obviously and directly upon our yearning to eat and take our ease and beget our kind, are founded upon our desire to appear superior, in some way or other, to our fellow men about us, and this desire for superiority, reduced to its lowest terms, is merely a desire to face the struggle for existence — to eat and beget — under more favorable conditions than those the world accords the average man. "Happiness is the feeling that power increases — that resistance is being overcome."

Nietzsche went to Basel firmly convinced that these fundamental ideas of Schopenhauer were profoundly true, though he soon essayed to make an amendment to them. This amendment consisted in changing Schopenhauer's "will to live" into "will to power." That which does not live, he argued, cannot exercise a will to live, and when a thing is already in existence, how can it strive after existence? Nietzsche voiced the argument many times, but its vacuity is apparent upon brief inspection. He started out, in fact, with an incredibly clumsy misinterpretation of Schopenhauer's phrase. The philosopher of pessimism, when he said "will to live" obviously meant, not will to begin living, but will to continue living. Now, this will to continue living, if we are to accept words at their usual meaning, is plainly identical, in every respect, with Nietzsche's will to power. Therefore, Nietzsche's amendment was nothing more than the coinage of a new phrase to express an old idea. The unity of the two philosophers and the identity of the two phrases are proved a thousand times by Nietzsche's own discourses. Like Schopenhauer he believed that all human ideas were the direct products of the unconscious and unceasing effort of all living creatures to remain alive. Like Schopenhauer he believed that abstract ideas, in man, arose out of concrete ideas, and that the latter arose out of experience, which, in turn, was nothing more or less than an ordered remembrance of the results following an endless series of endeavors to meet the conditions of existence and so survive. Like Schopenhauer, he believed that the criminal laws, the poetry, the cookery and the religion of a race were alike expressions of this unconscious groping for the line of least resistance.

As a philologist, Nietzsche's interest, very naturally, was fixed upon the literature of Greece and Rome, and so it was but natural that his first tests of Schopenhauer's doctrines should be made in that field. Some time before this, he had asked himself (as many another man had asked before him) why it was that the ancient Greeks, who were an efficient and vigorous people, living in a green and sunny land, should so delight in gloomy tragedies. One would fancy that a Greek, when he set out to spend a pleasant afternoon, would seek entertainment that was frivolous and gay. But instead, he often preferred to see one of the plays of Thespis, Æschylus, Phrynichus or Pratinus, in which the heroes fought hopeless battles with fate and died miserably, in wretchedness and despair. Nietzsche concluded that the Greeks had this liking for tragedy because it seemed to them to set forth, truthfully and understandably, the conditions of life as they found it: that it appeared to them as a reasonable and accurate picture of human existence. The gods ordered the drama on the real stage of the world; the dramatist ordered the drama on the mimic stage of the theatre — and the latter attained credibility and verisimilitude in proportion as it approached an exact imitation or reproduction of the former. Nietzsche saw that this quality of realism was the essence of all stage plays. "Only insofar as the dramatist," he said, "coalesces with the primordial dramatist of the world, does he reach the true function of his craft." "Man posits himself as the standard... A race cannot do otherwise than thus acquiesce in itself." In other words, man is interested in nothing whatever that has no bearing upon his own fate: he himself is his own hero. Thus the ancient Greeks were fond of tragedy because it reflected their life in miniature. In the mighty warriors who stalked the boards and defied the gods each Greek recognized himself. In the conflicts on the stage he saw replicas of that titanic conflict which seemed to him to be the eternal essence of human existence.

But why did the Greeks regard life as a conflict? In seeking an answer to this Nietzsche studied a growth of their civilization and of their race ideas. These race ideas, as among all other peoples, were visualized and crystallized in the qualities, virtues and opinions attributed to the racial gods. Therefore, Nietzsche undertook an inquiry into the nature of the gods set up by the Greeks, and particularly into the nature of the two gods who controlled the general scheme of Greek life, and, in consequence, of Greek art — for art, as we have seen, is nothing more or less than a race's view or opinion of itself, i.e. an expression of the things it sees and the conclusions it draws when it observes and considers itself. These gods were Apollo and Dionysus.

Apollo, according to the Greeks, was the inventor of music, poems and oratory, and as such, became the god of all art. Under his beneficent sway the Greeks became a race of artists and acquired all the refinement and culture that this implies. But the art that he taught them was essentially contemplative and subjective. It depicted, not so much things as they were, as things as they had been. Thus it became a mere record, and as such, exhibited repose as its chief quality. Whether it were expressed as sculpture, architecture, painting or epic poetry, this element of repose, or of action translated into repose, was uppermost. A painting of a man running, no matter how vividly it suggests the vitality and activity of the runner, is itself a thing inert and lifeless. Architecture, no matter how much its curves suggest motion and its hard lines the strength which may be translated into energy, is itself a thing immovable. Poetry, so long as it takes the form of the epic and is thus merely a chronicle of past actions, is as lifeless, at bottom, as a tax list.

The Greeks, during Apollo's reign as god of art, thus turned art into a mere inert fossil or record — a record either of human life itself or of the emotions which the vicissitudes of life arouse in the spectator. This notion of art was reflected in their whole civilization. They became singers of songs and weavers of metaphysical webs rather than doers of deeds, and the man who could carve a flower was more honored among them than the man who could grow one. In brief, they began to degenerate and go stale. Great men and great ideas grew few. They were on the downward road.

What they needed, of course, was the shock of contact with some barbarous, primitive people — an infusion of good red blood from some race that was still fighting for its daily bread and had had no time to grow contemplative and retrospective and fat. This infusion of red blood came in good time, but instead of coming from without (as it did years afterward in Rome, when the Goths swooped down from the North), it came from within. That is to say, there was no actual invasion of barbarian hordes, but merely an auto-reversion to simpler and more primitive ideas, which fanned the dormant energy of the Greeks into flame and so allowed them to accomplish their own salvation. This impulse came in the form of a sudden craze for a new god — Bacchus Dionysus.

Bacchus was a rude, boisterous fellow and the very antithesis of the quiet, contemplative Apollo. We remember him today merely as the god of wine, but in his time he stood, not only for drinking and carousing, but also for a whole system of art and a whole notion of civilization. Apollo represented the life meditative; Bacchus Dionysus represented the life strenuous. The one favored those forms of art by which human existence is halted and embalmed in some lifeless medium — sculpture, architecture, painting or epic poetry. The other was the god of life in process of actual being, and so stood for those forms of art which are not mere records or reflections of past existence, but brief snatches of present existence itself — dancing, singing, music and the drama.

It will be seen that this barbarous invasion of the new god and his minions made a profound change in the whole of Greek culture. Instead of devoting their time to writing epics, praising the laws, splitting philosophical hairs and hewing dead marble, the Greeks began to question all things made and ordained and to indulge in riotous and gorgeous orgies, in which thousands of maidens danced and hundreds of poets chanted songs of love and war, and musicians vied with cooks and vintners to make a grand delirium of joy. The result was that the entire outlook of the Greeks, upon history, upon morality and upon human life, was changed. Once a people of lofty introspection and elegant repose, they became a race of violent activity and strong emotions. They began to devote themselves, not to writing down the praises of existence as they had found it, but to the task of improving life and of widening the scope of present and future human activity and the bounds of possible human happiness.

But in time there came a reaction and Apollo once more triumphed. He reigned for awhile, unsteadily and uncertainly, and then, again, the pendulum swung to the other side. Thus the Greeks swayed from one god to the other.

During Apollo's periods of ascendancy they were contemplative and imaginative, and man, to them, seemed to reach his loftiest heights when he was most the historian. But when Dionysus was their best-beloved, they bubbled over with the joy of life, and man seemed, not an historian, but a maker of history — not an artist, but a work of art. In the end, they verged toward a safe middle ground and began to weigh, with cool and calm, the ideas represented by the two gods. When they had done so, they came to the conclusion that it was not well to give themselves unreservedly to either. To attain the highest happiness, they decided, humanity required a dash of both. There was need in the world for dionysians, to give vitality an outlet and life a purpose, and there was need, too, for apollonians, to build life's monuments and read its lessons. They found that true civilization meant a constant conflict between the two — between the dreamer and the man of action, between the artist who builds temples and the soldier who burns them down, between the priest and policeman who insist upon the permanence of laws and customs as they are and the criminal and reformer and conqueror who insist that they be changed.

When they had learned this lesson, the Greeks began to soar to heights of culture and civilization that, in the past, had been utterly beyond them, and so long as they maintained the balance between Apollo and Dionysus they continued to advance. But now and again, one god or the other grew stronger, and then there was a halt. When Apollo had the upper hand, Greece became too contemplative and too placid. When Dionysus was the victor, Greece became wild and thoughtless and careless of the desires of others, and so turned a bit toward barbarism. This seesawing continued for a long while, but Apollo was the final victor — if victor he may be called. In the eternal struggle for existence Greece became a mere looker-on. Her highest honors went to Socrates, a man who tried to reduce all life to syllogisms. Her favorite sons were rhetoricians, dialecticians and philosophical cobweb-spinners. She placed ideas above deeds. And in the end, as all students of history know, the state that once ruled the world descended to senility and decay, and dionysians from without overran it, and it perished in anarchy and carnage. But with this we have nothing to do.

Nietzsche noticed that tragedy was most popular in Greece during the best days of the country's culture, when Apollo and Dionysus were properly balanced, one against the other. This ideal balancing between the two gods was the result, he concluded, not of conscious, but of unconscious impulses. That is to say, the Greeks did not call parliaments and discuss the matter, as they might have discussed a question of taxes, but acted entirely in obedience to their racial instinct. This instinct — this will to live or desire for power — led them to feel, without putting it into words, or even, for a while, into definite thoughts, that they were happiest and safest and most vigorous, and so best able to preserve their national existence, when they kept to the golden mean. They didn't reason it out; they merely felt it.

But as Schopenhauer shows us, instinct, long exercised, means experience, and the memory of experience, in the end, crystallizes into what we call intelligence or reason. Thus the unconscious Greek feeling that the golden mean best served the race, finally took the form of an idea: i.e. that human life was an endless conflict between two forces, or impulses. These, as the Greeks saw them, were the dionysian impulse to destroy, to burn the candle, to "use up" life; and the apollonian impulse to preserve. Seeing life in this light, it was but natural that the Greeks should try to exhibit it in the same light on their stage. And so their tragedies were invariably founded upon some deadly and unending conflict — usually between a human hero and the gods. In a word, they made their stage plays set forth life as they saw it and found it, for, like all other human beings, at all times and everywhere, they were more interested in life as they found it than in anything else on the earth below or in the vasty void above.

When Nietzsche had worked out this theory of Greek tragedy and of Greek life, he set out, at once, to apply it to modern civilization, to see if it could explain certain ideas of the present as satisfactorily as it had explained one great idea of the past. He found that it could: that men were still torn between the apollonian impulse to conform and moralize and the dionysian impulse to exploit and explore. He found that all mankind might be divided into two classes: the apollonians who stood for permanence and the dionysians who stood for change. It was the aim of the former to live in strict obedience to certain invariable rules, which found expression as religion, law and morality. It was the aim of the latter to live under the most favorable conditions possible: to adapt themselves to changing circumstances, and to avoid the snares of artificial, permanent rules.

Nietzsche believed that an ideal human society would be one in which these two classes of men were evenly balanced — in which a vast, inert, religious, moral slave class stood beneath a small, alert, iconoclastic, immoral, progressive master class. He held that this master class — this aristocracy of efficiency — should regard the slave class as all men now regard the tribe of domestic beasts as an order of servitors to be exploited and turned to account. The aristocracy of Europe, though it sought to do this with respect to the workers of Europe, seemed to him to fail miserably, because it was itself lacking in true efficiency. Instead of practising a magnificent opportunism and so adapting itself to changing conditions, it stood for formalism and permanence. Its fetish was property in land and the worship of this fetish had got it into such a rut that it was becoming less and less fitted to survive, and was, indeed, fast sinking into helpless parasitism. Its whole color and complexion were essentially apollonic.

Therefore Nietzsche preached the gospel of Dionysus, that a new aristocracy of efficiency might take the place of this old aristocracy of memories and inherited glories. He believed that it was only in this way that mankind could hope to forge ahead. He believed that there was need in the world for a class freed from the handicap of law and morality, a class acutely adaptable and immoral; a class bent on achieving, not the equality of all men, but the production, at the top, of the superman.

The Origin of Morality

It may be urged with some reason, by those who have read the preceding chapter carefully, that the Nietzschean argument, so far, has served only to bring us face to face with a serious contradiction. We have been asked to believe that all human impulses are merely expressions of the primary instinct to preserve life by meeting the changing conditions of existence, and in the same breath we have been asked to believe, too, that the apollonian idea — which, like all other ideas, must necessarily be a result of this instinct — destroys adaptability and so tends to make life extra hazardous and difficult and progress impossible. Here we have our contradiction: the will to live is achieving, not life, but death. How are we to explain it away? How are we to account for the fact that the apollonian idea at the bottom of Christian morality, for example, despite its origin in the will to live, has an obvious tendency to combat free progress? How are we to account for the fact that the church, which is based upon this Christian morality, is, always has been and ever will be a bitter and implacable foe of good health, intellectual freedom, self-defense and every other essential factor of efficiency?

Nietzsche answers this by pointing out that an idea, while undoubtedly an effect or expression of the primary life instinct, is by no means identical with it. The latter manifests itself in widely different acts as conditions change: it is necessarily opportunistic and variable. The former, on the contrary, has a tendency to survive unchanged, even after its truth is transformed into falsity. That is to say, an idea which arises from a true and healthy instinct may survive long after this instinct itself, in consequence of the changing conditions of existence, has disappeared and given place to an instinct diametrically opposite. This survival of ideas we call morality. By its operation the human race is frequently saddled with the notions of generations long dead and forgotten. Thus we modern Christians still subscribe to the apollonian morality of the ancient Jews — our moral forebears — despite the fact that their ideas were evolved under conditions vastly different from those which confront us today. Thus the expressions of the life instinct, by obtaining an artificial and unnatural permanence, turn upon the instinct itself and defeat its beneficent purpose. Thus our contradiction is explained.

To make this rather complicated reasoning more clear it is necessary to follow Nietzsche through the devious twists and windings of his exhaustive inquiry into the origin of moral codes. In making this inquiry he tried to rid himself of all considerations of authority and reverence, just as a surgeon, in performing a difficult and painful operation, tries to rid himself of all sympathy and emotion. Adopting this plan, he found that a code of morals was nothing more than a system of customs; laws and ideas which had its origin in the instinctive desire of some definite race to live under conditions which best subserved its own welfare. The morality of the Egyptians, he found, was one thing, and the morality of the Goths was another. The reason for the difference lay in the fact that the environment of the Egyptians — the climate of their land, the nature of their food supply and the characteristics of the peoples surrounding them — differed from the environment of the Goths. The morality of each race was, in brief, its consensus of instinct, and once having formulated it and found it good, each sought to give it force and permanence. This was accomplished by putting it into the mouths of the gods. What was once a mere expression of instinct thus became the mandate of a divine law-giver. What was once a mere attempt to meet imminent — and usually temporary — conditions of existence, thus became a code of rules to be obeyed forever, no matter how much these conditions of existence might change. Wherefore, Nietzsche concluded that the chief characteristic of a moral system was its tendency to perpetuate itself unchanged, and to destroy all who questioned it or denied it.

Nietzsche saw that practically all members of a given race, including the great majority of those who violated these rules, were influenced into believing them — or at least into professing to believe them — utterly and unchangeably correct, and that it was the main function of all religions to enforce and support them by making them appear as laws laid down, at the beginning of the world, by the lord of the universe himself, or at some later period, by his son, messiah or spokesman. "Morality," he said, "not only commands innumerable terrible means for preventing critical hands being laid upon her: her security depends still more upon a sort of enchantment at which she is phenomenally skilled. That is to say, she knows how to enrapture. She appeals to the emotions; her glance paralyzes the reason and the will.... Ever since there has been talking and persuading on earth, she has been the supreme mistress of seduction." Thus "a double wall is put up against the continued testing, selection and criticism of values. On one hand is revelation, and on the other, veneration and tradition. The authority of the law is based upon two assumptions — first, that God gave it, and secondly, that the wise men of the past obeyed it." Nietzsche came to the conclusion that this universal tendency to submit to moral codes — this unreasonable, emotional faith in the invariable truths of moral regulations — was a curse to the human race and the chief cause of its degeneration, inefficiency and unhappiness. And then he threw down the gauntlet by denying that an ever-present deity had anything to do with framing such codes and by endeavoring to prove that, far from being eternally true, they commonly became false with the passing of the years. Starting out as expressions of the primary life-instinct's effort to adapt some individual or race to certain given conditions of existence, they took no account of the fact that these conditions were constantly changing, and that the thing which was advantageous at one time and to one race was frequently injurious at some other time and to another race.

This reduction of all morality to mere expressions of expedience engaged the philosopher during what he calls his "tunneling" period. To exhibit his precise method of "tunneling" let us examine, for example, a moral idea which is found in the code of every civilized country. This is the notion that there is something inherently and fundamentally wrong in the act of taking human life. We have good reason to believe that murder was as much a crime 5,000 years ago as it is today and that it took rank at the head of all conceivable outrages against humankind at the very dawn of civilization. And why? Simply because the man who took his neighbor's life made the life of everyone else in his neighborhood precarious and uncomfortable. It was plain that what he had done once he could do again, and so the peace and security of the whole district were broken.

Now, it is apparent that the average human being desires peace and security beyond all things, because it is only when he has them that he may satisfy his will to live — by procuring food and shelter for himself and by becoming the father of children. He is ill-fitted to fight for his existence; the mere business of living and begetting his kind consumes all of his energies: "the world, as a world," as Horace Greeley said, "barely makes a living." Therefore, it came to be recognized at the very beginning of civilization, that the man who killed other men was a foe to those conditions which the average man had to seek in order to exist — to peace and order and quiet and security. Out of this grew the doctrine that it was immoral to commit murder, and as soon as mankind became imaginative enough to invent personal gods, this doctrine was put into their mouths and so attained the force and authority of divine wisdom. In some such manner, said Nietzsche, the majority of our present moral concepts were evolved. At the start they were mere echoes of a protest against actions which made existence difficult and so outraged and opposed the will to live.

As a rule, said Nietzsche, such familiar protests as that against murder, which laid down the maxim that the community had rights superior to those of the individual, were voiced by the weak, who found it difficult to protect themselves, as individuals, against the strong. One strong man, perhaps, was more than a match, in the struggle for existence, for ten weak men and so the latter were at a disadvantage. But fortunately for them they could overcome this by combination, for they were always in an overwhelming majority, numerically, and in consequence they were stronger, taken together, than the phalanx of the strong. Thus it gradually became possible for them to enforce the rules that they laid down for their own protection — which rules always operated against the wishes — and, as an obvious corollary, against the best interests of — the strong. When the time arrived for fashioning religious systems, these rules were credited to the gods, and again the weak triumphed. Thus the desire of the weak among the world's early races of men, to protect their crops and wives against the forays of the strong, by general laws and divine decrees, instead of by each man fighting, for his own, has come down to us in the form of the Christian commandments: "Thou shalt not steal.... Thou shalt not covet thy neighbor's house.... Thou shalt not covet thy neighbor's wife, nor his manservant, nor his maidservant, nor his ox, nor his ass, nor anything that is thy neighbor's."

Nietzsche shows that the device of putting man-made rules of morality into the mouths of the gods — a device practiced by every nation in history — has vastly increased the respectability and force of all moral ideas. This is well exhibited by the fact that, even today and among thinking men, offenses which happen to be included in the scope of the Ten Commandments, either actually or by interpretation, are regarded with a horror which seldom, if ever, attaches to offenses obviously defined and delimited by merely human agencies. Thus, theft is everywhere looked upon as dishonorable, but cheating at elections, which is fully as dangerous to the body politic, is commonly pardoned by public opinion as a normal consequence of enthusiasm, and in some quarters is even regarded as an evidence of courage, not to say of a high and noble sense of gratitude and honor.

Nietzsche does not deny that human beings have a right to construct moral codes for themselves, and neither does he deny that they are justified, from their immediate standpoint, at least, in giving these codes the authority and force of divine commands. But he points out that this procedure is bound to cause trouble in the long run, for the reason that divine commands are fixed and invariable, and do not change as fast as the instincts and needs of the race. Suppose, for instance, that all acts of Parliament and Congress were declared to be the will of God, and that, as a natural consequence, the power to repeal or modify them were abandoned. It is apparent that the world would outgrow them as fast as it does today, but it is also apparent that the notion that they were infallible would paralyze and block all efforts, by atheistic reformers, to overturn or amend them. As a result, the British and American people would be compelled to live in obedience to rules which, on their very face, would often seem illogical and absurd.

Yet the same thing happens to notions of morality. They are devised, at the start, as measures of expediency, and then given divine sanction in order to lend them authority. In the course of time, perhaps, the race outgrows them, but none the less, they continue in force at least so long as the old gods are worshipped. Thus human laws become divine — and inhuman. Thus morality itself becomes immoral. Thus the old instinct whereby society differentiates between good things and bad, grows muddled and uncertain, and the fundamental purpose of morality — that of producing a workable scheme of living — is defeated. Thereafter it is next to impossible to distinguish between the laws that are still useful and those that have outlived their usefulness, and the man who makes the attempt — the philosopher who endeavors to show humanity how it is condemning as bad a thing that, in itself, is now good, or exalting as good a thing that, for all its former goodness, is now bad — this man is damned as a heretic and anarchist, and according as fortune serves him, is burned at the stake or merely read out of the human race.

Nietzsche found that all existing moral ideas might be divided into two broad classes, corresponding to the two broad varieties of human beings — the masters and the slaves. Every man is either a master or a slave, and the same is true of every race. Either it rules some other race or it is itself ruled by some other race. It is impossible to think of a man or of a people as being utterly isolated, and even were this last possible, it is obvious that the community would be divided into those who ruled and those who obeyed. The masters are strong and are capable of doing as they please; the slaves are weak and must obtain whatever rights they crave by deceiving, cajoling or collectively intimidating their masters. Now, since all moral codes, as we have seen, are merely collections of the rules laid down by some definite group of human beings for their comfort and protection, it is evident that the morality of the master class has for its main object the preservation of the authority and kingship of that class, while the morality of the slave class seeks to make slavery as bearable as possible and to exalt and dignify those things in which the slave can hope to become the apparent equal or superior of his master.

The civilization which existed in Europe before the dawn of Christianity was a culture based upon master-morality, and so we find that the theologians and moralists of those days esteemed a certain action as right only when it plainly subserved the best interests of strong, resourceful men. The ideal man of that time was not a meek and lowly sufferer, bearing his cross uncomplainingly, but an alert, proud and combative being who knew his rights and dared maintain them. In consequence we find that in many ancient languages, the words "good" and "aristocratic" were synonymous. Whatever served to make a man a nobleman — cunning, wealth, physical strength, eagerness to resent and punish injuries — was considered virtuous, praiseworthy and moral, and on the other hand, whatever tended to make a man sink to the level of the great masses — humility, lack of ambition, modest desires, lavish liberality and a spirit of ready forgiveness — was regarded as immoral and wrong.

"Among these master races," says Nietzsche, "the antithesis 'good and bad' signified practically the same as 'noble and contemptible!' The despised ones were the cowards, the timid, the insignificant, the self-abasing — the dog-species of men who allowed themselves to be misused — the flatterers and, above all, the liars. It is a fundamental belief of all true aristocrats that the common people are deceitful. 'We true ones,' the ancient Greek nobles called themselves.

"It is obvious that the designations of moral worth were at first applied to individual men, and not to actions or ideas in the abstract. The master type of man regards himself as a sufficient judge of worth. He does not seek approval: his own feelings determine his conduct. 'What is injurious to me,' he reasons, 'is injurious in itself.' This type of man honors whatever qualities he recognizes in himself: his morality is self-glorification. He has a feeling of plentitude and power and the happiness of high tension. He helps the unfortunate, perhaps, but it is not out of sympathy. The impulse, when it comes at all, rises out of his superabundance of power — his thirst to function. He honors his own power, and he knows how to keep it in hand. He joyfully exercises strictness and severity over himself and he reverences all that is strict and severe. 'Wotan has put a hard heart in my breast,' says an old Scandinavian saga. There could be no better expression of the spirit of a proud viking.

"The morality of the master class is irritating to the taste of the present day because of its fundamental principle that a man has obligations only to his equals; that he may act to all of lower rank and to all that are foreign as he pleases.... The man of the master class has a capacity for prolonged gratitude and prolonged revenge, but it is only among his equals. He has, too, great resourcefulness in retaliation; great capacity for friendship, and a strong need for enemies, that there may be an outlet for his envy, quarrelsomeness and arrogance, and that by spending these passions in this manner, he may be gentle towards his friends."

By this ancient herrenmoral, or master-morality, Napoleon Bonaparte would have been esteemed a god and the Man of Sorrows an enemy to society. It was the ethical scheme, indeed, of peoples who were sure of themselves and who had no need to make terms with rivals or to seek the good will or forbearance of anyone. In its light, such things as mercy and charity seemed pernicious and immoral, because they meant a transfer of power from strong men, whose proper business it was to grow stronger and stronger, to weak men, whose proper business it was to serve the strong. In a word, this master-morality was the morality of peoples who knew, by experience, that it was pleasant to rule and be strong. They knew that the nobleman was to be envied and the slave to be despised, and so they came to believe that everything which helped to make a man noble was good and everything which helped to make him a slave was evil. The idea of nobility and the idea of good were expressed by the same word, and this verbal identity survives in the English language today, despite the fact that our present system of morality, as we shall see, differs vastly from that of the ancient master races.

In opposition to this master-morality of the strong, healthy nations there was the sklavmoral, or slave-morality, of the weak nations. The Jews of the four or five centuries preceding the birth of Christ belonged to the latter class. Compared to the races around them, they were weak and helpless. It was out of the question for them to conquer the Greeks or Romans and it was equally impossible for them to force their laws, their customs or their religion upon their neighbors on other sides. They were, indeed, in the position of an army surrounded by a horde of irresistible enemies. The general of such an army, with the instinct of self-preservation strong within him, does not attempt to cut his way out. Instead he tries to make the best terms he can, and if the leader of the enemy insists upon making him and his vanquished force prisoners, he endeavors to obtain concessions which will make this imprisonment as bearable as possible. The strong man's object is to take as much as he can from his victim; the weak man's is to save as much as he can from his conqueror.

The fruit of this yearning of weak nations to preserve as much of their national unity as possible is the thing Nietzsche calls slave-morality. Its first and foremost purpose is to discourage, and if possible, blot out, all those traits and actions which are apt to excite the ire, the envy, or the cupidity of the menacing enemies round about. Revenge, pride and ambition are condemned as evils. Humility, forgiveness, contentment and resignation are esteemed virtues. The moral man is the man who has lost all desire to triumph and exult over his fellow-men — the man of mercy, of charity, of self-sacrifice.

The impotence which does not retaliate for injuries, says Nietzsche, "is falsified into 'goodness;' timorous abjectness becomes 'humility;' subjection to those one hates is called 'obedience,' and the one who desires and commands this impotence, abjectness and subjection is called God. The inoffensiveness of the weak, their cowardice (of which they have ample store); their standing at the door, their unavoidable time-serving and waiting — all these things get good names. The inability to get revenge is translated into an unwillingness to get revenge, and becomes forgiveness, a virtue.

"They are wretched — these mutterers and forgers — but they say that their wretchedness is of God's choosing and even call it a distinction that he confers upon them. The dogs which are liked best, they say, are beaten most. Their wretchedness is a test, a preparation, a schooling — something which will be paid for, one day, in happiness. They call that 'bliss.'"

By the laws of this slave-morality the immoral man is him who seeks power and eminence and riches — the millionaire, the robber, the fighter, the schemer. The act of acquiring property by conquest — which is looked upon as a matter of course by master-morality — becomes a crime and is called theft. The act of mating in obedience to natural impulses, without considering the desire of others, becomes adultery; the quite natural act of destroying one's enemies becomes murder.

Beyond Good and Evil

Despite the divine authority which gives permanence to all moral codes, this permanence is constantly opposed by the changing conditions of existence, and very often the opposition is successful. The slave-morality of the ancient Jews has come down to us, with its outlines little changed, as ideal Christianity, but such tenacious persistence of a moral scheme is comparatively rare. As a general rule, in truth, races change their gods very much oftener than we have changed ours, and have less faith than we in the independence of intelligence. In consequence they constantly revamp and modify their moral concepts. The same process of evolution affects even our own code, despite the extraordinary tendency to permanence just noted. Our scheme of things, in its fundamentals, has persisted for 2,500 years, but in matters of detail it is constantly in a state of flux. We still call ourselves Christians, but we have evolved many moral ideas that are not to be found in the scriptures and we have sometimes denied others that are plainly there. Indeed, as will be shown later on, the beatitudes would have wiped us from the face of the earth centuries ago had not our forefathers devised means of circumventing them without openly questioning them. Our progress has been made, not as a result of our moral code, but as a result of our success in dodging its inevitable blight.

All morality, in fact, is colored and modified by opportunism, even when its basic principles are held sacred and kept more or less intact. The thing that is a sin in one age becomes a virtue in the next. The ancient Persians, who were Zoroastrians, regarded murder and suicide, under any circumstances, as crimes. The modern Persians, who are Mohammedans, think that ferocity and foolhardiness are virtues. The ancient Japanese, to whom the state appeared more important than the man, threw themselves joyously upon the spears of the state's enemies. The modern Japanese, who are fledgling individualists, armor their ships with nickel steel and fight on land from behind bastions of earth and masonry. And in the same way the moral ideas that have grown out of Christianity, and even some of its important original doctrines, are being constantly modified and revised,

The Philosophy of Friedrich Nietzsche 61

despite the persistence of the fundamental notion of self-sacrifice at the bottom of them. In Dr. Andrew D. White's monumental treatise "On the Warfare of Science with Theology in Christendom" there are ten thousand proofs of it. Things that were crimes in the middle ages are quite respectable at present. Actions that are punishable by excommunication and ostracism in Catholic Spain today, are sufficient to make a man honorable in freethinking England. In France, where the church once stood above the king, it is now stripped of all rights not inherent in the most inconsequential social club. In [the German Empire] it [was] a penal offense to poke fun at the head of the state; in the United States it is looked upon by many as an evidence of independence and patriotism. "Many lands did I see," says Zarathustra, "and many peoples, and so I discovered the good and bad of many peoples.... Much that was regarded as good by one people was held in scorn and contempt by another. I found many things called bad here and adorned with purple honors there.... A catalogue of blessings is posted up for every people. Lo! it is the catalogue of their triumphs — the voice of their will to power!... Whatever enables them to rule and conquer and dazzle, to the dismay and envy of their neighbors, is regarded by them as the summit, the head, the standard of all things.... Verily, men have made for themselves all their good and bad. Verily they did not find it so — it did not come to them as a voice from heaven.... It is only through valuing that there comes value."

To proceed from the concrete to the general, and to risk a repetition, it is evident that all morality, as Nietzsche pointed out, is nothing more than an expression of expediency. A thing is called wrong solely because a definite group of people, at some specific stage of their career, have found it injurious to them. The fact that they have discovered grounds for condemning it in some pronunciamento of their god signifies nothing, for the reason that the god of a people is never anything more than a reflection of their ideas for the time being. As Prof. Pfleiderer has shown, Jesus Christ was a product of his age, mentally and spiritually as well as physically. Had there been no Jewish theology before him, he could not have sought or obtained recognition as a messiah, and the doctrines that he expressed — had he ever expressed them at all — would have fallen upon unheeding and uncomprehending ears.

Therefore it is plain that the Ten Commandments are no more immortal and immutable, in the last analysis, than the acts of Parliament. They have lasted longer, it is true, and they will probably continue in force for many years, but this permanence is only relative. Fundamentally they are merely expressions of expedience, like the rules of some great game, and it is easily conceivable that there may arise upon the earth, at some future day, a race to whom they will appear injurious, unreasonable and utterly immoral. "The time may come, indeed, when we will prefer the Memorabilia of Socrates to the Bible."

Admitting this, we must admit the inevitable corollary that morality in the absolute sense has nothing to do with truth, and that it is, in fact, truth's exact antithesis. Absolute truth necessarily implies eternal truth. The statement that a man and a woman are unlike was true on the day the first man and woman walked the earth and it will be true so long as there are men and women. Such a statement approaches very near our ideal of an absolute truth. But the theory that humility is a virtue is not an absolute truth, for while it was undoubtedly true in ancient Judea, it was not true in ancient Greece and is debatable, to say the least, in modern Europe and America. The Western Catholic Church, despite its extraordinarily successful efforts at permanence, has given us innumerable proofs that laws, in the long run, always turn upon themselves. The popes were infallible when they held that the earth was flat and they were infallible when they decided that it was round — and so we reach a palpable absurdity. Therefore, we may lay it down as an axiom that morality, in itself, is the enemy of truth, and that, for at least half of the time, (by the mathematical doctrine of probabilities,) it is necessarily untrue.

If this is so, why should any man bother about moral rules and regulations? Why should any man conform to laws formulated by a people whose outlook on the universe probably differed diametrically from his own? Why should any man obey a regulation which is denounced, by his common-sense, as a hodge-podge of absurdities, and why should he model his whole life upon ideals invented to serve the temporary needs of a forgotten race of some past age? These questions Nietzsche asked himself. His conclusion was a complete rejection of all fixed codes of morality, and with them of all gods, messiahs, prophets, saints, popes, bishops, priests, and rulers.

The proper thing for a man to do, he decided, was to formulate his own morality as he progressed from lower to higher things. He should reject the old conceptions of good and evil and substitute for them the human valuations, good and bad. In a word, he should put behind him the morality invented by some dead race to make its own progress easy and pleasant, and credited to some man-made god to give it authority, and put in the place of this a workable personal morality based upon his own power of distinguishing between the things which benefit him and the things which injure him. He should (to make the idea clearer) judge a given action solely by its effect upon his own welfare; his own desire or will-to-live; and that of his children after him. All notions of sin and virtue should banished from his mind. He should weigh everything in the scales of individual expedience.

Such a frank wielding of a razor-edged sword in the struggle for existence is frowned upon by our Jewish slave-morality. We are taught to believe that the only true happiness lies in self-effacement; that it is wrong to profit by the misfortune or weakness of another. But against this Nietzsche brings the undeniable answer that all life, no matter how much we idealize it, is, at bottom, nothing more or less than exploitation. The gain of one man is inevitably the loss of some other man. That the emperor may die of a surfeit the peasant must die of starvation. Among human beings, as well as among the bacilli in the hanging drop and the lions in the jungle, there is ever in progress this ancient struggle for existence. It is waged decently, perhaps, but it is none the less savage and unmerciful, and the devil always takes the hindmost.

"Life," says Nietzsche, "is essentially the appropriation, the injury, the vanquishing of the unadapted and weak. Its object is to obtrude its own forms and insure its own unobstructed functioning. Even an organization whose individuals forbear in their dealings with one another (a healthy aristocracy, for example) must, if it would live and not die, act hostilely toward all other organizations. It must endeavor to gain ground, to obtain advantages, to acquire ascendancy. And this is not because it is immoral, but because it lives, and all life is will to power."

Nietzsche argues from this that it is absurd to put the stigma of evil upon the mere symptoms of the great struggle. "In itself," he says, "an act of injury, violation, exploitation or annihilation cannot be wrong, for life operates, essentially and fundamentally, by injuring, violating, exploiting and annihilating, and cannot even be conceived of out of this character. One must admit, indeed, that, from the highest biological standpoint, conditions under which the so-called rights of others are recognized must ever be regarded as exceptional conditions — that is to say, as partial restrictions of the instinctive power-seeking will-to-live of the individual, made to satisfy the more powerful will-to-live of the mass. Thus small units of power are sacrificed to create large units of power. To regard the rights of others as being inherent in them, and not as mere compromises for the benefit of the mass-unit, would be to enunciate a principle hostile to life itself."

Nietzsche holds that the rights of an individual may be divided into two classes: those things he is able to do despite the opposition of his fellow men, and those things he is enabled to do by the grace and permission of his fellow men. The second class of rights may be divided again into two groups: those granted through fear and foresight, and those granted as free gifts. But how do fear and foresight operate to make one man concede rights to another man? It is easy enough to discern two ways. In the first place, the grantor may fear the risks of a combat with the grantee, and so give him what he wants without a struggle. In the second place, the grantor, while confident of his ability to overcome the grantee, may forbear because he sees in the struggle a certain diminution of strength on both sides, and in consequence, an impaired capacity for joining forces in effective opposition to some hostile third power.

And now for the rights obtained under the second head — by bestowal and concession. "In this case," says Nietzsche, "one man or race has enough power, and more than enough, to be able to bestow some of it on another man or race." The king appoints one subject viceroy of a province, and so gives him almost regal power, and makes another cup-bearer and so gives him a perpetual right to bear the royal cup. When the power of the grantee, through his inefficiency, decreases, the grantor either restores it to him or takes it away from him altogether. When the power of the grantee, on the contrary, increases, the grantor, in alarm, commonly seeks to undermine it and encroach upon it. When the power of the grantee remains at a level for a considerable time, his rights become "vested" and he begins to believe that they are inherent in him — that they constitute a gift from the gods and are beyond the will and disposal of his fellow men. As Nietzsche points out, this last happens comparatively seldom. More often, the grantor himself begins to lose power and so comes into conflict with the grantee, and not infrequently they exchange places. "National rights," says Nietzsche, "demonstrate this fact by their constant lapse and regenesis."

Nietzsche believed that a realization of all this would greatly benefit the human race, by ridding it of some of its most costly delusions. He held that so long as it sought to make the struggle for existence a parlor game, with rules laid down by some blundering god — that so long as it regarded its ideas of morality, its aspirations and its hopes as notions implanted by the creator in the mind of Father Adam — that so long as it insisted upon calling things by fanciful names and upon frowning down all effort to reach the ultimate verities — that just so long its progress would be fitful and slow. It was morality that burned the books of the ancient sages, and morality that halted the free inquiry of the Golden Age and substituted for it the credulous imbecility of the Age of Faith. It was a fixed moral code and a fixed theology which robbed the human race of a thousand years by wasting them upon alchemy, heretic-burning, witchcraft and sacerdotalism.

Nietzsche called himself an immoralist. He believed that all progress depended upon the truth and that the truth could not prevail while men yet enmeshed themselves in a web of gratuitous and senseless laws fashioned by their own hands. He was fond of picturing the ideal immoralist as "a magnificent blond beast" — innocent of "virtue" and "sin" and knowing only "good" and 'bad." Instead of a god to guide him, with commandments and the fear of hell, this immoralist would have his own instincts and intelligence. Instead of doing a given thing because the church called it a virtue or the current moral code required it, he would do it because he knew that it would benefit him or his descendants after him. Instead of refraining from a given action because the church denounced it as a sin and the law as a crime, he would avoid it only if he were convinced that the action itself, or its consequences, might work him or his an injury.

Such a man, were he set down in the world today, would bear an outward resemblance, perhaps, to the most pious and virtuous of his fellow-citizens, but it is apparent that his life would have more of truth in it and less of hypocrisy and cant and pretense than theirs. He would obey the laws of the land frankly and solely because he was afraid of incurring their penalties, and for no other reason, and he would not try to delude his neighbors and himself into believing that he saw anything sacred in them. He would have no need of a god to teach him the difference between right and wrong and no need of priests to remind him of this god's teachings. He would look upon the woes and ills of life as inevitable and necessary results of life's conflict, and he would make no effort to read into them the wrath of a peevish and irrational deity at his own or his ancestors' sins. His mind would be absolutely free of thoughts of sin and hell, and in consequence, he would be vast happier than the majority of persons about him. All in all, he would be a powerful influence for truth in his community, and as such, would occupy himself with the most noble and sublime task possible to mere human beings: the overthrow of superstition and unreasoning faith, with their long train of fears, horrors, doubts, frauds, injustice and suffering.

Under an ideal government — which Herbert Spencer defines as a government in which the number of laws has reached an irreducible minimum — such a man would prosper a great deal more than the priest-ridden, creed-barnacled masses about him. In a state wherein communistic society, with its levelling usages and customs, had ceased to exist, and wherein each individual of the master class was permitted to live his life as much as possible in accordance with his own notions of good and bad, such a man would stand forth from the herd in proportion as his instincts were more nearly healthy and infallible than the instincts of the herd. Ideal anarchy, in brief, would insure the success of those men who were wisest mentally and strongest physically, and the race would make rapid progress.

It is evident that the communistic and socialistic forms of government at present in fashion in the world oppose such a consummation as often as they facilitate it. Civilization, as we know it, makes more paupers than millionaires, and more cripples than Sandows. Its most conspicuous products, the church and the king, stand unalterably opposed to all progress. Like the frog of the fable, which essayed to climb out of a well, it slips back quite as often as it goes ahead.

And for these reasons Nietzsche was an anarchist — in the true meaning of that much-bespattered word — just as Herbert Spencer and Arthur Schopenhauer were anarchists before him.

The Superman

No doubt the reader who has followed the argument in the preceding chapters will have happened, before now, upon the thought that Nietzsche's chain of reasoning, so far, still has a gap in it. We have seen how he started by investigating Greek art in the light of the Schopenhauerean philosophy, how this led him to look into morality, how he revealed the origin of morality in transitory manifestations of the will to power, and how he came to the conclusion that it was best for a man to reject all ready-made moral ideas and to so order his life that his every action would be undertaken with some notion of making it subserve his own welfare or that of his children or children's children. But a gap remains and it may be expressed in the question: How is a man to define and determine his own welfare and that of the race after him?

Here, indeed, our dionysian immoralist is confronted by a very serious problem, and Nietzsche himself well understood its seriousness. Unless we have in mind some definite ideal of happiness and some definite goal of progress we had better sing the doxology and dismiss our congregation. Christianity has such an ideal and such a goal. The one is a Christ-like life on earth and the other is a place at the right hand of Jehovah in the hereafter. Mohammedanism, a tinsel form of Christianity, paints pictures of the same sort. Buddhism holds out the tempting bait of a race set free from the thrall of earthly desires, with an eternity of blissful nothingness. The other oriental faiths lead in the same direction and Schopenhauer, in his philosophy, laid down the doctrine that humanity would attain perfect happiness only when it had overcome its instinct of self-preservation — that is to say, when it had ceased to desire to live. Even Christian Science — that most grotesque child of credulous faith and incredible denial — offers us the double ideal of a mortal life entirely free from mortal pain and a harp in the heavenly band for all eternity.

What had Nietzsche to offer in place of these things? By what standard was his immoralist to separate the good — or beneficial — things of the world from the bad — or damaging — things? And what was the goal that the philosopher had in mind for his immoralist? The answer to the first question is to be found in Nietzsche's definition of the terms "good" and "bad." "All that elevates the sense of power, the will to power, and power itself" — this is how he defined "good." "All that proceeds from weakness" — this is how he defined "bad." Happiness, he held, is "the feeling that power increases — that resistance is being overcome." "I preach not contentedness," he said, "but more power; not peace, but war; not virtue, but efficiency. The weak and defective must go to the wall: that is the first principle of the dionysian charity. And we must help them to go."

To put it more simply, Nietzsche offers the gospel of prudent and intelligent selfishness, of absolute and utter individualism. "One must learn," sang Zarathustra, "how to love oneself, with a whole and hearty love, that one may find life with oneself endurable, and not go gadding about. This gadding about is familiar: it is called 'loving one's neighbor.'" His ideal was an aristocracy which regarded the proletariat merely as a conglomeration of draft animals made to be driven, enslaved and exploited. "A good and healthy aristocracy," he said, "must acquiesce, with a good conscience, in the sacrifice of a legion of individuals, who, for its benefit, must be reduced to slaves and tools. The masses have no right to exist on their own account: their sole excuse for living lies in their usefulness as a sort of superstructure or scaffolding, upon which a more select race of beings may be elevated." Rejecting all permanent rules of good and evil and all notions of brotherhood, Nietzsche held that the aristocratic individualist — and it was to the aristocrat only that he gave, unreservedly, the name of human being — must seek every possible opportunity to increase and exalt his own sense of efficiency, of success, of mastery, of power. Whatever tended to impair him, or to decrease his efficiency, was bad. Whatever tended to increase it — at no matter what cost to others — was good. There must be a complete surrender to the law of natural selection — that invariable natural law which ordains that the fit shall survive and the unfit shall perish. All growth must occur at the top. The strong must grow stronger, and that they may do so, they must waste no strength in the vain task of trying to lift up the weak.

The reader may interrupt here with the question we encountered at the start: how is the dionysian individualist to know whether a given action will benefit him or injure him? The answer, of course, lies in the obvious fact that, in every healthy man, instinct supplies a very reliable guide, and that, when instinct fails or is uncertain, experiment must solve the problem. As a general thing, nothing is more patent than the feeling of power — the sense of efficiency, of capacity, of mastery. Every man is constantly and unconsciously measuring himself with his neighbors, and so becoming acutely aware of those things in which he is their superior. Let two men clash in the stock market and it becomes instantly apparent that one is richer, or more resourceful or more cunning than the other. Let two men run after an omnibus and it becomes instantly apparent that one is swifter than the other. Let two men come together as rivals in love, war, drinking or holiness, and one is bound to feel that he has bested the other. Such contests are infinite in variety and in number, and all life, in fact, is made up of them. Therefore, it is plain that every man is conscious of his power, and aware of it when this power is successfully exerted against some other man. In such exertions, argues Nietzsche, lies happiness, and so his prescription for happiness consists in unrestrained yielding to the will to power. That all men worth discussing so yield, despite the moral demand for humility, is so plain that it scarcely needs statement. It is the desire to attain and manifest efficiency and superiority which makes one man explore the wilds of Africa and another pile up vast wealth and another write books of philosophy and another submit to pain and mutilation in the prize ring. It is this yearning which makes men take chances and risk their lives and limbs for glory. Everybody knows, indeed, that in the absence of such a primordial and universal emulation the world would stand still and the race would die. Nietzsche asks nothing more than that the fact be openly recognized and admitted; that every man yield to the yearning unashamed, without hypocrisy and without wasteful efforts to feed and satisfy the yearning of other men at the expense of his own.

It is evident, of course, that the feeling of superiority has a complement in the feeling of inferiority. Every man, in other words, sees himself, in respect to some talent possessed in common by himself and a rival, in one of three ways — he knows that he is superior, he knows that he is inferior, or he is in doubt. In the first case, says Nietzsche, the thing for him to do is to make his superiority still greater by yielding to its stimulation: to make the gap between himself and his rival wider and wider. In the second case, the thing for him to do is to try to make the gap smaller: to lift himself up or to pull his rival down until they are equal or the old disproportion is reversed. In the third case, it is his duty to plunge into a contest and risk his all upon the cast of the die. "I do not exhort you to peace," says Zarathustra, "but to victory!" If victory comes not, let it be defeat, death and annihilation- but, in any event, let there be a fair fight. Without this constant strife — this constant testing — this constant elimination of the unfit — there can be no progress. "As the smaller surrenders himself to the greater, so the greater must surrender himself to the will to power and stake life upon the issue. It is the mission of the greatest to run risk and danger — to cast dice with death." Power, in a word, is never infinite: it is always becoming.

Practically and in plain language, what does all this mean? Simply that Nietzsche preaches a mighty crusade against all those ethical ideas which teach a man to sacrifice himself for the theoretical good of his inferiors. A culture which tends to equalize, he says, is necessarily a culture which tends to rob the strong and so drag them down, for the strong cannot give of their strength to the weak without decreasing their store. There must be an unending effort to widen the gap; there must be a constant search for advantage, an infinite alertness. The strong man must rid himself of all idea that it is disgraceful to yield to his acute and ever present yearning for still more strength. There must be an abandonment of the old slave-morality and a transvaluation of moral values. The will to power must be emancipated from the bonds of that system of ethics which brands it with infamy, and so makes the one all-powerful instinct of every sentient creature loathsome and abominable.

It is only the under-dog, he says, that believes in equality. It is only the groveling and inefficient mob that seeks to reduce all humanity to one dead level, for it is only the mob that would gain by such leveling. "'There are no higher men,' says the crowd in the market place. 'We are all equal; man is man; in the presence of God we are all equal!' In the presence of God, indeed! But I tell you that God is dead!" So thunders Zarathustra. That is to say, our idea of brotherhood is part of the mob-morality of the ancient Jews, who evolved it out of their own helplessness and credited it to their god. We have inherited their morality with their god and so we find it difficult — in the mass — to rid ourselves of their point of view. Nietzsche himself rejected utterly the Judaic god and he believed that the great majority of intelligent men of his time were of his mind. That he was not far wrong in this assumption is evident to everyone. At the present time, indeed, it is next to impossible to find a sane man in all the world who believes in the actual existence of the deity described in the old testament. All theology is now an effort to explain away this god. Therefore, argues Nietzsche, it is useless to profess an insincere concurrence in a theistic idea at which our common sense revolts, and ridiculous to maintain the inviolability of an ethical scheme grounded upon this idea.

It may be urged here that, even if the god of Judea is dead, the idea of brotherhood still lives, and that, as a matter of fact, it is an idea inherent in the nature of man, and one that owes nothing to the rejected supernaturalism which once fortified and enforced it. That is to say, it may be argued that the impulse to self-sacrifice and mutual help is itself an instinct. The answer to this lies in the very patent fact that it is not. Nothing, indeed, is more apparent than the essential selfishness of man. In so far as they are able to defy or evade the moral code without shame or damage, the strong always exploit the weak. The rich man puts up the price of the necessities of life and so makes himself richer and the poor poorer. The emperor combats democracy. The political boss opposes the will of the people for his own advantage. The inventor patents his inventions and so increases his relative superiority to the common run of men. The ecclesiastic leaves a small parish for a larger one — because the pay is better or "the field offers wider opportunities," i.e. gives him a better chance to "save souls" and so increases his feeling of efficiency. The philanthropist gives away millions because the giving visualizes and makes evident to all men his virtue and power. It is ever the same in this weary old world: every slave would be a master if he could. Therefore, why deny it? Why make it a crime to do what every man's instincts prompt him to do? Why call it a sin to do what every man does, insofar as he can? The man who throws away his money or cripples himself with drink, or turns away from his opportunities — we call him a lunatic or a fool. And yet, wherein does he differ from the ideal holy man of our slave-morality — the holy man who tortures himself, neglects his body, starves his mind and reduces himself to parasitism, that the weak, the useless and unfit may have, through his ministrations, some measure of ease? Such is the argument of the dionysian philosophy. It is an argument for the actual facts of existence — however unrighteous and ugly those facts may be.

That the lifting up of the weak, in the long run, is an unprofitable and useless business is evident on very brief reflection. Philanthropy, considered largely, is inevitably a failure. Now and then we may transform an individual pauper or drunkard into a useful, producing citizen, but this happens very seldom. Nothing is more patent, indeed, than the fact that charity merely converts the unfit — who, in the course of nature, would soon die out and so cease to, encumber the earth — into parasites — who live on indefinitely, a nuisance and a burden to their betters. The "reformed" drunkard always goes back to his cups: drunkardness, as every physician knows, is as essentially incurable as congenital insanity. And it is the same with poverty. We may help a pauper to survive by giving him food and drink, but we cannot thereby make an efficient man of him — we cannot rid him of the unfitness which made him a pauper. There are, of course, exceptions to this, as to other rules, but the validity of the rule itself will not be questioned by any observant man. It goes unquestioned, indeed, by those who preach the doctrine of charity the loudest. They know it would be absurd to argue that helping the unfit is profitable to the race, and so they fall back, soon or late, upon the argument that charity is ordained of God and that the impulse to it is implanted in every decent man. Nietzsche flatly denies this. Charity, he says, is a man-made idea, with which the gods have nothing to do. Its sole effect is to maintain the useless at the expense of the strong. In the mass, the helped can never hope to discharge in full their debt to the helpers. The result upon the race is thus retrogression.

And now for our second question. What was the goal Nietzsche had in mind for his immoralist? What was to be the final outcome of his overturning of all morality? Did he believe the human race would progress until men became gods and controlled the sun and stars as they now control the flow of great rivers? Or did he believe that the end of it all would be annihilation? After the publication of Nietzsche's earlier books, with their ruthless tearing down of the old morality, these questions were asked by critics innumerable in all the countries of Europe. The philosopher was laughed at as a crazy iconoclast who destroyed without rebuilding. He was called a visionary and a lunatic, and it was reported and believed that he had no answer: that his philosophy was doomed to bear itself to the earth, like an arch without a keystone. But in April, 1883, he began the publication of *Also sprach Zarathustra* and therein his reply was written large.

"I teach you," cries Zarathustra, "the superman! Man is something that shall be surpassed. What, to man, is the ape? A joke or a shame. Man shall be the same to the superman: a joke or shame.... Man is a bridge connecting ape and superman.... The superman will be the final flower and ultimate expression of the earth. I conjure you to be faithful to the earth... to cease looking beyond the stars for your hopes and rewards. You must sacrifice yourself to the earth that one day it may bring forth the superman."

Here we hearken unto the materialist, the empiricist, the monist par excellence. And herein we perceive dimly the outlines of the superman. He will be rid of all delusions that hamper and oppress the will to power. He will be perfect in body and perfect in mind. He will know everything worth knowing and have strength and skill and cunning to defend himself against any conceivable foe. Because the prospect of victory will feed his will to power he will delight in combat, and his increasing capacity for combat will decrease his sensitiveness to pain. Conscious of his efficiency, he be happy; having no illusions regarding a heaven and a hell, he will be content. He will see life as something pleasant — something to be faced gladly and with a laugh. He will say "yes" alike to its pleasures and to its ills. Rid of the notion that there is anything filthy in living — that the flesh is abominable, and life an affliction — he will grow better and better fitted to meet the conditions of actual existence. He will be scornful, merciless and supremely fit. He will be set free from man's fear of gods and of laws, just as man has been set free from the ape's fear of lions and of open places.

To put it simply, the superman's thesis will be this: that he has been put into the world without his consent, that he must live in the world, that he owes nothing to the other people there, and that he knows nothing whatever of existence beyond the grave. Therefore, it will be his effort to attain the highest possible measure of satisfaction for the only unmistakable and genuinely healthy instinct within him: the yearning to live — to attain power — to meet and overcome the influences which would weaken or destroy him. "Keep yourselves up, my brethren," cautions Zarathustra, "learn to keep yourselves up! The sea is stormy and many seek to keep afloat by your aid. The sea is stormy and all are overboard. Well, cheer up and save yourselves, ye old seamen!... What is your fatherland? The land wherein your children will dwell.... Thus does your love to these remote ones speak: 'Disregard your neighbors! Man is something to be surpassed!' Surpass yourself at the expense of your neighbor. What you cannot seize, let no man give you.... Let him who can command, obey!" The idea, by this time, should be plain. The superman, in the struggle for existence, asks and gives no quarter. He believes that it is the destiny of sentient beings to progress upward, and he is willing to sacrifice himself that his race may do so. But his sacrifice must benefit, not his neighbor — not the man who should and must look out for himself — but the generations yet unborn.

It must be borne in mind that the superman will make a broad distinction between instinct and passion — that he will not mistake the complex thing we call love, with its costly and constant hurricanes of emotion, for the instinct of reproduction — that he will not mistake mere anger for war — that he will not mistake patriotism, with all its absurdities and illusions, for the homing instinct. The superman, in brief, will know how to renounce as well as how to possess, but his renunciation will be the child, not of faith or of charity, but of expediency. "Will nothing beyond your capacity," says Zarathustra. "Demand nothing of yourself that is beyond achievement!... The higher a thing is, the less often does it succeed. Be of good cheer! What matter! Learn to laugh at yourselves!... Suppose you have failed? Has not the future gained by your failure?" The superman, as Nietzsche was fond of putting it, must play at dice with death. He must have ever in mind no other goal but the good of the generations after him. He must be willing to battle with his fellows, as with illusions, that those who came after may not be afflicted by these enemies. He must be supremely unmoral and unscrupulous. His must be the gospel of eternal defiance.

Nietzsche, it will be observed, was unable to give any very definite picture of this proud, heaven-kissing superman. It is only in Zarathustra's preachments to "the higher man," a sort of bridge between man and superman, that we may discern the philosophy of the latter. On one occasion Nietzsche penned a passage which seemed to compare the superman to "the great blond beasts" which ranged Europe in the days of the mammoth, and from this fact many commentators have drawn the conclusion that he had in mind a mere two-legged brute, with none of the higher traits that we now speak of as distinctly human. But, as a matter of fact, he harbored no such idea. In another place, wherein he speaks of three metamorphoses of the race, under the allegorical names of the camel, the lion and the child, he makes this plain. The camel, a hopeless beast of burden, is man. But when the camel goes into the solitary desert, it throws off its burden and becomes a lion. That is to say, the heavy and hampering load of artificial dead-weight called morality is cast aside and the instinct to live — or, as Nietzsche insists upon regarding it, the will to power — is given free rein. The lion is the "higher man" — the intermediate stage between man and superman. The latter appears neither as camel nor lion, but as a little child. He knows a little child's peace. He has a little child's calm. Like a babe in utero, he is ideally adapted to his environment.

Zarathustra sees man "like a camel kneeling down to be heavy laden." What are his burdens? One is "to humiliate oneself." Another is "to love those who despise us." In the desert comes the first metamorphosis, and the "thou shalt" of the camel becomes the "I will" of the lion. And what is the mission of the lion? "To create for itself freedom for new creating." After the lion comes the child. It is "innocence and oblivion, a new starting, a play, a wheel rolling by itself, a prime motor, a holy asserting." The thought here is cast in the heightened language of mystic poetry, but its meaning, I take it, is not lost.

Nietzsche, even more than Schopenhauer, recognized the fact that great mental progress — in the sense that mental progress means an increased capacity for grappling with the conditions of existence — necessarily has to depend upon physical efficiency. In exceptional cases a great mind may inhabit a diseased body, but it is obvious that this is not the rule. A nation in which the average man had but one hand and the duration of life was but 20 years could not hope to cope with even the weakest nation of modern

Europe. So it is plain that the first step in the improvement of the race must be the improvement of the body. Jesus Christ gave expression to this need by healing the sick, and the chief end and aim of all modern science is that of making life more and more bearable. Every labor-saving machine ever invented by man has no other purpose than that of saving bodily wear and tear. Every religion aims to rescue man from the racking fear of hell and the strain of trying to solve the great problems of existence for himself. Every scheme of government that we know is, at bottom, a mere device for protecting human beings from injury and death.

Thus it will be seen that Nietzsche's program of progress does not differ from other programs quite so much as, at first sight, it may seem to do. He laid down the principle that, before anything else could be accomplished, we must have first looked to the human machine. As we have seen, the intellect is a mere symptom of the will to live. Therefore whatever removes obstacles to the free exercise of this will to live, necessarily promotes and increases intelligence. A race that was never incapacitated by illness would be better fitted than any other race for any conceivable intellectual pursuit: from making money to conjugating Greek verbs. Nietzsche merely states this obvious fact in an unaccustomed form.

His superman is to give his will to live — or will to power, as you please — perfect freedom. As a result, those individuals in whom this instinct most accurately meets the conditions of life on earth will survive, and in their offspring, by natural laws, the instinct itself will become more and more accurate. That is to say, there will appear in future generations individuals in whom this instinct will tend more and more to order the performance of acts of positive benefit and to forbid the performance of acts likely to result in injury. This injury, it is plain, may take the form of unsatisfied wants as well as of broken skulls. Therefore, the man — or superman — in whom the instinct reaches perfection will unconsciously steer clear of all the things which harass and batter mankind today — exhausting self-denials as well as exhausting passions. Whatever seems likely to benefit him, he will do; whatever seems likely to injure him he will avoid. When he is in doubt, he will dare — and accept defeat or victory with equal calm. His attitude, in brief, will be that of a being who faces life as he finds it, defiantly and unafraid — who knows how to fight and how to forbear — who sees things as they actually are, and not as they might or should be, and so wastes no energy yearning for the moon or in butting his head against stone walls. "This new table, O my brethren, I put over you: Be hard!."

Such was the goal that Nietzsche held before the human race. Other philosophers before him had attempted the same thing. Schopenhauer had put forward his idea of a race that had found happiness in putting away its desire to live. Comte had seen a vision of a race whose every member sought the good of all. The humanitarians of all countries had drawn pictures of Utopias peopled by beings who had outgrown all human instincts — who had outgrown the one fundamental, unquenchable and eternal instinct of every living thing: the desire to conquer, to live, to, remain alive. Nietzsche cast out all these fine ideals as essentially impossible. Man was of the earth, earthy, and his heavens and hells were creatures of his own vaporings. Only after he had ceased dreaming of them and thrown off his crushing burden of transcendental morality — only thus and then could he hope to rise out of the slough of despond in which he wallowed.

Eternal Recurrence

In the superman Nietzsche showed the world a conceivable and possible goal for all human effort. But there still remained a problem and it was this: When the superman at last appears on earth, what then? Will there be another super-superman to follow and a super-super-superman after that? In the end, will man become the equal of the creator of the universe, whoever or whatever He may be? Or will a period of decline come after, with a return down the long line, through the superman to man again, and then on to the anthropoid ape, to the lower mammals, to the asexual cell, and, finally, to mere inert matter, gas, ether and empty space?

Nietzsche answered these questions by offering the theory that the universe moved in regular cycles and that all which is now happening on earth, and in all the stars, to the uttermost, will be repeated, again and again, throughout eternity. In other words, he dreamed of a cosmic year, corresponding, in some fashion, to the terrestrial year. Man, who has sprung from the elements, will rise into superman, and perhaps infinitely beyond, and then, in the end, by catastrophe or slow decline, he will be resolved into the primary elements again, and the whole process will begin anew.

This notion, it must be admitted, was not original with Nietzsche and it would have been better for his philosophy and for his repute as an intelligent thinker had he never sought to elucidate it. In his early essay on history he first mentioned it and there he credited it to its probable inventors — the Pythagoreans. It was their belief that, whenever the heavenly bodies all returned to certain fixed relative positions, the whole history of the universe began anew. The idea seemed to fascinate Nietzsche, in whom, despite his worship of the actual, there was an ever-evident strain of mysticism, and he referred to it often in his later books. The pure horror of it — of the notion that all the world's suffering would have to be repeated again and again, that men would have to die over and over again for all infinity, that there was no stopping place or final goal — the horror of all this appealed powerfully to his imagination. Frau Andreas-Salomé tells us that he "spoke of it only in a low voice and with every sign of the profoundest emotion" and there is reason to believe that, at one time, he thought there might be some confirmation of it in the atomic theory, and that his desire to go to Vienna to study the natural sciences was prompted by a wish to investigate this notion. Finally he became convinced that there was no ground for such a belief in any of the known facts of science, and after that, we are told, his shuddering horror left him.

It was then possible for him to deal with the doctrine of eternal recurrence as a mere philosophical speculation, without the uncomfortable reality of a demonstrated scientific fact, and thereafter he spent much time considering it. In *Also sprach Zarathustra* he puts it into the brain of his prophet-hero, and shows how it well-nigh drove the latter mad.

"I will come back," muses Zarathustra, "with this sun, with this earth, with this eagle, with this serpent — not for a new life or a better life, but to the same life I am now leading. I will come back unto this same old life, in the greatest things and in the smallest, in order to teach once more the eternal recurrence of all things."

In the end, Nietzsche turned this fantastic idea into a device for exalting his superman. The superman is one who realizes that all of his struggles will be in vain, and that, in future cycles, he will have to go through them over and over again. Yet he has attained such a superhuman immunity to all emotion — to all ideas of pleasure and pain — that the prospect does not daunt him. Despite its horror, he faces it unafraid. It is all a part of life, and in consequence it is good. He has learned to agree to everything that exists — even to the ghastly necessity for living again and again. In a word, he does not fear an endless series of lives, because life, to him, has lost all the terrors which a merely human man sees in it.

"Let us not only endure the inevitable," says Nietzsche, "and still less bide it from ourselves: let us love it."

As Vernon Lee (Miss Violet Paget), has pointed out, this idea is scarcely to be distinguished from the fundamental tenet of stoicism. Miss Paget also says that it bears a close family resemblance to that denial of pain which forms the basis of Christian Science, but this is not true, for a vast difference exists between a mere denial of pain and a willingness to admit it, face it, and triumph over it. But the notion appears, in endless guises, in many philosophies and Goethe voiced it, after a fashion, in his maxim, "Entbehren sollst du" ("Man must do without"). The idea of eternal recurrence gives point, again, to a familiar anecdote. This concerns a joker who goes to an inn, eats his fill and then says to the innkeeper: "You and I will be here again in a million years: let me pay you then." "Very well," replies the quick-witted innkeeper, "but first pay me for the beefsteak you ate the last time you were here — a million years ago."

Despite Nietzsche's conclusion that the known facts of existence do not bear it out, and the essential impossibility of discussing it to profit, the doctrine of eternal recurrence is by no means unthinkable. The celestial cycle put forward, as an hypothesis, by modern astronomy — the progression, that is, from gas to molten fluid, from fluid to solid, and from solid, by catastrophe, back to gas again — is easily conceivable, and it is easily conceivable, too, that the earth, which has passed through an uninhabitable state into a habitable state, may one day become uninhabitable again, and so keep see-sawing back and forth through all eternity.

But what will be the effect of eternal recurrence upon the superman? The tragedy of it, as we have seen, will merely serve to make him heroic. He will defy the universe and say "yes" to life. Putting aside all thought of conscious existence beyond the grave, he will seek to live as nearly as possible in exact accordance with those laws laid down for the evolution of sentient beings on earth when the cosmos was first set spinning. But how will he know when he has attained this end? How will he avoid going mad with doubts about his own knowledge? Nietzsche gave much thought, first and last, to this epistemological problem, and at different times he leaned toward different schools, but his writing, taken as a whole, indicates that the fruit of his meditations was a thorough-going empiricism. The superman, indeed, is an empiricist who differs from Bacon only in the infinitely greater range of his observation and experiment. He learns by bitter experience and he generalizes from this knowledge. An utter and unquestioning materialist, he knows nothing of mind except as a function of body. To him speculation seems vain and foolish: his concern is ever with imminent affairs. That is to say, he believes a thing to be true when his eyes, his ears, his nose and his hands tell him it is true. And in this he will be at one with all those men who are admittedly above the mass today. Reject empiricism and you reject at one stroke, the whole sum of human knowledge.

When a man stubs his toe, for example, the facts that the injured member swells and that it hurts most frightfully appear to him as absolute certainties. If we deny that he actually knows these things and maintain that the spectacle of the swelling and the sensation of pain are mere creatures of his mind, we cast adrift from all order and common-sense in the universe and go sailing upon a stormy sea of crazy metaphysics and senseless contradictions. There are many things that we do not know, and in the nature of things, never can know. We do not know why phosphorus has a tendency to combine with oxygen, but the fact that it has we do know — and if we try to deny we do know it, we must deny that we are sentient beings, and in consequence, might regard life and the universe as mere illusions. No man with a sound mind makes any such denial. The things about us are real, just as our feeling that we are alive is real.(4)

From this it must be plain that the superman will have the same guides that we have, viz.: his instincts and senses. But in him they will be more accurate and more acute than in us, because the whole tendency of his scheme of things will be to fortify and develop them. If any race of Europe devoted a century to exercising its right arms, its descendants, in the century following, would have right arms like piston-rods. In the same way, the superman, by subordinating everything else to his instinct to live, will make it evolve into something very accurate and efficient. His whole concern, in brief, will be to live as long as possible and so to avoid as much as possible all of those things which shorten life — by injuring the body from without or by using up energy within. As a result he will cease all effort to learn why the world exists and will devote himself to acquiring knowledge how it exists. This knowledge how will be within his capacity even more than it is within our capacity today. Our senses, as we have seen, have given us absolute knowledge that stubbing the toe results in swelling and pain. The superman's developed senses will give him absolute knowledge about everything that exists on earth. He will know exactly how a tubercle bacillus attacks the lung tissue, he will know exactly how the blood fights the bacillus, and he will know exactly how to interfere in this battle in such a manner that the blood shall be invariably victorious. In a word, he will be the possessor of exact and complete knowledge regarding the working of all the benign and malignant forces in the world about him, but he will not bother himself about insoluble problems. He will waste no time speculating as to why tubercle bacilli were sent into the world: his instinct to live will be satisfied by his success in stamping them out.

The ideal superman then is merely a man in whom instinct works without interference — a man who feels that it is right to live and that the only knowledge worth while is that which makes life longer and more bearable. The superman's instinct for life is so strong that its mere exercise satisfies him, and so makes him happy. He doesn't bother about the unknown void beyond the grave: it is sufficient for him to know that he is alive and that being alive is pleasant. He is, in the highest sense, a utilitarian, and he believes to the letter in Auguste Comte's dictum that the only thing living beings can ever hope to accomplish on earth is to adapt themselves perfectly to the natural forces around them — to the winds and the rain, the hills and the sea, the thunderbolt and the germ of disease.

"I am a dionysian!" cries Nietzsche. "I am an immoralist!" He means simply that his ideal is a being capable of facing the horrors of life unafraid, of meeting great enemies and slaying them, of gazing down upon the earth in pride and scorn, of making his own way and bearing his own burdens. In the profane folk-philosophy of every healthy and vigorous people, we find some trace of this dionysian idea. "Let us so live day by day," says a distinguished American statesman, "that we can look any man in the eye and tell him to go to hell!" We get a subtle sort of joy out of this saying because it voices our racial advance toward individualism and away from revelation and rabbinism. We believe, at heart, in freedom, in toleration, in moral anarchy. We have put this notion into numerable homely forms.

Things have come to a hell of a pass

When a man can't wallop his own jackass.

So we phrase it. The superman, did he stalk the earth, would say the same thing.

Christianity

Nietzsche's astonishingly keen and fearless criticism of Christianity has probably sent forth wider ripples than any other stone he ever heaved into the pool of philistine contentment. He opened his attack in *Menschliches allzu Menschliches*, the first book of his maturity, and he was still at it, in full fuming and fury, in *Der Antichrist*, the last thing he was destined to write. The closing chapter of *Der Antichrist* — his swan song — contains his famous phillipic, beginning "I condemn." It recalls Zola's J' accuse letter in the Dreyfus case, but it is infinitely more sweeping and infinitely more uproarious and daring.

"I condemn Christianity," it begins. "I bring against it the most terrible of accusations that ever an accuser put into words. It is to me the greatest of all imaginable corruptions.... It has left nothing untouched by its depravity. It has made a worthlessness out of every value, a lie out of every truth, a sin out of everything straightforward, healthy and honest. Let anyone dare to speak to me of its humanitarian blessings! To do away with pain and woe is contrary to its principles. It lives by pain and woe: it has created pain and woe in order to perpetuate itself. It invented the idea of original sin.(1) It invented 'the equality of souls before God' — that cover for all the rancour of the useless and base.... It has bred the art of self-violation — repugnance and contempt for all good and cleanly instincts.... Parasitism is its praxis. It combats all good red-blood, all love and all hope for life, with its anæmic ideal of holiness. It sets up 'the other world' as a negation of every reality. The cross is the rallying post for a conspiracy against health, beauty, well-being, courage, intellect, benevolence — against life itself....

"This eternal accusation I shall write upon all walls: I call Christianity the one great curse, the one great intrinsic depravity,... for which no expedient is sufficiently poisonous, secret, subterranean, mean! I call it the one immortal shame and blemish upon the human race!"

So much for the philosopher's vociferous hurrah at the close of his argument. In the argument itself it is apparent that his indictment of Christianity contains two chief counts. The first is the allegation that it is essentially untrue and unreasonable, and the second is the theory that it is degrading. The first of these counts is not unfamiliar to the students of religious history. It was first voiced by that high priest who "rent his clothes" and cried "What need have we of any further witnesses? Ye have heard the blasphemy." It was voiced again by the Romans who threw converts to the lions, and after the long silence of the middle ages, it was piped forth again by Voltaire, Hume, the encyclopedists and Paine. After the philosophers and scientists who culminated in Darwin had rescued reason for all time from the transcendental nonsense of the cobweb-spinners and metaphysicians, Huxley came to the front with his terrific heavy artillery and those who still maintained that Christianity was historically true — Gladstone and the rest of the forlorn hope — were mowed down. David Strauss, Lessing, Eichhorn, Michaelis, Bauer, Meyer, Ritschl, Pfleidrer and a host of others joined in the chorus and in Nietzsche's early manhood the battle was practically won. By 1880 no reasonable man actually believed that there were devils in the swine, and it was already possible to deny the physical resurrection and still maintain a place in respectable society. Today a literal faith in the gospel narrative is confined to ecclesiastical *reactionarles, plous* old ladies and men about to be hanged.

Therefore, Nietzsche did not spend much time examining the historical credibility of Christianity. He did not try to prove, like Huxley, that the witnesses to the resurrection were superstitious peasants and hysterical women, nor did he seek to show, like Huxley again, that Christ might have been taken down from the cross before he was dead. He was intensely interested in all such inquiries, but he saw that, in the last analysis, they left a multitude of problems unsolved. The solution of these unsolved problems was the task that he took unto himself. Tunneling down, in his characteristic way, into the very foundations of the faith, he endeavored to prove that it was based upon contradictions and absurdities; that its dogmas were illogical and its precepts unworkable — and that its cardinal principles presupposed the acceptance of propositions which, to the normal human mind, were essentially unthinkable. This tunneling occupied much of Nietzsche's energy in *Menschliches allzu Menschliches*, and he returned to it again and again, in all of the other books that preceded *Der Antichrist*. His method of working may be best exhibited by a few concrete examples.

Prayer, for instance, is an excceedingly important feature of Christian worship and any form of worship in which it had no place would be necessarily unchristian. But upon what theory is prayer based? Examining the matter from all sides you will have to conclude that it is reasonable only upon two assumptions: first, that it is possible to change the infallible will and opinion of the deity, and secondly, that the petitioner is capable of judging what he needs. Now, Christianity maintains, as one of its main dogmas, that the deity is omniscient and all-wise, and, as another fundamental doctrine, that human beings are absolutely unable to solve their problems without heavenly aid i.e. that the deity necessarily knows what is best for any given man better than that man can ever hope to know it himself. Therefore, Christianity, in ordaining prayer, orders, as a condition of inclusion in its communion, an act which it holds to be useless. This contradiction, argues Nietzsche, cannot be explained away in terms comprehensible to the human intelligence.

Again Christianity holds that man is a mere creature of the deity's will, and yet insists that the individual be judged and punished for his acts. In other words, it tries to carry free will on one shoulder and determinism on the other, and its doctors and sages have themselves shown that they recognize the absurdity of this by their constant, but futile efforts to decide which of the two shall be abandoned. This contradiction is a legacy from Judaism, and Mohammedanism suffers from it, too. Those sects which have sought to remove it by an entire acceptance of determinism — under the name of predestination, fatalism, or what not — have become bogged in hopeless morasses of unreason and dogmatism. It is a cardinal doctrine of Presbyterianism, for instance, that "by the decree of God, for the manifestation of his glory, some men and angels are predestinated unto everlasting life and others foreordained to everlasting death...without any foresight of faith or good works, or perseverance in either of them, or any other thing in the creature, as conditions...." In other words, no matter how faithfully one man tries to follow in the footsteps of Christ, he may go to hell, and no matter how impiously another sins, he may be foreordained for heaven. That such a belief makes all religion, faith and morality absurd is apparent. That it is, at bottom, utterly unthinkable to a reasoning being is also plain.

Nietzsche devoted a great deal of time during his first period of activity to similar examinations of Christian ideas and he did a great deal to supplement the historical investigations of those English and German savants whose ruthless exposure of fictions and frauds gave birth to what we now call the higher criticism. But his chief service was neither in the field of historical criticism nor in that of the criticism of dogmas. Toward the end of his life he left the business of examining biblical sources to the archeologists and historians, whose equipment for the task was necessarily greater than his own, and the business of reducing Christian logic to contradiction and absurdity to the logicians. Thereafter, his own work took him a step further down and in the end he got to the very bottom of the subject. The answer of the theologians had been that, even if you denied the miracles, the gospels, the divinity of Christ and his very existence as an actual man, you would have to admit that Christianity itself was sufficient excuse for its own existence; that it had made the world better and that it provided a workable scheme of life by which men could live and die and rise to higher things. This answer, for awhile, staggered the agnostics and Huxley himself evidently came near being convinced that it was beyond rebuttal. But it only made Nietzsche spring into the arena more confident than ever. "Very well," he said, "we will argue it out. You say that Christianity has made the world better? I say that it has made it worse! You say that it is comforting and up-lifting? I say that it is cruel and degrading! You say that it is the best religion mankind has ever invented? I say it is the most dangerous!"

Having thus thrown down the gage of battle, Nietzsche proceeded to fight like a Tartar, and it is but common fairness to say that, for a good while, he bore the weight of his opponents' onslaught almost unaided. The world was willing enough to abandon its belief in Christian supernaturalism and as far back as the early 1880s the dignitaries of the Church of England — to employ a blunt but expressive metaphor — had begun to get in out of the wet. But the pietists still argued that Christianity remained the fairest flower of civilization and that it met a real and ever-present human want and made mankind better. To deny this took courage of a decidedly unusual sort — courage that was willing to face, not only ecclesiastical anathema and denunciation, but also the almost automatic opposition of every so-called respectable man.

But Nietzsche, whatever his deficiencies otherwise, certainly was not lacking in assurance, and so, when he came to write *Der Antichrist* he made his denial thunderous and uncompromising beyond expression. No medieval bishop ever pronounced more appalling curses. No back-woods evangelist ever laid down the law with more violent eloquence. The book is the shortest he ever wrote, but it is by long odds the most compelling. Beginning allegro, it proceeds from forte, by an uninterrupted crescendo to allegro con moltissimo molto fortissimo. The sentences run into mazes of italics, dashes and asterisks. It is German that one cannot read aloud without roaring and waving one's arm.

Christianity, says Nietzsche, is the most dangerous system of slave-morality the world has ever known. "It has waged a deadly war against the highest type of man. It has put a ban on all his fundamental instincts. It has distilled evil out of these instincts. It makes the strong and efficient man its typical outcast man. It has taken the part of the weak and the low; it has made an ideal out of its antagonism to the very instincts which tend to preserve life and well-being.... It has taught men to regard their highest impulses as sinful — as temptations." In a word, it tends to rob mankind of all those qualities which fit any living organism to survive in the struggle for existence.

As we shall see later on, civilization obscures and even opposes this struggle for existence, but it is in progress all the same, at all times and under all conditions. Every one knows, for instance, that one-third of the human beings born into the world every year die before they are five years old. The reason for this lies in the fact that they are, in some way or other, less fitted to meet the conditions of life on earth than the other two-thirds. The germ of cholera infantum is an enemy to the human race, and so long as it continues to exist upon earth it will devote all of its activity to attacking human infants and seeking to destroy them. It happens that some babies recover from cholera infantum, while others die of it. This is merely another way of saying that the former, having been born with a capacity for resisting the attack of the germ, or having been given the capacity artificially, are better fitted to survive, and that the latter, being incapable of making this resistance, are unfit.

All life upon earth is nothing more than a battle with the enemies of life. A germ is such an enemy, cold is such an enemy, lack of food is such an enemy, and others that may be mentioned are lack of water, ignorance of natural laws, armed foes and deficient physical strength. The man who is able to get all of the food he wants, and so can nourish his body until it becomes strong enough to combat the germs of disease; who gets enough to drink, who has shelter from the elements, who has devised means for protecting himself against the desires of other men — who yearn, perhaps, who take for themselves some of the things that he has acquired — such a man, it is obvious, is far better fitted to live than a man who has none of these things. He is far better fitted to survive, in a purely physical sense, because his body is nourished and protected, and he is far better fitted to attain happiness, because most of his powerful wants are satisfied.

Nietzsche maintains that Christianity urges a man to make no such efforts to insure his personal survival in the struggle for existence. The beatitudes require, he says, that, instead of trying to do so, the Christian shall devote his energies to helping others and shall give no thought to himself. Instead of exalting himself as much as possible above the common herd and thus raising his chances of surviving, and those of his children, above those of the average man, he is required to lift up this average man. Now, it is plain that every time he lifts up some one else, he must, at the same time, decrease his own store, because his own store is the only stock from which he can draw. Therefore, the tendency of the Christian philosophy of humility is to make men voluntarily throw away their own chances of surviving, which means their own sense of efficiency, which means their own "feeling of increasing power," which means their own happiness. As a substitute for this natural happiness, Christianity offers the happiness derived from the belief that the deity will help those who make the sacrifice and so restore them to their old superiority. This belief, as Nietzsche shows, is no more borne out by known facts than the old belief in witches. It is, in fact, proved to be an utter absurdity by all human experience.

"I call an animal, a species, an individual, depraved," he says, "when it loses its instincts, when it selects, when it prefers what is injurious to it.... Life itself is an instinct for growth, for continuance, for accumulation of forces, for power: where the will to power is wanting, there is decline." Christianity, he says, squarely opposes this will to power in the Golden Rule, the cornerstone of the faith. The man who confines his efforts to attain superiority over his fellow men to those acts which he would be willing to have them do toward him, obviously abandons all such efforts entirely. To put it in another form, a man can't make himself superior to the race in general without making every other man in the world, to that extent, his inferior. Now, if he follows the Golden Rule, he must necessarily abandon all efforts to make himself superior, because if he didn't he would be suffering all the time from the pain of seeing other men — whose standpoint the Rule requires him to assume — grow inferior. Thus his activity is restricted to one of two things: standing perfectly still or deliberately making himself inferior. The first is impossible, but Nietzsche shows that the latter is not, and that, in point of fact, it is but another way of describing the act of sympathy — one of the things ordered by the fundamental dogma of Christianity.

Sympathy, says Nietzsche, consists merely of a strong man giving up some of his strength to a weak man. The strong man, it is evident, is debilitated thereby, while the weak man, very often, is strengthened but little. If you go to a hanging and sympathize with the condemned, it is plain that your mental distress, without helping that gentleman, weakens, to a perceptible degree, your own mind and body, just as all other powerful emotions weaken them, by consuming energy, and so you are handicapped in the struggle for life to the extent of this weakness. You may get a practical proof of it an hour later by being overcome and killed by a foot-pad whom you might have been able to conquer, had you been feeling perfectly well, or by losing money to some financial rival for whom, under normal conditions, you would have been a match; and then again you may get no immediate or tangible proof of it at all. But your organism will have been weakened to some measurable extent, all the same, and at some time — perhaps on your death bed — this minute drain will make itself evident, though, of course, you may never know it.

"Sympathy," says Nietzsche, "stands in direct antithesis to the tonic passions which elevate the energy of human beings and increase their feeling of efficiency and power. It is a depressant. One loses force by sympathizing and any loss of force which has been caused by other means — personal suffering, for example — is increased and multiplied by sympathy. Suffering itself becomes contagious through sympathy and under certain circumstances it may lead to a total loss of life. If a proof of that is desired, consider the case of the Nazarene, whose sympathy for his fellow men brought him, in the end, to the cross.

"Again, sympathy thwarts the law of development, of evolution, of the survival of the fittest. It preserves what is ripe for extinction, it works in favor of life's condemned ones, it gives to life itself a gloomy aspect by the number of the ill-constituted it maintains in life.... It is both a multiplier of misery and a conservator of misery. It is the principal tool for the advancement of decadence. It leads to nothingness, to the negation of all those instincts which are at the basis of life.... But one does not say 'nothingness;' one says instead 'the other world' or 'the better life.'... This innocent rhetoric, out of the domain of religio-moral fantasy, becomes far from innocent when one realizes what tendency it conceals: the tendency hostile to life. "

The foregoing makes it patent that Nietzsche was a thorough-going and uncompromising biological monist. That is to say, he believed that man, while superior to all other animals because of his greater development, was, after all, merely an animal, like the rest of them; that the struggle for existence went on among human beings exactly as it went on among the lions in the jungle and the protozoa in the sea ooze, and that the law of natural selection ruled all of animated nature — mind and matter — alike. Indeed, it is but just to credit him with being the pioneer among modern monists of this school, for he stated and defended the doctrine of morphological universality at a time when practically all the evolutionists doubted it, and had pretty well proved its truth some years before Haeckel wrote his "Monism" and "The Riddle of the Universe."

To understand all of this, it is necessary to go back to Darwin and his first statement of the law of natural selection. Darwin proved, in The Origin of the Species, that a great many more individuals of any given species of living being are born into the world each year than can possibly survive. Those that are best fitted to meet the condition of existence live on; those that are worst fitted die. The result is that, by the influence of heredity, the survivors beget a new generation in which there is a larger percentage of the fit. One might think that this would cause a greater number to survive, but inasmuch as the food and room on earth are limited, a large number must always die. But all the while the half or third, or whatever the percentage may be, which actually do survive become more and more fit. In consequence, a species, generation after generation, tends to become more and more adapted to meet life's vicissitudes, or, as the biologists say, more and more adapted to its environment.

Darwin proved that this law was true of all the lower animals and showed that it was responsible for the evolution of the lower apes into anthropoid apes, and that it could account, theoretically, for a possible evolution of anthropoid apes into man. But in The Descent of Man he argued that the law of natural selection ceased when man became an intelligent being. Thereafter, he said, man's own efforts worked against those of nature. Instead of letting the unfit of his race die, civilization began to protect and preserve them. The result was that nature's tendency to make all living beings more and more sturdy was set aside by man's own conviction that mere sturdiness was not the thing most to be desired. From this Darwin argued that if two tribes of human beings lived side by side, and if, in one of them, the unfit were permitted to perish, while in the other there were many "courageous, sympathetic and faithful members, who were always ready to warn each other of danger, and to aid and defend one another" — that in such a case, the latter tribe would make the most progress, despite its concerted effort to defy a law of nature.

Darwin's disciples agreed with him in this and some of them went to the length of asserting that civilization, in its essence, was nothing more or less than a successful defiance of this sort. Herbert Spencer was much troubled by the resultant confusion and as one critic puts it the whole drift of his thought "appears to be inspired by the question: how to evade and veil the logical consequence of evolutionarism for human existence?" John Fiske, another Darwinian, accepted the situation without such disquieting doubt. "When humanity began to be evolved," he said, "an entirely new chapter in the history of the universe was opened. Henceforth the life of the nascent soul came to be first in importance and the bodily life became subordinated to it." Even Huxley believed that man would have to be excepted from the operation of the law of natural of society. "The ethical progress of society," he said, "depends, not on imitating the cosmic process and still less on running away from it, but in combating it." He saw that it was audacious thus to pit man against nature, but he thought that man was sufficiently important to make such an attempt and hoped "that the enterprise might meet with a certain measure of success."(16) And the other Darwinians agreed with him.(17)

As all the best critics of philosophy have pointed out, any philosophical system which admits such a great contradiction fails utterly to furnish workable standards of order in the universe, and so falls short of achieving philosophy's first aim. We must either believe with the scholastics that intelligence rules, or we must believe, with Haeckel, that all things happen in obedience to invariable natural laws. We cannot believe both. A great many men, toward the beginning of the 1890s, began to notice this fatal defect in Darwin's idea of human progress. In 1891 one of them pointed out the conclusion toward which it inevitably led. If we admitted, he said, that humanity had set at naught the law of natural selection, we must admit that civilization was working against nature's efforts to preserve the race, and that, in the end, humanity would perish. To put it more succinctly, man might defy the law of natural selection as much as he pleased, but he could never hope to set it aside. Soon or late, he would awaken to the fact that he remained a mere animal, like the rabbit and the worm, and that, if he permitted his body to degenerate into a thing entirely lacking in strength and virility, not all the intelligence conceivable could save him.

Nietzsche saw all this clearly as early as 1877. He saw that what passed for civilization, as represented by Christianity, was making such an effort to defy and counteract the law of natural selection, and he came to the conclusion that the result would be disaster. Christianity, he said, ordered that the strong should give part of their strength to the weak, and so tended to weaken the whole race. Self-sacrifice, he said, was an open defiance of nature, and so were all the other Christian virtues, in varying degree. He proposed, then, that before it was too late, humanity should reject Christianity, as the "greatest of all imaginable corruptions," and admit freely and fully, that the law of natural selection was universal and that the only way to make real progress was to conform to it.

It may be asked here how Nietzsche accounted for the fact that humanity had survived so long — for the fact that the majority of men were still physically healthy and that the race, as a whole, was still fairly vigorous. He answered this in two ways. First, he denied that the race was maintaining to the full its old vigor. "The European of the present," he said, "is far below the European of the Renaissance." It would be absurd, he pointed out, to allege that the average German of 1880 was as strong and as healthy — i.e. as well fitted to his environment — as the "blond beast" who roamed the Saxon lowlands in the days of the mammoth. It would be equally absurd to maintain that the highest product of modern civilization — the town-dweller — was as vigorous and as capable of becoming the father of healthy children as the intelligent farmer, whose life was spent in approximate accordance with all the more obvious laws of health.

Nietzsche's second answer was that humanity had escaped utter degeneration and destruction because, despite its dominance as a theory of action, few men actually practiced Christianity. It was next to impossible, he said, to find a single man who, literally and absolutely, obeyed the teachings of Christ. There were plenty of men who thought they were doing so, but all of them were yielding in only a partial manner. Absolute Christianity meant absolute disregard of self. It was obvious that a man who reached this state of mind would be unable to follow any gainful occupation, and so would find it impossible to preserve his own life or the lives of his children. In brief, said Nietzsche, an actual and utter Christian would perish today just as Christ perished, and so, in his own fate, would provide a conclusive argument against Christianity.

Nietzsche pointed out further that everything which makes for the preservation of the human race is diametrically opposed to the Christian ideal. Thus Christianity becomes the foe of science. The one argues that man should sit still and let God reign; the other that man should battle against the tortures which fate inflicts upon him, and try to overcome them and grow strong. Thus all science is unchristian because, in the last analysis, the whole purpose and effort of science is to arm man against loss of energy and death, and thus make him self-reliant and unmindful of any duty of propitiating the deity. That this antagonism between Christianity and the search for truth really exists has been shown in a practical way time and again. Since the beginning of the Christian era the church has been the bitter and tireless enemy of all science, and this enmity has been due to the fact that every member of the priest class has realized that the more a man learned the more he came to depend upon his own efforts, and the less he was given to asking help from above. In the ages of faith men prayed to the saints when they were ill. Today they send for a doctor. In the ages of faith battles were begun with supplications, and it was often possible to witness the ridiculous spectacle of both sides praying to the same God. Today every sane person knows that the victory goes to the wisest generals and largest battalions.

Nietzsche thus showed, first, that Christianity (and all other ethical systems having self-sacrifice as their basis) tended to oppose the law of natural selection and so made the race weaker; and secondly, that the majority of men, consciously or unconsciously, were aware of this, and so made no effort to be absolute Christians. If Christianity were to become universal, he said, and every man in the world were to follow Christ's precepts to the letter in all the relations of daily life, the race would die out in a generation. This being true — and it may be observed in passing that no one has ever successfully controverted it — there follows the converse: that the human race had best abandon the idea of self-sacrifice altogether and submit itself to the law of natural selection. If this is done, says Nietzsche, the result will be a race of supermen — of proud, strong dionysians — of men who will say "yes" to the world and will be ideally capable of meeting the conditions under which life must exist on earth.

In his efforts to account for the origin of Christianity, Nietzsche was less happy, and indeed came very near the borderline of the ridiculous. The faith of modern Europe, he said, was the result of a gigantic effort on the part of the ancient Jews to revenge themselves upon their masters. The Jews were helpless and inefficient and thus evolved a slave-morality. Naturally, as slaves, they hated their masters, while realizing, all the while, the unmanliness of the ideals they themselves had to hold to in order to survive. So they crucified Christ, who voiced these same ideals, and the result was that the outside world, which despised the Jews, accepted Christ as a martyr and prophet and thus swallowed the Jewish ideals without realizing it. In a word, the Jews detested the slave-morality which circumstances thrust upon them, and got their revenge by foisting it, in a sugar-coated pill, upon their masters.

It is obvious that this idea is sheer lunacy. That the Jews ever realized the degenerating effect of their own slave-morality is unlikely, and that they should take counsel together and plan such an elaborate and complicated revenge, is impossible. The reader of Nietzsche must expect to encounter such absurdities now and then. The mad German was ordinarily a most logical and orderly thinker, but sometimes the traditional German tendency to indulge in wild and imbecile flights of speculation cropped up in him.

Truth

At the bottom of all philosophy, of all science and of all thinking, you will find the one all-inclusive question: How is man to tell truth from error? The ignorant man solves this problem in a very simple manner: he holds that whatever he believes, he knows; and that whatever he knows is true. This is the attitude of all amateur and professional theologians, politicians and other numbskulls of that sort. The pious old maid, for example, who believes in the doctrine of the immaculate conception looks upon her faith as proof, and holds that all who disagree with her will suffer torments in hell. Opposed to this childish theory of knowledge is the chronic doubt of the educated man. He sees daily evidence that many things held to be true by nine-tenths of all men are, in reality, false, and he is thereby apt to acquire a doubt of everything, including his own beliefs.

At different times in the history of man, various methods of solving or evading the riddle have been proposed. In the age of faith it was held that, by his own efforts alone, man was unable, even partly, to distinguish between truth and error, but that he could always go for enlightenment to an infallible encyclopedia: the word of god, as set forth, through the instrumentality of inspired scribes, in the holy scriptures. If these scriptures said that a certain proposition was true, it was true, and any man who doubted it was either a lunatic or a criminal. This doctrine prevailed in Europe for many years and all who ventured to oppose it were in danger of being killed, but in the course of time the number of doubters grew so large that it was inconvenient or impossible to kill all of them, and so, in the end, they had to be permitted to voice their doubts unharmed.

The first man of this new era to inflict any real damage upon the ancient churchly idea of revealed wisdom was Nicolas of Cusa, a cardinal of the Roman Catholic Church, who lived in the early part of the fifteenth century. Despite his office and his time, Nicolas was an independent and intelligent man, and it became apparent to him, after long reflection, that mere belief in a thing was by no means a proof of its truth. Man, he decided was prone to err, but in the worst of his errors, there was always some kernel of truth, else he would revolt against it as inconceivable. Therefore, he decided, the best thing for man to do was to hold all of his beliefs lightly and to reject them whenever they began to appear as errors. The real danger, he said, was not in making mistakes, but in clinging to them after they were known to be mistakes.

It seems well nigh impossible that a man of Nicolas' age and training should have reasoned so clearly, but the fact remains that he did, and that all of modern philosophy is built upon the foundations he laid. Since his time a great many other theories of knowledge have been put forward, but all have worked, in a sort of circle, back to Nicolas. It would be interesting, perhaps, to trace the course and history of these variations and denials, but such an enterprise is beyond the scope of the present inquiry. Nicolas by no means gave the world a complete and wholly credible system of philosophy. Until the day of his death scholasticism was dominant in the world that he knew, and it retained its old hold upon human thought, in fact, for nearly two hundred years thereafter. Not until Descartes, in 1619, made his famous resolution "to take nothing for the truth without clear knowledge that it is such," did humanity in general begin to realize, as Huxley says, that there was sanctity in doubt. And even Descartes could not shake himself free of the supernaturalism and other balderdash which yet colored philosophy. He laid down, for all time, the emancipating doctrine that "the profession of belief in propositions, of the truth of which there is no sufficient evidence, is immoral" — a doctrine that might well be called the Magna Charta of human thought. — but it should not be forgotten that he also laid down other doctrines and that many of them were visionary and silly. The philosophers after him rid their minds of the old ideas but slowly and there were frequent reversions to the ancient delusion that a man's mind is a function of his soul — whatever that may be — and not of his body. It was common, indeed, for a philosopher to set out with sane, debatable, conceivable ideas — and then to go soaring into the idealistic clouds. Only in our own time have men come to understand that the ego, for all its seeming independence, is nothing more than the sum of inherited race experience — that a man's soul, his conscience and his attitude of mind are things he has inherited from his ancestors, just as he has inherited his two eyes, his ten toes and his firm belief in signs, portents and immortality. Only in our own time have men ceased seeking a golden key to all riddles, and sat themselves down to solve one riddle at a time.

Those metaphysicians who fared farthest from the philosopher of Cusa evolved the doctrine that, in themselves, things have no existence at all, and that we can think of them only in terms of our impressions of them. The color green, for example, may be nothing but a delusion, for all we can possibly know of it is that, under certain conditions, our optic nerves experience a sensation of greenness. Whether this sensation of greenness is a mere figment of our imagination or the reflection of an actual physical state, is something that we cannot tell. It is impossible, in a word, to determine whether there are actual things around us, which produce real impressions upon us, or whether our idea of these things is the mere result of subjective impressions or conditions. We know that a blow on the eyes may cause us to see a flash of light which does not exist and that a nervous person may feel the touch of hands and hear noises which are purely imaginary. May it not be possible, also, that all other sensations have their rise within us instead of without, and that in saying that objects give us impressions we have been confusing cause and effect?

Such is the argument of those metaphysicians who doubt, not only the accuracy of human knowledge, but also the very capacity of human beings to acquire knowledge. It is apparent, on brief reflection, that this attitude, while theoretically admissible, is entirely impracticable, and that, as a matter of fact, it gives us no more substantial basis for intelligent speculation than the old device of referring all questions to revelation. To say that nothing exists save in the imagination of living beings is to say that this imagination itself does not exist. This, of course, is an absurdity, because every man is absolutely certain that he himself is a real thing and that his mind is a real thing, too, and capable of thought. In place of such cob-web spinning, modern philosophers — driven to it, it may be said, in parenthesis, by the scientists — have gone back to the doctrine that, inasmuch as we can know nothing of anything save through the impressions it makes upon us, these impressions must be accepted provisionally as accurate, so, long as they are evidently normal and harmonize one with the other.

That is to say, our perceptions, corrected by our experience and our common sense, must serve as guides for us, and we must seize every opportunity to widen their range and increase their accuracy. For millions of years they have been steadily augmenting our store of knowledge. We know, for instance, that when fire touches us it causes an impression which we call pain and that this impression is invariably the same, and always leads to the same results, in all normal human beings. Therefore, we accept it as an axiom that fire causes pain. There are many other ideas that may be and have been established in the same manner: by the fact that they are universal among sane men. But there is also a multitude of things which produce different impressions upon different men, and here we encounter the problem of determining which of these impressions is right and which is wrong. One man, observing the rising and setting of the sun, concludes that it is a hall of fire revolving about the earth. Another man, in the face of the same phenomena, concludes that the earth revolves around the sun. How, then, are we to determine which of these men has drawn the proper conclusion?

As a matter of fact, it is impossible in such a case, to come to any decision which can be accepted as utterly and absolutely true. But all the same the scientific empiric method enables us to push the percentage of error nearer and nearer to the irreducible minimum. We can observe the phenomenon under examination from a multitude of sides and compare the impression it produces with the impressions produced by kindred phenomena regarding which we know more. Again, we can put this examination into the hands of men specially trained and fitted for such work — men whose conclusions we know, by previous experience, to be above the average of accuracy. And so, after a long time, we can formulate some idea of the thing under inspection which violates few or none of the other ideas held by us. When we have accomplished this, we have come as near to the absolute truth as it is possible for human beings to come.

I need not point out that this method does not contemplate a mere acceptance of the majority vote. Its actual effect, indeed, is quite the contrary, for it is only a small minority of human beings who may be said, with any truth, to be capable of thought. It is probable, for example, that nine-tenths of the people in Christendom today believe that Friday is an unlucky day, while only the remaining tenth hold that one day is exactly like another. But despite this, it is apparent that the idea of the latter will survive and that, by slow degrees, it will be forced upon the former. We know that it is true, not because it is accepted by all men or by the majority of men — for, as a matter of fact, we have seen that it isn't — but because we realize that the few who hold to it are best capable of distinguishing between actual impressions and mere delusions.

Again, the scientific method tends to increase our knowledge by the very fact that it discourages unreasoning faith. The scientist realizes that most of his so-called facts are probably errors and so he is willing to harbor doubts of their truth and to seek for something better. Like Socrates he boldly says "I know that I am ignorant." He realizes, in fact, that error, when it is constantly under fire, is bound to be resolved in the long run into something approximating the truth. As Nicolas pointed out 500 years ago, nothing is utterly and absolutely true and nothing is utterly and absolutely false. There is always a germ of truth in the worst error, and there is always a residuum of error in the soundest truth. Therefore, an error is fatal only when it is hidden from the white light of investigation. Herein lies the difference between the modern scientist and the moralist. The former holds nothing sacred, not even his own axioms; the latter lays things down as law and then makes it a crime to doubt them.

It is in this way — by submitting every idea to a searching, pitiless unending examination — that the world is increasing its store of what may be called, for the sake of clearness, absolute knowledge. Error always precedes truth, and it is extremely probable that the vast majority of ideas held by men of today — even the sanest and wisest men — are delusions, but with the passing of the years our stock of truth grows larger and larger. "A conviction," says Nietzsche, "always has its history — its previous forms, its tentative forms, its states of error. It becomes a conviction, indeed, only after having been not a conviction, and then hardly a conviction. No doubt falsehood is one of these embryonic forms of conviction. Sometimes only a change of persons is needed to transform one into the other. That which, in the son, is a conviction, was, in the father, still a falsehood. The tendency of intelligent men, in a word, is to approach nearer and nearer the truth, by the processes of rejection, revision and invention. Many old ideas are rejected by each new generation, but there always remain a few that survive. We no longer believe with the cave-men that the thunder is the voice of an angry god and the lightning the flash of his sword, but we still believe, as they did, that wood floats upon water, that seeds sprout and give forth plants, that a roof keeps off the rain and that a child, if it lives long enough, will inevitably grow into a man or a woman. Such ideas may be called truths. If we deny them we must deny at once that the world exists and that we exist ourselves.

Nietzsche's discussion of these problems is so abstruse and so much complicated by changes in view that it would be impossible to make an understandable summary of it in the space available here. In his first important book, *Menschliches allzu Menschliches*, he devoted himself, in the main, to pointing out errors made in the past, without laying down any very definite scheme of thought for the future. In the early stages of human progress, he said, men made the mistake of regarding everything that was momentarily pleasant or beneficial as absolutely and eternally true. Herein they manifested the very familiar human weakness for rash and hasty generalization, and the equally familiar tendency to render the ideas of a given time and place perpetual and permanent by erecting them into codes of morality and putting them into the mouths of gods. This, he pointed out, was harmful, for a thing might be beneficial to the men of today and fatal to the men of tomorrow. Therefore, he argued that while a certain idea's effect was a good criterion, humanly speaking, of its present or current truth, it was dangerous to assume that this effect would be always the same, and that, in consequence, the idea itself would remain true forever.

Not until the days of Socrates, said Nietzsche, did men begin to notice this difference between imminent truth and eternal truth. The notion that such a distinction existed made its way very slowly, even after great teachers began to teach it, but in the end it was accepted by enough men to give it genuine weight. Since that day philosophy and science, which were once merely different names for the same thing, have signified two separate things. It is the object of philosophy to analyze happiness, and by means of the knowledge thus gained, to devise means for safe-guarding and increasing it. In consequence, it is necessary for philosophy to generalize — to assume that the thing which makes men happy today will make them happy tomorrow. Science, on the contrary, concerns itself, not with things of the uncertain future, but with things of the certain present. Its object is to examine the world as it exists today, to uncover as many of its secrets as possible, and to study their effect upon human happiness. In other words, philosophy first constructs a scheme of happiness and then tries to fit the world to it, while science studies the world with no other object in view than the increase of knowledge, and with full confidence that, in the long run, this increase of knowledge will increase efficiency and in consequence happiness.

It is evident, then, that science, for all its contempt for fixed schemes of happiness, will eventually accomplish with certainty what philosophy — which most commonly swims into the ken of the average man as morality — is now trying to do in a manner that is not only crude and unreasonable, but also necessarily unsuccessful. In a word, just so soon as man's store of knowledge grows so large that he becomes complete master of the natural forces which work toward his undoing, he will be perfectly happy. Now, Nietzsche believed, as we have seen in past chapters, that man's instinctive will to power had this same complete mastery over his environment as its ultimate object, and so he concluded that the will to power might be relied upon to lead man to the truth. That is to say, he believed that there was, in every man of the higher type (the only type he thought worth discussing) an instinctive tendency to seek the true as opposed to the false, that this instinct, as the race progressed, grew more and more accurate, and that its growing accuracy explained the fact that, despite the opposition of codes of morality and of the iron hand of authority, man constantly increased his store of knowledge. A thought, he said, arose in a man without his initiative or volition, and was nothing more or less than an expression of his innate will to obtain power over his environment by accurately observing and interpreting it. It was just as reasonable, he said, to say it thinks as to say I think, because every intelligent person knew that a man couldn't control his thoughts. Therefore, the fact that these thoughts, in the long run and considering the human race as a whole, tended to uncover more and more truths proved that the will to power, despite the danger of generalizing from its manifestations, grew more and more accurate and so worked in the direction of absolute truth. Nietzsche believed that mankind was ever the slave of errors, but he held that the number of errors tended to decrease. When, at last, truth reigned supreme and there were no more errors, the superman would walk the earth.

Now it is impossible for any man to note the workings of the will to power save as it is manifested in his own instincts and thoughts, and therefore Nietzsche, in his later books, urges that every man should be willing, at all times, to pit his own feelings against the laws laid down by the majority. A man should steer clear of rash generalization from his own experience, but he should be doubly careful to steer clear of the generalizations of others. The greatest of all dangers lies in subscribing to a thesis without being certain of its truth. "This not-wishing-to-see what one sees...is a primary requisite for membership in a party, in any sense whatsoever. Therefore, the party man becomes a liar by necessity." The proper attitude for a human being, indeed, is chronic dissent and skepticism. "Zarathustra is a skeptic.... Convictions are prisons.... The freedom from every kind of permanent conviction, the ability to search freely, belong to strength.... The need of a belief, of something that is unconditioned...is a sign of weakness. The man of belief is necessarily a dependent man.... His instinct gives the highest honor to self-abnegation. He does not belong to himself, but to the author of the idea he believes." It is only by skepticism, argues Nietzsche, that we can hope to make any progress. If all men accepted without question, the dictata of some one supreme sage, it is plain that there could be no further increase of knowledge. It is only by constant turmoil and conflict and exchange of views that the minute granules of truth can be separated from the vast muck heap of superstition and error. Fixed truths, in the long run, are probably more dangerous to intelligence than falsehoods.(8)

This argument, I take it, scarcely needs greater elucidation. Every intelligent man knows that if there had been no brave agnostics to defy the wrath of the church in the middle ages, the whole of Christendom would still wallow in the unspeakably foul morass of ignorance which had its center, during that black time, in an infallible sovereign of sovereigns. Authority, at all times and everywhere, means sloth and degeneration. It is only doubt that creates. It is only the minority that counts.

The fact that the great majority of human beings are utterly incapable of original thought, and so must, perforce, borrow their ideas or submit tamely to some authority, explains Nietzsche's violent loathing and contempt for the masses. The average, self-satisfied, conservative, orthodox, law-abiding citizen appeared to him to be a being but little raised above the cattle in the barn-yard. So violent was this feeling that every idea accepted by the majority excited, for that very reason, his suspicion and opposition. "What everybody believes," he once said, "is never true." This may seem like a mere voicing of brobdingnagian egotism, but as a matter of fact, the same view is held by every man who has spent any time investigating the history of ideas. "Truth," said Dr. Osler a while ago, "scarcely ever carries the struggle for acceptance at its first appearance." The masses are always a century or two behind. They have made a virtue of their obtuseness and call it by various fine names: conservatism, piety, respectability, faith. The nineteenth century witnessed greater human progress than all the centuries before it saw or even imagined, but the majority of white men of today still believe in ghosts, still fear the devil, still hold that the number 13 is unlucky and still picture the deity as a patriarch in a white beard, surrounded by a choir of resplendent amateur musicians. "We think a thing," says Prof. Henry Sidgwick, "because all other people think so; or because, after all, we do think so; or because we are told so, and think we must think so; or because we once thought so, and think we still think so; or because, having thought so, we think we will think so."

Naturally enough, Nietzsche was an earnest opponent of the theological doctrine of free will. He held, as we have seen, that every human act was merely the effect of the will to power reacting against environment, and in consequence he had to reject absolutely the notion of volition and responsibility. A man, he argued, was not an object in vacuo and his acts, thoughts, impulses and motives could not be imagined without imagining some cause for them. If this cause came from without, it was clearly beyond his control, and if it came from within it was no less so, for his whole attitude of mind, his instinctive habits of thoughts, his very soul, so-called, were merely attributes that had been handed down to him, like the shape of his nose and the color of his eyes, from his ancestors. Nietzsche held that the idea of responsibility was the product and not the cause of the idea of punishment, and that the latter was nothing more than a manifestation of primitive man's will to power — to triumph over his fellows by making them suffer the handicap and humiliation of pain. "Men were called free," he said, "in order that they might be condemned and punished.... When we immoralists try to cleanse psychology, history, nature and sociology of these notions, we find that our chief enemies are the theologians, who, with their preposterous idea of 'a moral order of the world,' go on tainting the innocence of man's struggle upward with talk of punishment and guilt. Christianity is, indeed, a hangman's metaphysic." As a necessary corollary of this, Nietzsche denied the existence of any plan in the cosmos. Like Haeckel, he believed that but two things existed — energy and matter; and that all the phenomena which make us conscious of the universe were nothing more than symptoms of the constant action of the one upon the other. Nothing ever happened without a cause, he said, and no cause was anything other than the effect of some previous cause. "The destiny of man," he said, "cannot be disentangled from the destiny of everything else in existence, past, present and future.... We are a part of the whole, we exist in the whole.... There is nothing which could judge, measure or condemn our being, for that would be to judge, measure and condemn the whole.... But there is nothing outside of the whole.... The concept of God has hithero made our existence a crime.... We deny God, we deny responsibility by denying God: it is only thereby that we save man."

Herein, unluckily, Nietzsche fell into the trap which has snapped upon Haeckel and every other supporter of atheistic determinism. He denied that the human will was free and argued that every human action was inevitable, and yet he spent his whole life trying to convince his fellow men that they should do otherwise than as they did in fact. In a word, he held that they had no control whatever over their actions, and yet, like Moses, Mohammed and St. Francis, he thundered at them uproariously and urged them to turn from their errors and repent.

Civilization

On the surface, at least, the civilization of today seems to be moving slowly toward two goals. One is the eternal renunciation of war and the other is universal brotherhood: one is "peace on earth" and the other is "good will to men." Five hundred years ago a statesman's fame rested frankly and solely upon the victories of his armies; today we profess to measure him by his skill at keeping these armies in barracks. And in the internal economy of all civilized states we find today some pretence at unrestricted and equal suffrage. In times past it was the chief concern of all logicians and wiseacres to maintain the proposition that God reigned. At present, the dominant platitude of Christendom — the corner-stone of practically every political party and the stock-in- trade of every politician — is the proposition that the people rule.

Nietzsche opposed squarely both the demand for peace and the demand for equality, and his opposition was grounded upon two arguments. In the first place, he said, both demands were rhetorical and insincere and all intelligent men knew that neither would ever be fully satisfied. In the second place, he said, it would be ruinous to the race if they were. That is to say, he believed that war was not only necessary, but also beneficial, and that the natural system of castes was not only beneficent, but also inevitable. In the demand for universal peace he saw only the yearning of the weak and useless for protection against the righteous exploitation of the useful and strong. In the demand for equality he saw only the same thing. Both demands, he argued, controverted and combated that upward tendency which finds expression in the law of natural selection.

"The order of castes," said Nietzsche, "is the dominating law of nature, against which no merely human agency may prevail. In every healthy society there are three broad classes, each of which has its own morality, its own work, its own notion of perfection and its own sense of mastery. The first class comprises those who are obviously superior to the mass intellectually; the second includes those whose eminence is chiefly muscular, and the third is made up of the mediocre. The third class, very naturally, is the most numerous, but the first is the most powerful.

"To this highest caste belongs the privilege of representing beauty, happiness and goodness on earth.... Its members accept the world as they find it and make the best of it.... They find their happiness in those things which, to lesser men, would spell ruin — in the labyrinth, in severity toward themselves and others, in effort. Their delight is self-governing: with them asceticism becomes naturalness, necessity, instinct. A difficult task is regarded by them as a privilege; to play with burdens which would crush others to death is their recreation. They are the most venerable species of men. They are the most cheerful, the most amiable. They rule because they are what they are. They are not at liberty to be second in rank.

"The second caste includes the guardians and keepers of order and security — the warriors, the nobles, the king — above all, as the highest types of warrior, the judges and defenders of the law. They execute the mandates of the first caste, relieving the latter of all that is course and menial in the work of ruling.

"At the bottom are the workers — the men of handicraft, trade, agriculture and the greater part of art and science. It is the law of nature that they should be public utilities — that they should be wheels and functions. The only kind of happiness of which they are capable makes intelligent machines of them. For the mediocre, it is happiness to be mediocre. In them the mastery of one thing — i.e. specialism — is an instinct.

"It is unworthy of a profound intellect to see in mediocrity itself an objection. It is, indeed, a necessity of human existence, for only in the presence of a horde of average men is the exceptional man a possibility....

"Whom do I hate most among the men of today? The socialist who undermines the workingman's healthy instincts, who takes from him his feeling of contentedness with his existence, who makes him envious, who teaches him revenge.... There is no wrong in unequal rights — it lies in the vain pretension to equal rights."

It is obvious from this that Nietzsche was an ardent believer in aristocracy, but it is also obvious that he was not a believer in the thing which passes for aristocracy in the world today. The nobility of Europe belongs, not to his first class, but to his second class. It is essentially military and legal, for in themselves its members are puny and inefficient, and it is only the force of law that maintains them in their inheritance.

The fundamental doctrine of civilized law, as we know it today, is the proposition that what a man has once acquired shall belong to him and his heirs forever, without need on his part or theirs to defend it personally against predatory rivals. This transfer of the function of defense from the individual to the state naturally exalts the state's professional defenders — that is, her soldiers and judges — and so it is not unnatural to find the members of this class, and their parasites, in control of most of the world's governments and in possession of a large share of the world's wealth, power and honors. To Nietzsche this seemed grotesquely illogical and unfair. He saw that this ruling class expended its entire energy in combating experiment and change and that the aristocracy it begot and protected — an aristocracy often identical, very naturally, with itself — tended to become more and more unfit and helpless and more and more a bar to the ready recognition and unrestrained functioning of the only true aristocracy — that of efficiency.

Nietzsche pointed out that one of the essential absurdites of a constitutional aristocracy was to be found in the fact that it hedged itself about with purely artificial barriers. Next only to its desire to maintain itself without actual personal effort was its jealous endeavor to prevent accessions to its ranks. Nothing, indeed, disgusts the traditional belted earl quite so much as the ennobling of some upstart brewer or iron-master. This exclusiveness, from Nietzsche's point of view, seemed ridiculous and pernicious, for a true aristocracy must be ever willing and eager to welcome to its ranks — and to enroll in fact, all who display those qualities which automatically make a man extraordinarily fit and efficient. There should always be, he said, a free and constant interchange of individuals between the three natural castes of men. It should be always possible for an abnormally efficient man of the slave class to enter the master class, and, by the same token, accidental degeneration or incapacity in the master class should be followed by swift and merciless reduction to the ranks of slaves. Thus, those aristocracies which presented the incongruous spectacle of imbeciles being intrusted with the affairs of government seemed to him utterly abhorrent, and those schemes of caste which made a mean birth an offset to high intelligence seemed no less so.

So long as man's mastery of the forces of nature is incomplete, said Nietzsche, it will be necessary for the vast majority of human beings to spend their lives in either supplementing those natural forces which are partly under control or in opposing those which are still unleashed. The business of tilling the soil, for example, is still largely a matter of muscular exertion, despite the vast improvement in farm implements, and it will probably remain so for centuries to come. Since such labor is necessarily mere drudgery, and in consequence unpleasant, it is plain that it should be given over to men whose realization of its unpleasantness is least acute. Going further, it is plain that this work will be done with less and less revolt and less and less driving, as we evolve a class whose ambition to engage in more inviting pursuits grows smaller and smaller. In a word, the ideal plough-man is one who has no thought of anything higher and better than ploughing. Therefore, argued Nietzsche, the proper performance of the manual labor of the world makes it necessary that we have a laboring class, which means a class content to obey without fear or question.

This doctrine brought down upon Nietzsche's head the pious wrath of all the world's humanitarians, but empiric experiment has more than once proved its truth. The history of the hopelessly futile and fatuous effort to improve the negroes of the Southern United States by education affords one such proof. It is apparent, on brief reflection, that the negro, no matter how much he is educated, must remain, as a race, in a condition of subservience; that he must remain the inferior of the stronger and more intelligent white man so long as he retains racial differentiation. Therefore, the effort to educate him has awakened in his mind ambitions and aspirations which, in the very nature of things, must go unrealized, and so, while gaining nothing whatever materially, he has lost all his old contentment, peace of mind and happiness. Indeed, it is a commonplace of observation in the United States that the educated and refined negro is invariably a hopeless, melancholy, embittered and despairing man.

Nietzsche, to resume, regarded it as absolutely essential that there be a class of laborers or slaves — his "third caste" — and was of the opinion that such a class would exist upon earth so long as the human race survived. Its condition, compared to that of the ruling class, would vary but slightly, he thought, with the progress of the years. As man's mastery of nature increased, the laborer would find his task less and less painful, but he would always remain a fixed distance behind those who ruled him. Therefore, Nietzsche, in his philosophy, gave no thought to the desires and aspirations of the laboring class, because, as we have just seen, he held that a man could not properly belong to this class unless his desires and aspirations were so faint or so well under the control of the ruling class that they might be neglected. All of the Nietzschean doctrines and ideas apply only to the ruling class. It was at the top, he argued, that mankind grew. It was only in the ideas of those capable of original thought — that progress had its source. William the Conqueror was of far more importance, though he was but a single man, than all the other Normans of his generation taken together.

Nietzsche was well aware that his "first caste" was necessarily small in numbers and that there was a strong tendency for its members to drop out of it and seek ease and peace in the castes lower down. "Life," he said, "is always hardest toward the summit — the cold increases, the responsibility increases."(3) But to the truly efficient man these hardships are but spurs to effort. His joy is in combating and in overcoming — in pitting his will to power against the laws and desires of the rest of humanity. "I do not advise you to labor," says Zarathustra, "but to fight. I do not advise you to compromise and make peace, but to conquer. Let your labor be fighting and your peace victory.... You say that a good cause will hallow even war? I tell you that a good war hallows every cause. War and courage have done more great things than charity. Not your pity, but your bravery lifts up those about you. Let the little girlies tell you that 'good' means 'sweet' and 'touching.' I tell you that 'good' means 'brave.'... The slave rebels against hardships and calls his rebellion superiority. Let your superiority be an acceptance of hardships. Let your commanding be an obeying.... Let your highest thought be: 'Man is something to be surpassed.'... I do not advise you to love your neighbor — the nearest human being. I advise you rather to flee from the nearest and love the furthest human being. Higher than love to your neighbor is love to the higher man that is to come in the future.... Propagate yourself upward. Thus live your life. What are many years worth? I do not spare you.... Die at the right time!"

The average man, said Nietzsche is almost entirely lacking in this gorgeous, fatalistic courage and sublime egotism. He is ever reluctant to pit his private convictions and yearnings against those of the mass of men. He is either afraid to risk the consequences of originality or fearful that, since the majority of his fellows disagree with him, he must be wrong. Therefore, no matter how strongly an unconventional idea may possess a man, he commonly seeks to combat it and throttle it, and the ability to do this with the least possible expenditure of effort we call self-control. The average man, said Nietzsche, has the power of self-control well developed, and in consequence he seldom contributes anything positive to the thought of his age and almost never attempts to oppose it.

We have seen in the preceding chapter that if every man, without exception, were of this sort, all human progress would cease, because the ideas of one generation would be handed down unchanged to the next and there would be no effort whatever to improve the conditions of existence by the only possible method — constant experiment with new ideas. Therefore, it follows that the world must depend for its advancement upon those revolutionists who, instead of overcoming their impulse to go counter to convention, give it free rein. Of such is Nietzsche's "first caste" composed. It is plain that among the two lower castes, courage of this sort is regarded, not as an evidence of strength, but as a proof of weakness. The man who outrages conventions is a man who lacks self-control, and the majority, by a process we have examined in our consideration of slave-morality, has exalted self-control, which, at bottom, is the antithesis of courage, into a place of honor higher than that belonging, by right, to courage itself.

But Nietzsche pointed out that the act of denying or combating accepted ideas is a thing which always tends to inspire other acts of the same sort. It is true enough that a revolutionary idea, so soon as it replaces an old convention and obtains the sanction of the majority, ceases to be revolutionary and becomes itself conventional, but all the same the mere fact that it has succeeded gives courage to those who harbor other revolutionary ideas and inspires them to give these ideas voice. Thus, it happens that courage breeds itself, and that, in times of great conflict, of no matter what sort, the world produces more than an average output of originality, or, as we more commonly denominate it, genius. In this manner Nietzsche accounted for a fact that had been noticed by many men before him: that such tremendous struggles as the French Revolution and the American Civil War are invariably followed by eras of diligent inquiry, of bold overturning of existing institutions and of marked progress. People become accustomed to unrestrained combat and so the desirability of self-control becomes less insistent.

Nietzsche had a vast contempt for what he called "the green-grazing happiness of the herd." Its strong morality and its insistence upon the doctrine that whatever is, is right — that "God's in his heaven; all's well with the world" — revolted him. He held that the so-called rights of the masses had no justifiable existence, since everything they asserted as a right was an assertion, more or less disguised, of the doctrine that the unfit should survive. "There are," he said, "only three ways in which the masses appear to me to deserve a glance: first, as blurred copies of their betters, printed on bad paper and from worn out plates; secondly, as a necessary opposition to stimulate the master class, and thirdly, as instruments in the hands of the master class. Further than this I hand them over to statistics — and the devil." Kant's proposal that the morality of every contemplated action be tested by the question, "Suppose everyone did as I propose to do?" seemed utterly ridiculous to Nietzsche because he saw that "everyone" always opposed the very things which meant progress; and Kant's corollary that the sense of duty contemplated in this dictum was "the obligation to act in reverence for law," proved to Nietzsche merely that both duty and law were absurdities. "Contumely," he said, "always falls upon those who break through some custom or convention. Such men, in fact, are called criminals. Everyone who overthrows an existing law is, at the start, regarded as a wicked man. Long afterward, when it is found that this law was bad and so cannot be re-established, the epithet is changed. All history treats almost exclusively of wicked men who, in the course of time, have come to be looked upon as good men. All progress is the result of successful crimes."(6)

Dr. Turck, Miss Paget, M. Nordau and other critics see in all this good evidence that Nietzsche was a criminal at heart. At the bottom of all philosophies, says Miss Paget, there is always one supreme idea. Sometimes it is a conception of nature, sometimes it is a religious faith and sometimes it is a theory of truth. In Nietzsche's case it is "my taste." He is always irritated: "I dislike," "I hate," "I want to get rid of" appear on every page of his writings. He delights in ruthlessness, his fellow men disgust him, his physical senses are acute, he has a sick ego. For that reason he likes singularity, the lonely Alps, classic literature and Bizet's "clear yellow" music. Turck argues that Nietzsche was a criminal because he got pleasure out of things which outraged the majority of his fellow men, and Nordau, in supporting this idea, shows that it is possible for a man to experience and approve criminal impulses and still never act them: that there are criminals of the chair as well as of the dark lantern and sandbag. The answer to all of this, of course, is the fact that the same method of reasoning would convict every original thinker the world has ever known of black felony: that it would make Martin Luther a criminal as well as Jack Sheppard, John the Baptist as well as the Borgias, and Galileo as well as Judas Iscariot; that it would justify the execution of all the sublime company of heroes who have been done to death for their opinions, from Jesus Christ down the long line.

Women and Marriage

Nietzsche's faithful sister, with almost comical and essentially feminine disgust, bewails the fact that, as a very young man, the philosopher became acquainted with the baleful truths set forth in Schopenhauer's immortal essay "On Women." That this daring work greatly influenced him is true, and that he subscribed to its chief arguments all the rest of his days is also true, but it is far from true to say that his view of the fair sex was borrowed bodily from Schopenhauer or that he would have written otherwise than as he did if Schopenhauer had never lived. Nietzsche's conclusions regarding women were the inevitable result, indeed, of his own philosophical system. It is impossible to conceive a man who held his opinions of morality and society laying down any other doctrines of femininity and matrimony than those he scattered through his books.

Nietzsche believed that there was a radical difference between the mind of man and the mind of woman and that the two sexes reacted in diametrically different ways to those stimuli which make up what might be called the clinical picture of human society. It is the function of man, he said, to wield a sword in humanity's battle with everything that makes life on earth painful or precarious. It is the function of woman, not to fight herself, but to provide fresh warriors for the fray. Thus the exercise of the will to exist is divided between the two: the man seeking the welfare of the race as he actually sees it and the woman seeking the welfare of generations yet unborn. Of course, it is obvious that this division is by no means clearly marked, because the man, in struggling for power over his environment, necessarily improves the conditions under which his children live, and the woman, working for her chilidren, often benefits herself. But all the same the distinction is a good one and empiric observation bears it out. As everyone who has given a moment's thought to the subject well knows, a man's first concern in the world is to provide food and shelter for himself and his family, while a woman's foremost duty is to bear and rear children. "Thus," said Nietzsche, "would I have man and woman: the one fit for warfare, the other fit for giving birth; and both fit for dancing with head and legs" — that is to say: both capable of doing their share of the race's work, mental and physical, with conscious and superbundant efficiency.

Nietzsche points out that, in the racial economy, the place of woman may be compared to that of a slave-nation, while the position of man resembles that of a master-nation. We have seen how a weak nation, unable, on account of its weakness, to satisfy its will to survive and thirst for power by forcing its authority upon other nations, turns to the task of keeping these other nations, as much as possible, from enforcing their authority upon it. Realizing that it cannot rule, but must serve, it endeavors to make the conditions of its servitude as bearable as possible. This effort is commonly made in two ways: first by ostensibly renouncing its desire to rule, and secondly, by attempts to inoculate its powerful neighbors with its ideas in subterranean and roundabout ways, so as to avoid arousing their suspicion and opposition. It becomes, in brief, humble and cunning, and with its humility as a cloak, it seeks to pit its cunning against the sheer might of those it fears.

The position of women in the world is much the same. The business of bearing and rearing children is destructive to their physical strength, and in consequence makes it impossible for them to prevail by force when their ideas and those of men happen to differ. To take away the sting of this incapacity, they make a virtue of it, and it becomes modesty, humility, self-sacrifice and fidelity; to win in spite of it they cultivate cunning, which commonly takes the form of hypocrisy, cajolery, dissimulation and more or less masked appeals to the masculine sexual instinct. All of this is so often observed in every-day life that it has become commonplace. A woman is physically unable to force a man to do as she desires, but her very inability to do so becomes a sentimental weapon against him, and her blandishments do the rest. The spectacle of a strong man ruled by a weak woman is no rare one certainly, and Samson was neither the first nor last giant to fall before a Delilah. There is scarcely a household in all the world, in truth, in which the familiar drama is not being acted and reacted day after day.

Now, it is plain from the foregoing that, though women's business in the world is of such a character that it inevitably leads to physical degeneration, her constant need to overcome the effects of this degeneration by cunning produces constant mental activity, which, by the law of exercise, should produce, in turn, great mental efficiency. This conclusion, in part, is perfectly correct, for women, as a sex, are shrewd, resourceful and acute; but the very fact that they are always concerned with imminent problems and that, in consequence, they are unaccustomed to dealing with the larger riddles of life, makes their mental attitude essentially petty. This explains the circumstance that despite their mental suppleness, they are not genuinely strong intellectually. Indeed, the very contrary is true. Women's constant thought is, not to lay down broad principles of right and wrong; not to place the whole world in harmony with some great scheme of justice; not to consider the future of nations; not to make two blades of grass grow where one grew before; but to deceive, influence, sway and please men. Normally, their weakness makes masculine protection necessary to their existence and to the exercise of their overpowering maternal instinct, and so their whole effort is to obtain this protection in the easiest way possible. The net result is that feminine morality is a morality of opportunism and imminent expediency, and that the normal woman has no respect for, and scarcely any conception of abstract truth. Thus is proved the fact noted by Schopenhauer and many other observers: that a woman seldom manifests any true sense of justice or of honor.

It is unnecessary to set forth this idea in greater detail, because everyone is familiar with it and proofs of its accuracy are supplied in infinite abundance by common observation. Nietzsche accepted it as demonstrated. When he set out to pursue the subject further, he rejected entirely the Schopenhauerean corollary that man should ever regard woman as his enemy, and should seek, by all means within his power, to escape her insidious influence. Such a notion naturally outraged the philosopher of the superman. He was never an advocate of running away: to all the facts of existence he said "yes." His ideal was not resignation or flight, but an intelligent defiance and opposition. Therefore, he argued that man should accept woman as a natural opponent arrayed against him for the benevolent purpose of stimulating him to constant efficiency. Opposition, he pointed out, was a necessary forerunner of function, and in consequence the fact that woman spent her entire effort in a ceaseless endeavor to undermine and change the will of man, merely served to make this will alert and strong, and so increased man's capacity for meeting and overcoming the enemies of his existence.

A man conscious of his strength, observes Nietzsche, need have no fear of women. It is only the man who finds himself utterly helpless in the face of feminine cajolery that must cry, "Get thee behind me, Satan!" and flee. "It is only the most sensual men," he says, "who have to shun women and torture their bodies." The normal, healthy man, despite the strong appeal which women make to him by their subtle putting forward of the sexual idea — visually as dress, coquetry and what not — still keeps a level head. He is strong enough to weather the sexual storm. But the man who cannot do this, who experiences no normal reaction in the direction of guardedness and caution and reason, must either abandon himself utterly as a helpless slave to woman's instinct of race-preservation, and so become a bestial voluptuary, or avoid temptation altogether and so become a celibate.

There is nothing essentially evil in woman's effort to combat and control man's will by constantly suggesting the sexual idea to him, because it is necessary, for the permanence of the race, that this idea be presented frequently and powerfully. Therefore, the conflict between masculine and feminine ideals is to be regarded, not as a lamentable battle, in which one side is right and the other wrong, but a convenient means of providing that stimulation-by-opposition — without which all function, and in consequence all progress, would cease. "The man who regards women as an enemy to be avoided," says Nietzsche, "betrays an unbridled lust which loathes not only itself, but also its means."

There are, of course, occasions when the feminine influence, by its very subtlety, works harm to the higher sort of men. It is dangerous for a man to love too violently and it is dangerous, too, for him to be loved too much. "The natural inclination of women to a quiet, uniform and peaceful existence" — that is to say, to a slave-morality — "operates adversely to the heroic impulse of the masculine free spirit. Without being aware of it, women act like a person who would remove stones from the path of a mineralogist, lest his feet should come in contact with them — forgetting entirely that he is faring forth for the very purpose of coming in contact with them.... The wives of men with lofty aspirations cannot resign themselves to seeing their husbands suffering, impoverished and slighted, even though it is apparent that this suffering proves, not only that its victim has chosen his attitude aright, but also that his aims — some day, at least — will be realized. Women always intrigue in secret against the higher souls of their husbands. They seek to cheat the future for the sake of a painless and agreeable present." In other words, the feminine vision is ever limited in range. Your typical woman cannot see far ahead; she cannot reason out the ultimate effect of a complicated series of causes; her eye is always upon the present or the very near future. Thus Nietzsche reaches, by a circuitous route, a conclusion supported by the almost unanimous verdict of the entire masculine sex, at all times and everywhere.

Nietzsche quite agrees with Schopenhauer (and with nearly everyone else who has given the matter thought) that the thing we call love is grounded upon physical desire, and that all of those arts of dress and manner in which women excel are mere devices for arousing this desire in man, but he points out, very justly, that a great many other considerations also enter into the matter. Love necessarily presupposes a yearning to mate, and mating is its logical consequence, but the human imagination has made it more than that. The man in love sees in his charmer, not only an attractive instrument for satisfying his comparatively rare and necessarily brief impulses to dalliance, but also a worthy companion, guide, counsellor and friend. The essence of love is confidence — confidence in the loved one's judgment, honesty and fidelity and in the persistence of her charm. So large do these considerations loom among the higher classes of men that they frequently obscure the fundamental sexual impulse entirely. It is a commonplace, indeed, that in the ecstasies of amorous idealization, the notion of the function itself becomes obnoxious. It may be impossible to imagine a man loving a woman without having had, at some time, conscious desire for her, but all the same it is undoubtedly true that the wish for marriage is very often a wish for close and constant association with the one respected, admired and trusted rather than a yearning for the satisfaction of desire.

All of this admiration, respect and trust, as we have seen, may be interpreted as confidence, which, in turn, is faith. Now, faith is essentially unreasonable, and in the great majority of cases, is the very antithesis of reason. Therefore, a man in love commonly endows the object of his affection with merits which, to the eye of a disinterested person, she obviously lacks. "Love...has a secret craving to discover in the loved one as many beautiful qualities as possible and to raise her as high as possible." "Whoever idolizes a person tries to justify himself by idealizing; and thus becomes an artist (or self-deceiver) in order to have a clear conscience." Again there is a tendency to illogical generalization. "Everything which pleases me once, or several times, is pleasing of and in itself." The result of this, of course, is quick and painful disillusion. The loved one is necessarily merely human and when the ideal gives way to the real, reaction necessarily follows. "Many a married man awakens one morning to the consciousness that his wife is far from attractive." — And it is only fair to note that the same awakening is probably the bitter portion of most married women, too.

In addition, it is plain that the purely physical desire which lies at the bottom of all human love, no matter how much sentimental considerations may obscure it, is merely a passion and so, in the very nature of things, is intermittent and evanescent. There are moments when it is over-powering, but there are hours, days, weeks and months when it is dormant. Therefore, we must conclude with Nietzsche, that the thing we call love, whether considered from its physical or psychical aspect, is fragile and short-lived.

Now, inasmuch as marriage, in the majority of cases, is a permanent institution (as it is, according to the theory of our moral code, in all cases), it follows that, in order to make the relation bearable, something must arise to take the place of love. This something, as we know, is ordinarily tolerance, respect, camaraderie, or a common interest in the well-being of the matrimonial firm or in the offspring of the marriage. In other words, the discovery that many of the ideal qualities seen in the life-companion through the rosy glasses of love do not exist is succeeded by a common-sense and unsentimental decision to make the best of those real ones which actually do exist.

From this it is apparent that a marriage is most apt to be successful when the qualities imagined in the beloved are all, or nearly all, real: that is to say, when the possibility of disillusion is at an irreducible minimum. This occurs sometimes by accident, but

Nietzsche points out that such accidents are comparatively rare. A man in love, indeed, is the worst possible judge of his inamorata's possession of those traits which will make her a satisfactory wife, for, as we have noted, he observes her through an ideal haze and sees in her innumerable merits which, to the eye of an unprejudiced and accurate observer, she does not possess. Nietzsche, at different times, pointed out two remedies for this. His first plan proposed that marriages for love be discouraged, and that we endeavor to insure the permanence of the relation by putting the selection of mates into the hands of third persons likely to be dispassionate and far-seeing: a plan followed with great success, it may be recalled, by most ancient peoples and in vogue, in a more or less disguised form, in many European countries today. "It is impossible," he said, "to found a permanent institution upon an idiosyncrasy. Marriage, if it is to stand as the bulwark of civilization, cannot be founded upon the temporary and unreasonable thing called love. To fulfil its mission, it must be founded upon the impulse to reproduction, or race permanence; the impulse to possess property (women and children are property); and the impulse to rule, which constantly organizes for itself the smallest unit of sovereignty, the family, and which needs children and heirs to maintain, by physical force, whatever measure of power, riches and influence it attains."

Nietzsche's second proposal was nothing more or less than the institution of trial marriage, which, when it was proposed years later by an American sociologist, caused all the uproar which invariably rises in the United States whenever an attempt is made to seek absolute truth. "Give us a term," said Zarathustra, "and a small marriage, that we may see whether we are fit for the great marriage." The idea here, of course, is simply this: that, when a man and a woman find it utterly impossible to live in harmony, it is better for them to separate at once than to live on together, making a mock of the institution they profess to respect, and begetting children who, in Nietzsche's phrase, cannot be regarded other than as mere "scapegoats of matrimony." Nietzsche saw that this notion was so utterly opposed to all current ideals and hypocrisies that it would be useless to argue it, and so he veered toward his first proposal. The latter, despite its violation of one of the most sacred illusions of the Anglo-Saxon race, is by no means a mere fantasy of the chair. Marriages in which love is subordinated to mutual fitness and material considerations are the rule in many countries today, and have been so for thousands of years, and if it be urged that, in France, their fruit has been adultery, unfruitfulness and degeneration, it may be answered that, in Turkey, Japan and India, they have become the cornerstones of quite respectable civilizations.

Nietzsche believed that the ultimate mission and function of human marriage was the breeding of a race of supermen and he saw very clearly that fortuitous pairing would never bring this about. "Thou shalt not only propagate thyself," said Zarathustra, "but propagate thyself upward. Marriage should be the will of two to create that which is greater than either. But that which the many call marriage — alas! what call I that? Alas! that soul-poverty of two! Alas! that soul-filth of two! Alas! that miserable dalliance of two! Marriage they call it — and they say that marriages are made in heaven. I like them not: these animals caught in heavenly nets...Laugh not at such marriages! What child has not reason to weep over its parents?" It is the old argument against haphazard breeding. We select the sires and dams of our race-horses with most elaborate care, but the strains that mingle in our children's veins get there by chance. "Worthy and ripe for begetting the superman this man appeared to me, but when I saw his wife earth seemed a madhouse. Yea, I wish the earth would tremble in convulsions when such a saint and such a goose mate! This one fought for truth like a hero — and then took to heart a little dressed-up lie. He calls it his marriage. That one was reserved in intercourse and chose his associates fastidiously — and then spoiled his company forever. He calls it his marriage. A third sought for a servant with an angel's virtues. Now he is the servant of a woman. Even the most cunning buys his wife in a sack."

As has been noted, Nietzsche was by no means a declaimer against women. A bachelor himself and constitutionally suspicious of all who walked in skirts, he nevertheless avoided the error of damning the whole sex as a dangerous and malignant excrescence upon the face of humanity. He saw that woman's mind was the natural complement of man's mind; that womanly guile was as useful, in its place, as masculine truth; that man, to retain those faculties which made him master of the earth, needed a persistent and resourceful opponent to stimulate them and so preserve and develop them. So long as the institution of the family remained a premise in every sociological syllogism, so long as mere fruitfulness remained as much a merit among intelligent human beings as it was among peasants and cattle — so long, he saw, it would be necessary for the stronger sex to submit to the parasitic opportunism of the weaker.

But he was far from exalting mere women into goddesses, after the sentimental fashion of those virtuosi of illusion who pass for law-givers in the United States, and particularly in the southern part thereof. Chivalry, with its ridiculous denial of obvious facts, seemed to him unspeakable and the good old sub-Potomac doctrines that a woman who loses her virtue is, ipso facto, a victim and not a criminal or particeps criminis, and that a "lady," by virtue of being a "lady," is necessarily a reluctant and helpless quarry in the hunt of love — these ancient and venerable fallacies would have made him laugh. He admitted the great and noble part that women had to play in the world-drama, but he saw clearly that her methods were essentially deceptive, insincere and pernicious, and so, he held that she should be confined to her proper rôle and that any effort she made to take a hand in other matters should be regarded with suspicion, and when necessary, violently opposed. Thus Nietzsche detested the idea of women's suffrage almost as much as he detested the idea of chivalry. The participation of women in large affairs, he argued, could lead to but one result: the contamination of the masculine ideals of justice, honor and truth by the feminine ideals of dissimulation, equivocation and intrigue. In women, he believed, there was an entire absence of that instinctive liking for a square deal and a fair fight which one finds in all men — even the worst.

Hence, Nietzsche believed that, in his dealings with women, man should be wary and cautious. "Let men fear women when she loveth: for she sacrificeth all for love and nothing else hath value to her.... Man is for woman a means: the end is always the child.... Two things are wanted by the true man: danger and play. Therefore he seeketh woman as the most dangerous toy within his reach.... Thou goest to women? Don't forget thy whip!" This last sentence has helped to make Nietzsche a stench in the nostrils of the orthodox, but the context makes his argument far more than a mere effort at sensational epigram. He is pointing out the utter unscrupulousness which lies at the foundation of the maternal instinct: an unscrupulousness familiar to every observer of humanity. Indeed, it is so potent a factor in the affairs of the world that we have, by our ancient device of labelling the inevitable the good, exalted it to the dignity and estate of a virtue. But all the same, we are instinctively conscious of its inherent opposition to truth and justice, and so our law books provide that a woman who commits a crime in her husband's presence is presumed to have been led to it by her desire to work what she regards as her good, which means her desire to retain his protection and good will. "Man's happiness is: 'I will.' Woman's happiness is: 'He will.'"

Maternity, thought Nietzsche, was a thing even more sublime than paternity, because it produced a more keen sense of race responsibility. "Is there a state more blessed," he asked, "than that of a woman with child?... Even worldly justice does not allow the judge and hangman to lay hold on her."(12) He saw, too, that woman's insincere masochism(13) spurred man to heroic efforts and gave vigor and direction to his work by the very fact that it bore the outward aspect of helplessness. He saw that the resultant stimulation of the will to power was responsible for many of the world's great deeds, and that, if woman served no other purpose, she would still take an honorable place as the most splendid reward — greater than honors or treasures — that humanity could bestow upon its victors. The winning of a beautiful and much-sought woman, indeed, will remain as great an incentive to endeavor as the conquest of a principality so long as humanity remains substantially as it is today.

It is unfortunate that Nietzsche left us no record of his notions regarding the probable future of matrimony as an institution. We have renson to believe that he agreed with Schopenhauer's analysis of the "lady," i.e. the woman elevated to splendid, but complete parasitism. Schopenhauer showed that this pitiful creature was the product of the monogamous ideal, just as the prostitute was the product of the monogamous actuality. In the United States and England, unfortunately, it is impossible to discuss such matters with frankness, or to apply to them the standards of absolute truth, on account of the absurd axiom that monogamy is ordained of God — with which maxim there appears the equally absurd corollary: that the civilization of a people is to be measured by the degree of dependence of its women. Luckily for posterity this last revolting doctrine is fast dying, though its decadence is scarcely noticed and wholly mis-understood. We see about us that women are becoming more and more independent and self-sufficient and that, as individuals, they have less and less need to seek and retain the good will and protection of individual men, but we overlook the fact that this tendency is fast under-mining the ancient theory that the family is a necessary and impeccable institution and that without it progress would be impossible. As a matter of fact, the idea of the family, as it exists today, is based entirely upon the idea of feminine helplessness. So soon as women are capable of making a living for themselves and their children, without the aid of the fathers of the latter, the old corner-stone of the family — the masculine defender and bread-winner — will find his occupation gone, and it will become ridiculous to force him, by law or custom, to discharge duties for which there is no longer need. Wipe out your masculine defender, and your feminine parasite — haus-frau — and where is your family?

This tendency is exhibited empirically by the rising revolt against those fetters which the family idea has imposed upon humanity: by the growing feeling that divorce should be a matter of individual expedience; by the successful war of cosmopolitanism upon insularity and clannishness and upon all other costly outgrowths of the old idea that because men are of the same blood they must necessarily love one another; and by the increasing reluctance among civilized human beings to become parents without some reason more logical than the notion that parenthood, in itself, is praiseworthy. It seems plain, in a word, that so soon as any considerable portion of the women of the world become capable of doing men's work and of thus earning a living for themselves and their children without the aid of men, there will be in full progress a dangerous, if unconscious, war upon the institution of marriage. It may be urged in reply that this will never happen, because of the fact that women are physically unequal to men, and that in consequence of their duty of child-bearing, they will ever remain so, but it may be answered to this that use will probably vastly increase their physical fitness; that science will rob child-bearing of most of its terrors within a comparatively few years; and that the woman who seeks to go it alone will have only herself and her child to maintain, whereas, the man of today has not only himself and his child, but also the woman. Again, it is plain that the economic handicap of child-bearing is greatly overestimated. At most, the business of maternity makes a woman utterly helpless for no longer than three months, and in the case of a woman who has three children, this means nine months in a lifetime. It is entirely probable that alcohol alone, not to speak of other enemies of efficiency, robs the average man of quite that much productive activity during his three score years and ten.

All of this, of course, is mere speculation, and it is presented as such, and not as prophecy. To it a thousand answers are possible: that woman, growing independent, will fall a prey to alcohol, promiscuousness and all the other evils from which man now protects her, only to be a slave to them himself; that man's lead in the race toward absolute efficiency is too long to be overcome; or that, in case woman makes the gains indicated, man will degenerate, and there will follow a transvaluation of the sexes, with woman the producer and man the parasite: a condition of affairs obviously identical, in all its essentials, with that which obtains today.

Government

Like Spencer before him, Nietzsche believed, as we have seen, that the best possible system of government was that which least interfered with the desires and enterprises of the efficient and intelligent individual. That is to say, he held that it would be well to establish, among the members of his first caste of human beings, a sort of glorified anarchy. Each member of this caste should be at liberty to work out his own destiny for himself. There should be no laws regulating and circumscribing his relations to other members of his caste, except the easily-recognizable and often-changing laws of common interest, and above all, there should be no laws forcing him to submit to, or even to consider, the wishes and behests of the two lower castes. The higher man, in a word, should admit no responsibility whatever to the lower castes. The lowest of all he should look upon solely as a race of slaves bred to work his welfare in the most efficient and uncomplaining manner possible, and the military caste should seem to him a race designed only to carry out his orders and so prevent the slave caste marching against him.

It is plain from this that Nietzsche stood squarely opposed to both of the two schemes of government which, on the surface, at least, seem to prevail in the western world to-day. For the monarchial ideal and for the democratic ideal he had the same words of contempt. Under an absolute monarchy, he believed, the military or law-enforcing caste was unduly exalted, and so its natural tendency to permanence was increased and its natural opposition to all experiment and progress was made well nigh irresistible. Under a communistic democracy, on the other hand, the mistake was made of putting power into the hands of the great, inert herd, which was necessarily and inevitably ignorant, credulous, superstitious, corrupt and wrong. The natural tendency of the herd, said Nietzsche, was to combat change and progress as bitterly and as ceaselessly as the military-judicial caste, and when, by some accident, it rose out of its rut and attempted experiments, it nearly always made mistakes, both in its premises and its conclusions and so got hopelessly bogged in error and imbecility. Its feeling for truth seemed to him to be almost nil; its mind could never see beneath misleading exteriors. "In the market place," said Zarathustra, "one convinces by gestures, but real reasons make the populace distrustful."

That this natural incompetence of the masses is an actual fact was observed by a hundred philosophers before Nietzsche, and fresh proofs of it are spread copiously before the world every day. Wherever universal suffrage, or some close approach to it, is the primary axiom of government, the thing known in the United States as "freak legislation" is a constant evil. On the statute books of the great majority of American states there are laws so plainly opposed to all common-sense that they bear an air of almost pathetic humor. One state legislature, in in an effort to prevent the corrupt employment of insurance funds, passes laws so stringent that, in the face of them, it is utterly impossible for an insurance company to transact a profitable business. Another considers an act contravening rights guaranteed specifically by the state and national constitutions; yet another passes a law prohibiting divorce under any circumstances whatever. And the spectacle is by no means confined to the American states. In the Australian Commonwealth, mob-rule has burdened the statutes with regulations which make difficult, if not impossible, the natural development of the country's resources and trade. If, in England and Germany, the effect of universal suffrage has been less apparent, it is because in these countries the two upper castes have solved the problem of keeping the proletariat, despite its theoretical sovereignty, in proper leash and bounds.

The possibility of exercising this control seemed to Nietzsche to be the saving grace of all modern forms of government, just as their essential impossibility appeared as the saving grace alike of Christianity and of communistic civilization. In England, as we have seen, the military-judicial caste, despite the Reform Act of 1867, has retained its old dominance, and in Germany, despite the occasional success of the socialists, it is always possible for the military aristocracy, by appealing to the vanity of the bourgeoisie, to win in a stand-up fight. In America, the proletariat, when it is not engaged in functioning in its own extraordinary manner, is commonly the tool, either of the first of Nietzsche's castes or of the second. That is to say, the average legislature has its price, and this price is often paid by those who believe that old laws, no matter how imperfect they may be, are better than harum-scarum new ones. Naturally enough, the most intelligent and efficient of Americans — members of the first caste — do not often go to a state capital with corruption funds and openly buy legislation, but nevertheless their influence is frequently felt. President Roosevelt, for one, has more than once forced his views upon a reluctant proletariat and even enlisted it under his banner — as in his advocacy of centralization, a truly dionysian idea, for example — and in the southern states the educated white class — which there represents, though in a melancholy fashion, the Nietzschean first caste — has found it easy to take from the black masses their very right to vote, despite the fact that they are everywhere in a great majority numerically, and so, by the theory of democracy, represent whatever power lies in the state. Thus it is apparent that Nietzsche's argument against democracy, like his argument against brotherhood, is based upon the thesis that both are rejected instinctively by all those men whose activity works for the progress of the human race.

It is obvious, of course, that the sort of anarchy preached by Nietzsche differs vastly from the beery, collarless anarchy preached by Herr Most and his unwashed followers. The latter contemplates a suspension of all laws in order that the unfit may escape the natural and rightful exploitation of the fit, whereas the former reduces the unfit to de facto slavery and makes them subject to the laws of a master class, which, in so far as the relations of its own members, one to the other, are concerned, recognizes no law but that of natural selection. To the average American or Englishman the very name of anarchy causes a shudder, because it invariably conjures up a picture of a land terrorized by low-browed assassins with matted beards, carrying bombs in one hand and mugs of beer in the other. But as a matter of fact, there is no reason whatever to believe that, if all laws were abolished tomorrow, such swine would survive the day. They are incompetents under our present paternalism and they would be incompetents under dionysian anarchy. The only difference between the two states is that the former, by its laws, protects men of this sort, whereas the latter would work their speedy annihilation. In a word, the dionysian state would see the triumph, not of drunken loafers, but of the very men whose efforts are making for progress today: those strong, free, self-reliant, resourceful men whose capacities are so much greater than the mobs' that they are often able to force their ideas upon it, despite its theoretical right to rule them and its actual endeavor so to do. Nietzschean anarchy would create an aristocracy of efficiency. The strong man — which means the intelligent, ingenious and far-seeing man — would acknowledge no authority but his own will and no morality but his own advantage. As we have seen in previous chapters, this would re-establish the law of natural selection firmly upon its disputed throne, and so the strong would grow ever stronger and more efficient, and the weak would grow ever more obedient and tractile.

It may be well at this place to glance briefly at an objection that bas been urged against Nietzsche's argument by many critics, and particularly by those in the socialistic camp. Led to it, no doubt, by their too literal acceptance of Marx's materialistic conception of history, they have assumed that Nietzsche's higher man must necessarily belong to the class denominated, by our after-dinner speakers and leader writers, "captains of industry," and to this class alone. That is to say, they have regarded the higher man as identical with the pushing, grasping buccaneer of finance, because this buccaneer has seemed to them to be the only man of today who is truly "strong, free, self-reliant and resourceful" and the only one who actually "acknowledges no authority but his own will." As a matter of fact, all of these assumptions are in error. For one thing, the "captain of industry" is not uncommonly the reverse of a dionysian, and without the artificial aid of our permanent laws, he might often perish in the struggle for existence. For another thing, it is an obvious fact that the men who go most violently counter to the view of the herd, and who battle most strenuously to prevail against it — our true criminals and transvaluers and breakers of the law — are not such men as Rockefeller, but men such as Pasteur; not such men as Morgan and Hooley, but sham-smashers and truth-tellers and mob-fighters after the type of Huxley, Lincoln, Bismarck, Darwin, Virchow, Haeckel, Hobbes, Macchiavelli, Harvey and Jenner, the father of vaccination.

Jenner, to choose one from the long list, was a real dionysian, because he boldly pitted his own opinion against the practically unanimous opinion of all the rest of the human race. Among those members of the ruling class in England who came after him — those men, that is, who made vaccination compulsory — the dionysian spirit was still more apparent. The masses themselves did not want to be vaccinated, because they were too ignorant to understand the theory of inoculation and too stupid to be much impressed by its unvisualized and — for years, at least — impalpable benefits. Yet their rulers forced them, against their will, to bare their arms. And why was this done? Was it because the ruling class was possessed by a boundless love for humanity and so yearned to lavish upon it a wealth of Christian devotion? Not at all. The real motive of the law makers was to be found in two considerations. In the first place, a proletariat which suffered from epidemics of small-pox was a crippled mob whose capacity for serving its betters, in the fields and factories of England, was sadly decreased. In the second place experience proved that when small-pox raged in the slums, it had an unhappy habit of stretching out its arms in the direction of mansion and castle, too. Therefore, the proletariat was vaccinated and small-pox was stamped out —

not because the ruling class loved the workers, but because it wanted to make them work for it as continuously as possible and to remove or reduce their constant menace to its life and welfare. In so far as it took the initiative in these proceedings, the military ruling-class of England raised itself to the eminence of Nietzsche's first caste. That Jenner himself, when he put forward his idea and led the military caste to carry it into execution, was an ideal member of the first caste, is plain. The goal before him was fame ever-lasting — and he gained it.

I have made this rather long digression because the opponents of Nietzsche have voiced their error a thousand times and have well-nigh convinced a great many persons of its truth. It is apparent enough, of course, that a great many men whose energy is devoted to the accumulation of money are truly dionysian in their methods and aims, but it is apparent, too, that a great many others are not. Nietzsche himself was well aware of the dangers which beset a race enthralled by commercialism, and he sounded his warning against them. Trade, being grounded upon security, tends to work for permanence in laws and customs, even after the actual utility of these laws and customs is openly questioned. This is shown by the persistence of free trade in England and of protectionism in the United States, despite the fact that the conditions of existence, in both countries, have materially changed since the two systems were adopted, and there is now good ground, in each, for demanding reform. So it is plain that Nietzsche did not cast his higher man in the mold of a mere millionaire. It is conceivable that a careful analysis might prove Mr. Morgan to be a dionysian, but it is certain that his character as such would not be grounded upon his well-known and oft-repeated plea that existing institutions be permitted to remain as they are.

Yet again, a great many critics of Nietzsche mistake his criticism of existing governmental institutions for an argument in favor of their immediate and violent abolition. When he inveighs against monarchy or democracy, for instance, it is concluded that he wants to assassinate all the existing rulers of the world, overturn all existing governments and put chaos, carnage, rapine and anarchy in their place. Such a conclusion, of course, is a grievous error. Nietzsche by no means believed that reforms could be instituted in a moment or that the characters and habits of thought of human beings could be altered by a lightning stroke. His whole philosophy, in truth, was based upon the idea of slow evolution, through infinitely laborious and infinitely protracted stages. All he attempted to do was to indicate the errors that were being made in his own time and to point out the probable character of the truths that would be accepted in the future. He believed that it was only by constant skepticism, criticism and opposition that progress could be made, and that the greatest of all dangers was inanition. Therefore, when he condemned all existing schemes of government, it meant no more than that he regarded them as based upon fundamental errors, and that he hoped and believed that, in the course of time, these errors would be observed, admitted and swept away, to make room for other errors measurably less dangerous, and in the end for truths. Such was his mission, as he conceived it: to attack error wherever he saw it and to proclaim truth whenever he found it. It is only by such iconoclasm and proselyting that humanity can be helped. It is only after a mistake is perceived and admitted that it can be rectified.

Nietzsche's argument for the "free spirit " by no means denies the efficacy of co-operation in the struggle upward, but neither does it support that blind fetishism which sees in co-operation the sole instrument of human progress. In one of his characteristic thumb-nail notes upon evolution he says: "The most important result of progress in the past is the fact that we no longer live in constant fear of wild beasts, barbarians, gods and our own dreams." It may be argued, in reference to this, that organized government is to be thanked for our deliverance, but a moment's thought will show the error of the notion. Humanity's war upon wild beasts was fought and won by individualists, who had in mind no end but their personal safety and that of their children, and the subsequent war upon barbarians would have been impossible, or at least unsuccessful, had it not been for the weapons invented and employed during the older fight against beasts. Again, it is apparent that our emancipation from the race's old superstitions regarding gods and omens has been achieved, not by communal effort, but by individual effort. Knowledge and not government brought us the truth that made us free. Government, in its very essence, is opposed to all increase of knowledge. Its tendency is always toward permanence and against change. It is unthinkable without some accepted scheme of law or morality, and such schemes, as we have seen, stand in direct antithesis to every effort to find the absolute truth. Therefore, it is plain that the progress of humanity, far from being the result of government, has been made entirely without its aid and in the face of its constant and bitter opposition. The code of Hammurabi, the laws of the Medes and Persians, the Code Napoleon and the English common law have retarded the search for the ultimate verities almost as much, indeed, as the Ten Commandments.

Nietzsche denies absolutely that there is inherent in mankind a yearning to gather into communities. There is, he says, but one primal instinct in human beings (as there is in all other animals), and that is the desire to remain alive. All those systems of thought which assume the existence of a "natural morality " are wrong. Even the tendency to tell the truth, which seems to be inborn in every civilized white man, is not "natural," for there have been — and are today — races in which it is, to all intents and purposes, entirely absent. And so it is with the so-called social instinct. Man, say the communists, is a gregarious animal and can be happy only in company with his fellows, and in proof of it they cite the fact that loneliness is everywhere regarded as painful and that, even among the lower animals, there is an impulse toward association. The facts set forth in the last sentence are indisputable, but they by no means prove the existence of an elemental social feeling sufficiently strong to make its satisfaction an end in itself. In other words, while it is plain that men flock together, just as birds flock together, it is going too far to say that the mere joy of flocking — the mere desire to be with others — is at the bottom of the tendency. On the contrary, it is quite possible to show that men gather in communities for the same reason that deer gather in herds: because each individual realizes (unconsciously, perhaps) that such a combination materially aids him in the business of self-protection. One deer is no match for a lion, but fifty deer make him impotent.

Nietzsche shows that, even after communities are formed, the strong desire of every individual to look out for himself, regardless of the desires of others, persists, and that, in every herd there are strong members and weak members. The former, whenever the occasion arises, sacrifice the latter: by forcing the heavy, killing drudgery of the community upon them or by putting them, in time of war, into the forefront of the fray. The result is that the weakest are being constantly weeded out and the strongest are always becoming stronger and stronger. "Hence," says Nietzsche, "the first 'state' made its appearance in the form of a terrible tyranny, a violent and unpitying machine, which kept grinding away until the primary raw material, the man-ape, was kneaded and fashioned into alert, efficient man."

Now, when a given state becomes appreciably more efficient than the states about it, it invariably sets about enslaving them. Thus larger and larger states are formed, but always there is a ruling master-class and a serving slave-class. "This," says Nietzsche, "is the origin of the state on earth, despite the fantastic theory which would found it upon some general agreement among its members. He who can command, he who is a master by nature, he who, in deed and gesture, behaves violently — what need has he for agreements? Such beings come as fate comes, without reason or pretext.... Their work is the instinctive creation of forms: they are the most unconscious of all artists; wherever they appear, something new is at once created — a governmental organism which lives; in which the individual parts and functions are differentiated and brought into correlation, and in which nothing at all is tolerable unless some utility with respect to the whole is implanted in it. They are innocent of guilt, of responsibility, of charity — these born rulers. They are ruled by that terrible art-egotism which knows itself to be justified by its work, as the mother knows herself to be justified by her child."

Nietzsche points out that, even after nations have attained some degree of permanence and have introduced ethical concepts into their relations with one another, they still give evidence of that same primary will to power which is responsible, at bottom, for every act of the individual man. "The masses, in any nation," he says, "are ready to sacrifice their lives, their goods and chattels, their consciences and their virtue, to obtain that highest of pleasures — the feeling that they rule, either in reality or in imagination, over others. On these occasions they make virtues of their instinctive yearnings, and so they enable an ambitious or wisely provident prince to rush into a war with the good conscience of his people as his excuse. The great conquerors have always had the language of virtue on their lips: they have always had crowds of people around them who felt exalted and would not listen to any but the most exalted sentiments.... When man feels the sense of power, he feels and calls himself good, and at the same time those who have to endure the weight of his power call him evil. Such is the curious mutability of moral judgments!... Hesiod, in his fable of the world's ages, twice pictured the age of the Homeric heroes and made two out of one. To those whose ancestors were under the iron heel of the Homeric despots, it appeared evil; while to the grandchildren of these despots it appeared good. Hence the poet had no alternative but to do as he did: his audience was composed of the descendants of both classes."

Nietzsche saw naught but decadence and illusion in humanitarianism and nationalism. To profess a love for the masses seemed to him to be ridiculous and to profess a love for one race or tribe of men, in preference to all others, seemed to him no less so. Thus he denied the validity of two ideals which lie at the base of all civilized systems of government, and constitute, in fact, the very conception of the state. He called himself, not a German, but "a good European."

"We good Europeans," he said, "are not French enough to 'love mankind.' A man must be afflicted by an excess of Gallic eroticism to approach mankind with ardour. Mankind! Was there ever a more hideous old woman among all the old women? No, we do not love mankind!... On the other hand, we are not German enough to advocate nationalism and race-hatred, or to take delight in that national blood-poisoning which sets up quarantines between the nations of Europe. We are too unprejudiced for that — too perverse, too fastidious, too well-informed, too much travelled. We prefer to live on mountains — apart, unseasonable.... We are too diverse and mixed in race to be patriots. We are, in a word, good Europeans — the rich heirs of millenniums of European thought....

"We rejoice in everything, which like ourselves, loves danger, war and adventure — which does not make compromises, nor let itself be captured, conciliated or faced.... We ponder over the need of a new order of things — even of a new slavery, for the strengthening and elevation of the human race always involves the existence of slaves....

"The horizen is unobstructed.... Our ships can start on their voyage once more in the face of danger.... The sea — our sea! — lies before us!"

Crime and Punishment

Nietzsche says that the thing which best differentiates man from the other animals is his capacity for making and keeping a promise. That is to say, man has a trained and efficient memory and it enables him to project an impression of today into the future. Of the millions of impressions which impinge upon his consciousness every day, he is able to save a chosen number from the oblivion of forgetfulness. An animal lacks this capacity almost entirely. The things that it remembers are far from numerous and it is devoid of any means of reinforcing its memory. But man has such a means and it is commonly called conscience. At bottom it is based upon the principle that pain is always more enduring than pleasure. Therefore, "in order to make an idea stay it must be burned into the memory; only that which never ceases to hurt remains fixed." Hence all the world's store of tortures and sacrifices. At one time they were nothing more than devices to make man remember his pledges to his gods. Today they survive in the form of legal punishments, which are nothing more, at bottom, than devices to make a man remember his pledges to his fellow men.

From all this Nietzsche argues that our modern law is the outgrowth of the primitive idea of barter — of the idea that everything has an equivalent and can be paid for — that when a man forgets or fails to discharge an obligation in one way he may wipe out his sin by discharging it in some other way. "The earliest relationship that ever existed," he says, "was the relationship between buyer and seller, creditor and debtor. On this ground man first stood face to face with man. No stage of civilization, however inferior, is without the institution of bartering. To fix prices, to adjust values, to invent equivalents, to exchange things — all this has to such an extent preoccupied the first and earliest thought of man, that it may be said to constitute thinking itself. Out of it sagacity arose, and out of it, again, arose man's first pride — his first feeling of superiority over the animal world. Perhaps, our very word man (manus) expresses something of this. Man calls himself the being who weighs and measures."

Now besides the contract between man and man, there is also a contract between man and the community. The community agrees to give the individual protection and the individual promises to pay for it in labor and obedience. Whenever he fails to do so, he violates his promise, and the community regards the contract as broken. Then "the anger of the outraged creditor -or community — withdraws its protection from the debtor — or law-breaker — and he is laid open to all the dangers and disadvantages of life in a state of barbarism. Punishment, at this stage of civilization, is simply the image of a man's normal conduct toward a hated, dis-armed and cast-down enemy, who has forfeited not only all claims to protection, but also all claims to mercy. This accounts for the fact that war (including the sacrificial cult of war) has furnished all the forms in which punishment appears in history."

It will be observed that this theory grounds all ideas of justice and punishment upon ideas of expedience. The primeval creditor forced his debtor to pay because he knew that if the latter didn't pay he (the creditor) would suffer. In itself, the debtor's effort to get something for nothing was not wrong, because, as we have seen in previous chapters, this is the ceaseless and unconscious endeavor of every living being, and is, in fact, the most familiar of all manifestations of the primary will to live, or more understandably, of the will to acquire power over environment. But when the machinery of justice was placed in the hands of the state, there came a transvaluation of values. Things that were manifestly costly to the state were called wrong, and the old individualistic standards of good and bad — i. e. beneficial and harmful — became the standards of good and evil — i.e. right and wrong.

In this way, says Nietzsche, the original purpose of punishment has become obscured and forgotten. Starting out as a mere means of adjusting debts, it has become a machine for enforcing moral concepts. Moral ideas came into the world comparatively late, and it was not until man had begun to be a speculative being that he invented gods, commandments and beatitudes. But the institution of punishment was in existence from a much earlier day. Therefore, it is apparent that the moral idea, — the notion that there is such a thing as good and such a thing as evil, — far from being the inspiration of punishment, was engrafted upon it at a comparatively late period. Nietzsche says that man, in considering things as they are today, is very apt to make this mistake about their origins. He is apt to conclude, because the human eye is used for seeing, that it was created for that purpose, whereas it is obvious that it may have been created for some other purpose and that the function of seeing may have arisen later on. In the same way, man believes that punishment was invented for the purpose of enforcing moral ideas, whereas, as a matter of fact, it was originally an instrument of expediency only, and did not become a moral machine until a code of moral laws was evolved.

To show that the institution of punishment itself is older than the ideas which now seem to lie at the base of it, Nietzsche cites the fact that these ideas themselves are constantly varying. That is to say, the aim and purpose of punishment are conceived differently by different races and individuals. One authority calls it a means of rendering the criminal helpless and harmless and so preventing further mischief in future. Another says that it is a means of inspiring others with fear of the law and its agents. Another says that it is a device for destroying the unfit. Another holds it to be a fee exacted by society from the evil-doer for protecting him against the excesses of private revenge. Still another looks upon it as society's declaration of war against its enemies. Yet another says that it is a scheme for making the criminal realize his guilt and repent. Nietzsche shows that all of these ideas, while true, perhaps, in some part, are fallacies at bottom. It is ridiculous, for instance, to believe that punishment makes the law-breaker acquire a feeling of guilt and sinfulness. He sees that he was indiscreet in committing his crime, but he sees, too, that society's method of punishing his indiscretion consists in committing a crime of the same sort against him. In other words, he cannot hold his own crime a sin without also holding his punishment a sin — which leads to an obvious absurdity. As a matter of fact, says Nietzsche, punishment really does nothing more than "augment fear, intensify prudence and subjugate the passions." And in so doing it tames man, but does not make him better. If he refrains from crime in future, it is because he has become more prudent and not because he has become more moral. If he regrets his crimes of the past, it is because his punishment, and not his so-called conscience, hurts him.

But what, then, is conscience? That there is such a thing every reasonable man knows. But what is its nature and what is its origin? If it is not the regret which follows punishment, what is it? Nietzsche answers that it is nothing more than the old will to power, turned inward. In the days of the cave men, a man gave his will to power free exercise. Any act which increased his power over his environment, no matter how much it damaged other men, seemed to him good. He knew nothing of morality. Things appeared to him, not as good or evil, but as good or bad — beneficial or harmful. But when civilization was born, there arose a necessity for controlling and regulating this will power. The individual had to submit to the desire of the majority and to conform to nascent codes of morality. The result was that his will to power, which once spent itself in battles with other individuals, had to be turned upon himself. Instead of torturing others, he began to torture his own body and mind. His ancient delight in cruelty and persecution (a characteristic of all healthy animals) remained, but he could not longer satisfy it upon his fellow men and so he turned it upon himself, and straightway became a prey to the feeling of guilt, of sinfulness, of wrong-doing — with all its attendant horrors.

Now, one of the first forms that this self-torture took was primitive man's accusation against himself that he was not properly grateful for the favors of his god. He saw that many natural phenomena benefited him, and he thought that these phenomena occurred in direct obedience to the deity's command. Therefore, he regarded himself as the debtor of the deity, and constantly accused himself of neglecting to discharge this debt, because he felt that, by so accusing, he would be most apt to discharge it in full, and thus escape the righteous consequences of insufficient payment. This led him to make sacrifices — to place food and drink upon his god's altar, and in the end, to sacrifice much more valuable things, such, for instance, as his first born child. The more vivid the idea of the deity became and the more terrible he appeared, the more man tried to satisfy and appease him. In the early days, it was sufficient to sacrifice a square meal or a baby. But when Christianity — with its elaborate and certain theology — arose, it became necessary for a man to sacrifice himself.

Thus arose the Christian idea of sin. Man began to feel that be was in debt to his creator hopelessly and irretrievably, and that, like a true bankrupt, he should offer all that he had in partial payment. So he renounced everything that made life on earth bearable and desirable and built up an ideal of poverty and suffering. Sometimes he hid himself in a cave and lived like an outcast dog — and then he was called a saint. Sometimes he tortured himself with whips and poured vinegar into his wounds — and then he was a flagellant of the middle ages. Sometimes, he killed his sexual instinct and his inborn desire for property and power — and then he became a penniless celibate in a cloister.

Nietzsche shows that this idea of sin, which lies at the bottom of all religions, was and is an absurdity; that nothing, in itself, is sinful, and that no man is, or can be, a sinner. If we could rid ourselves of the notion that there is a God in Heaven, to whom we owe a debt, we would rid ourselves of the idea of sin. Therefore, argues Nietzsche, it is evident that skepticism, while it makes no actual change in man, always makes him feel better. It makes him lose his fear of hell and his consciousness of sin. It rids him of that most horrible instrument of senseless and costly torture — his conscience. "Atheism," says Nietzsche, " will make a man innocent."

Education

Education, as everyone knows, has two main objects: to impart knowledge and to implant culture. It is the object of a teacher, first of all, to bring before his pupil as many concrete facts about the universe — the fruit of long ages of inquiry and experience — as the latter may be capable of absorbing in the time available. After that, it is the teacher's aim to make his pupil's habits of mind sane, healthy and manly, and his whole outlook upon life that of a being conscious of his efficiency and eager and able to solve new problems as they arise. The educated man, in a word, is one who knows a great deal more than the average man and is constantly increasing his area of knowledge, in a sensible, orderly logical fashion; one who is wary of sophistry and leans automatically and almost instinctively toward clear thinking.

Such is the purpose of education, in its ideal aspect. As we observe the science of teaching in actual practice, we find that it often fails utterly to attain this end. The concrete facts that a student learns at the average school are few and unconnected, and instead of being led into habits of independent thinking he is trained to accept authority. When he takes his degree it is usually no more than a sign that he has joined the herd. His opinion of Napoleon is merely a reflection of the opinion expressed in the books he has studied; his philosophy of life is simply the philosophy of his teacher — tinctured a bit, perhaps, by that of his particular youthful idols. He knows how to spell a great many long words and he is familiar with the table of logarithms, but in the readiness and accuracy of his mental processes he has made comparatively little progress. If he was illogical and credulous and a respecter of authority as a freshman he remains much the same as a graduate. In consequence, his usefulness to humanity has been increased but little, if at all, for, as we have seen in previous chapters, the only man whose life is appreciably more valuable than that of a good cow is the man who thinks for himself, clearly and logically, and lends some sort of hand, during his lifetime, in the eternal search for the ultimate verities.

The cause for all this lies, no doubt, in the fact that school teachers, taking them by and large, are probably the most ignorant and stupid class of men in the whole group of mental workers. Imitativeness being the dominant impulse in youth, their pupils acquire some measure of their stupidity, and the result is that the influence of the whole teaching tribe is against everything included in genuine education and culture.

That this is true is evident on the surface and a moment's analysis furnishes a multitude of additional proofs. For one thing, a teacher, before he may begin work, must sacrifice whatever independence may survive within him upon the altar of authority. He becomes a cog in the school wheel and must teach only the things countenanced and approved by the powers above him, whether those powers be visible in the minister of education, as in Germany; in the traditions of the school, as in England, or in the private convictions of the millionaire who provides the cash, as in the United States. As Nietzsche points out, the schoolman's thirst for the truth is always conditioned by his yearning for food and drink and a comfortable bed. His archetype is the university philosopher, who accepts the state's pay. and so surrenders that liberty to inquire freely which alone makes philosophy worth while.

"No state," says Nietzsche, "would ever dare to patronize such men as Plato and Schopenhauer. And why? Simply because the state is always afraid of them. They tell the truth.... Consequently, the man who submits to be a philosopher in the pay of the state must also submit to being looked upon by the state as one who has waived his claim to pursue the truth into all its fastnesses. So long as he holds his place, he must acknowledge something still higher than the truth — and that is the state....

"The sole criticism of a philosophy which is possible and the only one which proves anything — namely, an attempt to live according to it — is never put forward in the universities. There the only thing one hears of is a wordy criticism of words. And so the youthful mind, without much experience in life, is confronted by fifty verbal systems and fifty criticisms of them, thrown together and hopelessly jumbled. What demoralization! What a mockery of education! It is openly acknowledged, in fact, that the object of education is not the acquirement of learning, but the successful meeting of examinations. No wonder then, that the examined student says to himself 'Thank God, I am not a philosopher, but a Christian and a citizen!...'

"Therefore, I regard it as necessary to progress that we withdraw from philosophy all governmental and academic recognition and support.... Let philosophers spring up naturally, deny therein every prospect of appointment, tickle them no longer with salaries — yea, persecute them! Then, you will see marvels! They will then flee afar and seek a roof anywhere. Here a parsonage will open its doors; there a schoolhouse. One will appear upon the staff of a newspaper, another will write manuals for young ladies' schools. The most rational of them will put his hand to the plough and the vainest will seek favor at court. Thus we shall get rid of bad philosophers."

The argument here is plain enough. The professional teacher must keep to his rut. The moment he combats the existing order of things he loses his place. Therefore he is wary, and his chief effort is to transmit the words of authority to his pupils unchanged. Whether he be a philosopher, properly so-called, or something else matters not. In a medical school wherein Chauveau's theory of immunity was still maintained it would be hazardous for a professor of pathology to teach the theory of Ehrlich. In a Methodist college in Indiana it would be foolhardy to dally with the doctrine of apostolic succession. Everywhere the teacher must fashion his teachings according to the creed and regulations of his school and he must even submit to authority in such matters as text books and pedagogic methods. Again, his very work itself makes him an unconscious partisan of authority, as against free inquiry. During the majority of his waking hours he is in close association with his pupils, who are admittedly his inferiors, and so, he rapidly acquires the familiar, self-satisfied professorial attitude of mind. Other forces tend to push him in the same direction and the net result is that all his mental processes are based upon ideas of authority. He believes and teaches a thing, not because he is convinced by free reasoning that it is true, but because it is laid down as an axiom in some book or was laid down at some past time, by himself.

In all this, of course, I am speaking of the teacher properly so-called — of the teacher, that is, whose sole aim and function is teaching. The university professor whose main purpose in life is original research and whose pupils are confined to graduate students engaged in much the same work, is scarcely a professional teacher, in the customary meaning of the word. The man I have been discussing is him who spends all or the greater part of his time in actual instruction. Whether that work be done in a primary school, a secondary school or in the undergraduate department of a college or university does not matter. In all that relates to it, he is essentially and almost invariably a mere perpetuator of doctrines. In some cases, naturally enough, these doctrines are truths, but in a great many other cases they are errors. An examination of the physiology, history and "English" books used in the public schools of America will convince anyone that the latter proposition is amply true.

Nietzsche's familiarity with these facts is demonstrated by numerous passages in his writings. "Never," he says, "is either real proficiency or genuine ability the result of toilsome years at school." The study of the classics, he says, can never lead to more than a superficial acquaintance with them, because the very modes of thought of the ancients, in many cases, are unintelligible to men of today. But the student who has acquired what is looked upon in our colleges as a mastery of the humanities is acutely conscious of his knowledge, and so the things that he cannot understand are ascribed by him to the dullness, ignorance or imbecility of the ancient authors. As a result he harbors a sort of subconscious contempt for the learning they represent and concludes that learning cannot make real men happy, but is only fit for the futile enthusiasm of "honest, poor and foolish old book-worms."

Nietzsche's own notion of an ideal curriculum is substantially that of Spencer. He holds that before anything is put forward as a thing worth teaching it should be tested by two questions: Is it a fact? and, Is the presentation of it likely to make the pupil measurably more capable of discovering other facts? In consequences, he holds the old so-called "liberal" education in abomination, and argues in favor of a system of instruction based upon the inculcation of facts of imminent value and designed to instill into the pupil orderly and logical habits of mind and a clear and accurate view of the universe. The educated man, as he understands the term, is one who is above the mass, both in his thirst for knowledge and in his capacity for differentiating between truth and its reverse. It is obvious that a man who has studied biology and physics, with their insistent dwelling upon demonstrable facts, has proceeded further in this direction than the man who has studied Greek mythology and metaphysics, with their constant trend toward unsupported and gratuitous assumption and their essential foundation upon undebatable authority.

Nietzsche points out, in his early essay upon the study of history, that humanity is much too prone to consider itself historically. That is to say, there is too much tendency to consider man as he has seemed rather than man as he has been — to dwell upon creeds and manifestoes rather than upon individual and racial motives, characters and instincts. The result is that history piles up misleading and useless records and draws erroneous conclusions from them. As a science in itself, it bears but three useful aspects — the monumental, the antiquarian and the critical. Its true monuments are not the constitutions and creeds of the past — for these, as we have seen, are always artificial and unnatural — but the great men of the past — those fearless free spirits who achieved immortality by their courage and success in pitting their own instincts against the morality of the majority. Such men, he says, are the only human beings whose existence is of interest to posterity. "They live together as timeless contemporaries:" they are the land-marks along the weary road the human race has traversed. In its antiquarian aspect, history affords us proof that the world is progressing, and so gives the men of the present a definite purpose and justifiable enthusiasm. In its critical aspect, history enables us to avoid the delusions of the past, and indicates to us the broad lines of evolution. Unless we have in mind some definite program of advancement, he says, all learning is useless. History, which merely accumulates records, without "an ideal of humanistic culture" always in mind, is mere pedantry and scholasticism.

All education, says Nietzsche, may be regarded as a continuation of the process of breeding. The two have the same object: that of producing beings capable of surviving in the struggle for existence. A great many critics of Nietzsche have insisted that since the struggle for existence means a purely physical contest, he is in error, for education does not visibly increase a man's chest expansion or his capacity for lifting heavy weights. But it is obvious none the less that a man who sees things as they are, and properly estimates the world about him, is far better fitted to achieve some measure of mastery over his environment than the man who is a slave to delusions. Of two men, one of whom believes that the moon is made of green cheese and that it is possible to cure smallpox by merely denying that it exists, and the other of whom harbors no such superstitions, it is plain that the latter is more apt to live long and acquire power.

A further purpose of education is that of affording individuals a means of lifting themselves out of the slave class and into the master class. That this purpose is accomplished — except accidently — by the brand of education ladled out in the colleges of today is far from true. To transform a slave into a master we must make him intelligent, self-reliant, resourceful, independent and courageous. It is evident enough, I take it, that a college directed by an ecclesiastic and manned by a faculty of asses — a very fair, and even charitable, picture of the average small college in the United States — is not apt to accomplish this transformation very often. Indeed, it is a commonplace observation that a truly intelligent youth is aided but little by the average college education, and that a truly stupid one is made, not less, but more stupid. The fact that many graduates of such institutions exhibit dionysian qualities in later life merely proves that they are strong enough to weather the blight they have suffered. Every sane man knows that, after a youth leaves college, he must devote most of his energies during three or four years, to ridding himself of the fallacies, delusions and imbecilities inflicted upon him by messieurs, his professors.

The intelligent man, in the course of his life, nearly always acquires a vast store of learning, because his mind is constantly active and receptive, but intelligence and mere learning are by no means synonymous, despite the popular notion that they are. Disregarding the element of sheer good luck — which is necessarily a small factor — it is evident that the man who, in the struggle for wealth and power, seizes a million dollars for himself, is appreciably more intelligent than the man who starves. That this achievement, which is admittedly difficult, requires more intelligence again, than the achievement of mastering the Latin language, which presents so few difficulties that it is possible to any healthy human being with sufficient leisure and patience, is also evident. In a word, the illiterate contractor, who says, "I seen" and "I done" and yet manages to build great bridges and to acquire a great fortune, is immeasurably more vigorous intellectually, and immeasurably more efficient and respectable, as a man, than the college professor who laughs at him and presumes to look down upon him. A man's mental powers are to be judged, not by his ability to accomplish things that are possible to every man foolish enough to attempt them, but by his capacity for doing things beyond the power of other men. Education, as we commonly observe it today, works toward the former, rather than toward the latter end.

Sundry Ideas

Death. — It is Schopenhauer's argument in his essay "On Suicide," that the possibility of easy and painless self-destruction is the only thing that constantly and considerably ameliorates the horror of human life. Suicide is a means of escape from the world and its tortures — and therefore it is good. It is an ever-present refuge for the weak, the weary and the hopeless. It is, in Pliny's phrase, "the greatest of all blessings which Nature gives to man," and one which even God himself lacks, for "he could not compass his own death, if he willed to die." In all of this exaltation of surrender, of course, there is nothing whatever in common with the dionysian philosophy of defiance. Nietzsche's teaching is all in the other direction. He urges, not surrender, but battle; not flight, but war to the end. His curse falls upon those "preachers of death" who counsel "an abandonment of life" — whether this abandonment be partial, as in asceticism, or actual, as in suicide. And yet Zarathustra sings the song of "free death" and says that the higher man must learn "to die at the right time." Herein an inconsistency appears, but it is on the surface only. Schopenhauer regards suicide as a means of escape, Nietzsche sees in it as a means of good riddance. It is time to die, says Zarathustra, when the purpose of life ceases to be attainable — when the fighter breaks his sword arm or falls into his enemy's hands. And it is time to die, too, when the purpose of life is attained — when the fighter triumphs and sees before him no more worlds to conquer. "He who hath a goal and an heir wisheth death to come at the right time for goal and heir." One who has "waxed too old for victories," one who is "yellow and wrinkled," one with a "toothless mouth " — for such an one a certain and speedy death. The earth has no room for cumberers and pensioners. For them the highest of duties is the payment of nature's debt, that there may be more room for those still able to wield a sword and bear a burden in the heat of the day. The best death is that which comes in battle "at the moment of victory;" the second best is death in battle in the hour of defeat. "Would that a storm came," sings Zarathustra, "to shake from the tree of life all those apples that are putrid and gnawed by worms. It is cowardice that maketh them stick to their branches" — cowardice which makes them afraid to die. But there is another cowardice which makes men afraid to live, and this is the cowardice of the Schopenhauerean pessimist. Nietzsche has no patience with it. To him a too early death seems as abominable as a death postponed too long. "Too early died that Jew whom the preachers of slow death revere. Would that he had remained in the desert and far away from the good and just! Perhaps he would have learned how to live and how to love the earth — and even how to laugh. He died too early. He himself would have revoked his doctrine, had he reached mine age!", Therefore Nietzsche pleads for an intelligent regulation of death. One must not die too soon and one must not die too late."Natural death," he says, "is destitute of rationality. It is really irrational death, for the pitiable substance of the shell determines how long the kernel shall exist. The pining, sottish prison-warder decides the hour at which his noble prisoner is to die.... The enlightened regulation and control of death belongs to the morality of the future. At present religion makes it seem immoral, for religion presupposes that when the time for death comes, God gives the command."

The Attitude at Death. — Nietzsche rejects entirely that pious belief in signs and portents which sees a significance in death-bed confessions and "dying words." The average man, he says, dies pretty much as he has lived, and in this Dr. Osler and other unusually competent and accurate observers agree with him. When the dying man exhibits unusual emotions or expresses ideas out of tune with his known creed, the explanation is to be found in the fact that, toward the time of death the mind commonly gives way and the customary processes of thought are disordered. "The way in which a man thinks of death, in the full bloom of his life — and strength, is certainly a good index of his general character and habits of mind, but at the hour of death itself his attitude is of little importance or significance. The exhaustion of the last hours — especially when an old man is dying — the irregular or insufficient nourishment of the brain, the occasional spasms of severe physical pain, the horror and novelty of the whole situation, the atavistic return of early impressions and superstitions, and the feeling that death is a thing unutterably vast and important and that bridges of an awful kind are about to be crossed — all of these things make it irrational to accept a man's attitude at death as an indication of his character during life. Moreover, it is not true that a dying man is more honest than a man in full vigor. On the contrary, almost every dying man is led, by the solemnity of those at his bedside, and by their restrained or flowing torrents of tears, to conscious or unconscious conceit and make-believe. He becomes, in brief, an actor in a comedy.... No doubt the seriousness with which every dying man is treated has given many a poor devil his only moment of real triumph and enjoyment. He is, ipso facto, the star of the play, and so, he is indemnified for a life of privation and subservience."

The Origin of Philosophy. — Nietzsche believed that introspection and self-analysis, as they were ordinarily manifested, were signs of disease, and that the higher man and superman would waste little time upon them. The first thinkers, he said, were necessarily sufferers, for it was only suffering that made a man think and only disability that gave him leisure to do so. "Under primitive conditions," he said, "the individual, fully conscious of his power, is ever intent upon transforming it into action. Sometimes this action takes the form of hunting, robbery, ambuscade, maltreatment or murder, and at other times it appears as those feebler imitations of those things which alone are countenanced by the community. But when the individual's power declines — when he feels fatigued, ill, melancholy or satiated, and in consequence, temporarily lacks the yearning to function — he is a comparatively better and less dangerous man. That is to say, he contents himself with thinking instead of doing, and so puts into thought and words "his impressions and feelings regarding his companions, his wife or his gods." Naturally enough, since his efficiency is lowered and his mood is gloomy his judgments are evil ones. He finds fault and ponders revenges. He gloats over enemies or envies his friends. "In such a state of mind he turns prophet and so, adds to his store of superstitions or devises new acts of devotion or prophesies the downfall of his enemies. Whatever he thinks, his thoughts reflect his state of mind: his fear and weariness are more than normal; his tendency to action and enjoyment are less than normal. Herein we see the genesis of the poetic, thoughtful, priestly mood. Evil thoughts must rule supreme therein.... In later stages of culture, there arose a caste of poets, thinkers, priests and medicine men who all acted the same as, in earlier years, individuals used to act in their comparatively rare hours of illness and depression. These persons led sad, inactive lives and judged maliciously.... The masses, perhaps, yearned to turn them out of the community, because they were parasites, but in this enterprise there was great risk, because these men were on terms of familiarity with the gods and so possessed vast and mysterious power. Thus the most ancient philosophers were viewed. The masses hearkened unto thern in proportion to the amount of dread they inspired. In such a way contemplation made its appearance in the world, with an evil heart and a troubled head. It was both weak and terrible, and both secretly abhorred and openly worshipped.... Pudenda origo!"

Priestcraft. — So long as man feels capable of taking care of himself he has no need of priests to intercede for him with the deity. Efficiency is proverbially identified with impiety: it is only when the devil is sick that the devil a monk would be. Therefore "the priest must be regarded as the saviour, shepherd and advocate of the sick.... It is his providence to rule over the sufferers." In order that he may understand them and appeal to them he must be sick himself, and to attain this end there is the device of asceticism. The purpose of asceticism, as we have seen, is to make a man voluntarily destroy his own efficiency. But the priest must have a certain strength, nevertheless, for he must inspire both confidence and dread in his charges, and must be able to defend them — against whom? "Undoubtedly against the sound and strong.... He must be the natural adversary and despiser of all barbarous, impetuous, unbridled, fierce, violent, beast-of-prey healthiness and power." Thus he must fashion himself into a new sort of fighter — "a new zoological terror, in which the polar bear, the nimble and cool tiger and the fox are blended into a unity as attractive as it is awe-inspiring." He appears in the midst of the strong as "the herald and mouthpiece of mysterious powers, with the determination to sow upon the soil, whenever and wherever possible, the seeds of suffering, dissension and contradiction.... Undoubtedly he brings balms and balsams with him, but he must first inflict the wound, before he may act as physician.... It is only the unpleasantness of disease that is combated by him — not the cause, not the disease itself!" He dispenses, not specifics, but narcotics. He brings surcease from sorrow, not by showing men how to attain the happiness of efficiency, but by teaching them that their sufferings have been laid upon them by a god who will one day repay them with bliss illimitable."

God. — "A god who is omniscient and omnipotent and yet neglects to make his wishes and intentions certainly known to his creatures — certainly this is not a god of goodness. One who for thousands of years has allowed the countless scruples and doubts of men to afflict them and yet holds out terrible consequences for involuntary errors — certainly this is not a god of justice. Is he not a cruel god if he knows the truth and yet looks down upon millions miserably searching for it? Perhaps he is good, but is unable to communicate with his creatures more intelligibly. Perhaps he is wanting in intelligence — or in eloquence. So much the worse! For, in that case, he may be mistaken in what he calls the truth. He may, indeed, be a brother to the 'poor, duped devils' below him. If so, must he not suffer agonies on seeing his creatures, in their struggle for knowledge of him, submit to tortures for all eternity? Must it not strike him with grief to realize that he cannot advise them or help them, except by uncertain and ambiguous signs?... All religions bear traces of the fact that they arose during the intellectual immaturity of the human race — before it had learned the obligation to speak the truth. Not one of them makes it the duty of its god to be truthful and understandable in his communications with man."

Self-Control. — Self-control, says Nietzsche, consists merely in combating a given desire with a stronger one. Thus the yearning to commit a murder may be combated and overcome by the yearning to escape the gallows and to retain the name and dignity of a law-abiding citizen. The second yearning is as much unconscious and instinctive as the first, and in the battle between them the intellect plays but a small part. In general there are but six ways in which a given craving may be overcome. First, we may avoid opportunities for its gratification and so, by a long disuse, weaken and destroy it. Secondly, we may regulate its gratification, and by thus encompassing its flux and reflux within fixed limits, gain intervals during which it is faint. Thirdly, we may intentionally give ourselves over to it and so wear it out by excess — provided we do not act like the rider who lets a runaway horse gallop itself to death and, in so doing, breaks his own neck, — which unluckily is the rule in this method. Fourthly, by an intellectual trick, we may associate gratification with an unpleasant idea, as we have associated sexual gratification, for example, with the idea of indecency. Fifthly, we may find a substitute in some other craving that is measurably less dangerous. Sixthly, we may find safety in a general war upon all cravings, good and bad alike, after the manner of the ascetic, who, in seeking to, destroy his sensuality, at the same time destroys his physical strength, his reason and, not infrequently, his life.

The Beautiful. — Man's notion of beauty is the fruit of his delight in his own continued existence. Whatever makes this existence easy, or is associated, in any manner, with life or vigor, seems to him to be beautiful. "Man mirrors himself in things. He counts everything beautiful which reflects his likeness. The word 'beautiful' represents the conceit of his species.... Nothing is truly ugly except the degenerating man. But other things are called ugly, too, when they happen to weaken or trouble man. They remind him of impotence, deterioration and danger: in their presence he actually suffers a loss of power. Therefore he calls them ugly. Whenever man is at all depressed he has an intuition of the proximity of something 'ugly.' His sense of power, his will to power, his feeling of pride and efficiency — all sink with the ugly and rise with the beautiful. The ugly is instinctively understood to be a sign and symptom of degeneration. That which reminds one, in the remotest degree, of degeneracy seems ugly. Every indication of exhaustion, heaviness, age, or lassitude, every constraint — such as cramp or paralysis — and above all, every odor, color or counterfeit of decomposition — though it may be no more than a far-fetched symbol — calls forth the idea of ugliness. Aversion is thereby excited — man's aversion to the decline of his type." The phrase "art for art's sake" voices a protest against subordinating art to morality — that is, against making it a device for preaching sermons — but as a matter of fact, all art must praise and glorify and so must lay down values. It is the function of the artist, indeed, to select, to choose, to bring into prominence. The very fact that he is able to do this makes us call him an artist. And when do we approve his choice? Only when it agrees with our fundamental instinct — only when it exhibits "the desirableness of life." "Therefore art is the great stimulus to life. We cannot conceive it as being purposeless or aimless. 'Art for art's sake' is a phrase without meaning."

Liberty. — The worth of a thing often lies, not in what one attains by it, but in the difficulty one experiences in getting it. The struggle for political liberty, for example, has done more than any other one thing to develop strength, courage and resourcefulness in the human race, and yet liberty itself, as we know it today, is nothing more or less than organized morality, and as such, is necessarily degrading and degenerating. "It under-mines the will to power, it levels the racial mountains and valleys, it makes man small, cowardly and voluptuous. Under political liberty the herd-animal always triumphs." But the very fight to attain this burdensome equality develops the self-reliance and unconformity which stand opposed to it, and these qualities often persist. Warfare, in brief, makes men fit for real, as opposed to political freedom. "And what is freedom? The will to be responsible for one's self. The will to keep that distance which separates man from man. The will to become indifferent to hardship, severity, privation and even to life. The will to sacrifice men to one's cause and to sacrifice one self, too.... The man who is truly free tramples under foot the contemptible species of well-being dreamt of by shop-keepers, Christians, cows, women, Englishmen and other democrats. How is freedom to be measured? By the resistance it has to overcome — by the effort required to maintain it. We must seek the highest type of freemen where the highest resistance must be constantly overcome: five paces from tyranny, close to the threshold of thraldom.... Those peoples who were worth something, who became worth something, never acquired their greatness under political liberty. Great danger made something of them — danger of that sort which first teaches us to know our resources, our virtues, our shields and swords, our genius — which compels us to be strong."

Science. — The object of all science is to keep us from drawing wrong inferences — from jumping to conclusions. Thus it stands utterly opposed to all faith and is essentially iconoclastic and skeptical. "The wonderful in science is the reverse of the wonderful in juggling. The juggler tries to make us see a very simple relation between things which, in point of fact, have no relation at all. The scientist, on the contrary, compels us to abandon our belief in simple casualities and to see the enormous complexity of phenomena. The simplest things, indeed, are extremely complex — a fact which will never cease to make us wonder." The effect of science is to show the absurdity of attempting to reach perfect happiness and the impossibility of experiencing utter woe. "The gulf between the highest pitch of happiness and the lowest depth of misery has been created by imaginary things." That is to say, the heights of religious exaltation and the depths of religious fear and trembling are alike creatures of our own myth-making. There is no such thing as perfect and infinite bliss in heaven and there is no such thing as eternal damnation in hell. Hereafter our highest happiness must be less than that of the martyrs who saw the heavenly gates opening for them, and our worst woe must be less than that of those medieval sinners who died shrieking and trembling and with the scent of brim-stone in their noses. "This space is being reduced further and further by science, just as through science we have learned to make the earth occupy less and less space in the universe, until it now seems infinitely small and our whole solar system appears as a mere point."

The Jews. — For the Jewish slave-morality which prevails in the western world today, under the label of Christianity, Nietzsche had, as we know, the most violent aversion and contempt, but he saw very clearly that this same morality admirably served and fitted the Jews themselves; that it had preserved them through long ages and against powerful enemies, and that its very persistence proved alike its own ingenuity and the vitality of its inventors as a race. "The Jews," said Nietzsche, "will either become the masters of Europe or lose Europe, as they once lost Egypt. And it seems to be improbable that they will lose again. In Europe, for eighteen centuries, they have passed through a school more terrible than that known to any other nation, and the experiences of this time of stress and storm have benefited the individual even more than the community. In consequence, the resourcefulness and alertness of the modern Jew are extraordinary.... In times of extremity, the people of Israel less often sought refuge in drink or suicide than any other race of Europe. Today, every Jew finds in the history of his forebears a voluminous record of coolness and perseverance in terrible predicaments —

of artful cunning and clever fencing with chance and misfortune. The Jews have hid their bravery under the cloak of submissiveness; their heroism in facing contempt surpasses that of the saints. People tried to make them contemptible for twenty centuries by refusing them all honors and dignities and by pushing them down into the mean trades. The process did not make them cleaner, alas! but neither did it make them contemptible. They have never ceased to believe themselves qualified for the highest of activities. They have never failed to show the virtues of all suffering peoples. Their manner of honoring their parents and their children and the reasonableness of their marriage customs make them conspicuous among Europeans. Besides, they have learned how to derive a sense of power from the very trades forced upon them. We cannot help observing, in excuse for their usury, that without this pleasant means of inflicting torture upon their oppressors, they might have lost their self-respect ages ago, for self-respect depends upon being able to make reprisals. Moreover, their vengeance has never carried them too far, for they have that liberality which comes from frequent changes of place, climate, customs and neighbors. They have more experience of men than any other race and even in their passions there appears a caution born of this experience. They are so sure of themselves that, even in their bitterest straits, they never earn their bread by manual labor as common workmen, porters or peasants.... Their manners, it may be admitted, teach us that they have never been inspired by chivalrous, noble feelings, nor their bodies girt with beautiful arms: a certain vulgarity always alternates with their submissiveness. But now they are intermarrying with the gentlest blood of Europe, and in another hundred years they will have enough good manners to save them from making themselves ridiculous, as masters, in the sight of those they have subdued." It was Nietzsche's belief that the Jews would take the lead before long, in the intellectual progress of the world. He thought that their training, as a race, fitted them for this leadership." Where," he asked, "shall the accumulated wealth of great impressions which forms the history of every Jewish family — that great wealth of passions, virtues, resolutions, resignations, struggles and victories of all sorts — where shall it find an outlet, if not in great intellectual functioning?" The Jews, he thought, would be safe guides for mankind, once they were set free from their slave-morality and all need of it. "Then again," he said, "the old God of the Jews may rejoice in Himself, in His creation and in His chosen people — and all of us will rejoice with Him."

The Gentleman. — A million sages and diagnosticians, in all ages of the world, have sought to define the gentleman, and their definitions have been as varied as their own minds. Nietzsche's definition is based upon the obvious fact that the gentleman is ever a man of more than average influence and power, and the further fact that this superiority is admitted by all. The vulgarian may boast of his bluff honesty, but at heart he looks up to the gentleman, who goes through life serene and imperturbable. There is in the latter, in truth, an unmistakable air of fitness and efficiency, and it is this which makes it possible for him to be gentle and to regard those below him with tolerance. "The demeanor of high-born persons," says Nietzsche, "shows plainly that in their minds the consciousness of power is ever-present. Above all things, they strive to avoid a show of weakness, whether it takes the form of inefficiency or of a too-easy yielding to passion or emotion. They never sink exhausted into a chair. On the train, when the vulgar try to make themselves comfortable, these higher folk avoid reclining. They do not seem to get tired after hours of standing at court. They do not furnish their houses in a comfortable, but in a spacious and dignified manner, as if they were the abodes of a greater and taller race of beings. To a provoking speech, they reply with politeness and self-possession — and not as if horrified, crushed, abashed, enraged or out of breath, after the manner of plebeians. The aristocrat knows how to preserve the appearance of ever-present physical strength, and he knows, too, how to convey the impression that his soul and intellect are a match to all dangers and surprises, by keeping up an unchanging serenity and civility, even under the most trying circumstances."

Dreams. — Dreams are symptoms of the eternal law of compensation. In our waking hours we develop a countless horde of yearnings, cravings and desires, and by the very nature of things, the majority of them must go ungratified. The feeling that something is wanting, thus left within us, is met and satisfied by our imaginary functionings during sleep. That is to say, dreams represent the reaction of our yearnings upon the phenomena actually encountered during sleep — the motions of our blood and intestines, the pressure of the bedclothes, the sounds of church-bells, domestic animals, etc., and the state of the atmosphere. These phenomena are fairly constant, but our dreams vary widely on successive nights. Therefore, the variable factor is represented by the yearnings we harbor as we go to bed. Thus, the man who loves music and must go without it all day, hears celestial harmonies in his sleep. Thus the slave dreams of soaring like an eagle. Thus the prisoner dreams that he is free and the sailor that he is safely at home. Inasmuch as the number of our conscious and un-conscious desires, each day, is infinite, there is an infinite variety in dreams. But always the relation set forth may be predicated.

Nietzsche vs. Wagner

Nietzsche believed in heroes and, in his youth, was a hero worshipper. First Arthur Schopenhauer's bespectacled visage stared from his shrine and after that the place of sacredness and honor was held by Richard Wagner. When the Wagner of the philosopher's dreams turned into a Wagner of very prosaic flesh and blood, there came a time of doubt and stress and suffering for poor Nietzsche. But he had courage as well as loyalty, and in the end he dashed his idol to pieces and crunched the bits underfoot. Faith, doubt, anguish, disillusion — it is not a rare sequence in this pitiless and weary old world.

Those sapient critics who hold that Nietzsche discredited his own philosophy by constantly writing against himself, find their chief ammunition in his attitude toward the composer of Tristan und Isolde. In the decade from 1869 to 1878 the philosopher was the king of German Wagnerians. In the decade from 1879 to 1889, he was the most bitter, the most violent, the most resourceful and the most effective of Wagner's enemies. On their face these things seem to indicate a complete change of front and a careful examination bears out the thought. But the same careful examination reveals another fact: that the change of front was made, not by Nietzsche, but by Wagner.

As we have seen, the philosopher was an ardent musician from boyhood and so it was not unnatural that he should be among the first to recognize Wagner's genius. The sheer musicianship of the man overwhelmed him and he tells us that from the moment the piano transcription of Tristan und Isolde was printed he was a Wagnerian. The music was bold and daring: it struck out into regions that the süsslich sentimentality of Donizetti and Bellini and the pallid classicism of Beethoven and Bach had never even approached. In Wagner Nietzsche saw a man of colossal originality and sublime courage, who thought for himself and had skill at making his ideas comprehensible to others. The opera of the past had been a mere potpourri of songs, strung together upon a filament of banal recitative. The opera of Wagner was a symmetrical and homogeneous whole, in which the music was unthinkable without the poetry and the poetry impossible without the music.

Nietzsche, at the time, was saturated with Schopenhauer's brand of individualism, and intensely eager to apply it to realities. In Wagner lie saw a living, breathing individualist — a man who scorned the laws and customs of his craft and dared to work out his own salvation in his own way. And when fate made it possible for him to meet Wagner, he found the composer preaching as well as practising individualism. In a word, Wagner was well nigh as enthusiastic a Schopenhauerean as Nietzsche himself. His individualism almost touched the boundary of anarchy. He had invented a new art of music and he was engaged in the exciting task of smashing the old one to make room for it.

Nietzsche met Wagner in Leipsic and was invited to visit the composer at his home near Tribschen, a suburb of Lucerne. He accepted, and on May 15, 1869, got his first glimpse of that queer household in which the erratic Richard, the ingenious Cosima and little Siegfried lived and had their being. When he moved to Basel, he was not far from Tribschen and so he fell into the habit of going there often and staying long. He came, indeed, to, occupy the position of an adopted son, and spent the Christmas of 1869 and that of 1870 under the Wagner rooftree. This last fact alone is sufficient to show the intimate footing upon which he stood. Christmas, among the Germans, is essentially a family festival and mere friends are seldom asked to share its joys.

Nietzsche and Wagner had long and riotous disputations at Tribschen, but in all things fundamental they agreed. Together they accepted Schopenhauer's data and together they began to diverge from his conclusions. Nietzsche saw in Wagner that old dionysian spirit which had saved Greek art. The music of the day was colorless and coldblooded. A too rigid formalism stood in the way of all expression of actual life. Wagner proposed to batter this formalism to pieces and Nietzsche was his prophet and claque.

It was this enthusiasm, indeed, which determined the plan of Die Geburt der Tragödie. Nietzsche had conceived it as a mere treatise upon the philosophy of the Greek drama. His ardor as an apostle, his yearning to convert the stolid Germans, his wild desire to do something practical and effective for Wagner, made him turn it into a gospel of the new art. To him Wagner was Dionysus, and the whole of his argument against Apollo was nothing more than an argument against classicism and for the Wagnerian romanticism. It was a bomb-shell and its explosion made Germany stare, but another — perhaps many more — were needed to, shake the foundations of philistinism. Nietzsche loaded the next one carefully and hurled it at him who stood at the very head of that self-satisfied conservatism which lay upon all

Germany. This man was David Strauss. Strauss was the prophet of the good-enough. He taught that German art was sound, that German culture was perfect. Nietzsche saw in him the foe of Dionysus and made an example of him. In every word of that scintillating philippic there was a plea for the independence and individualism, and outlawry that the philosopher saw in Wagner.

Unluckily the disciple here ran ahead of the master and before long Nietzsche began to realize that he and Wagner were drifting apart. So long as they met upon the safe ground of Schopenhauer's data, the two agreed, but after Nietzsche began to work out his inevitable conclusions, Wagner abandoned him. To put it plainly, Wagner was the artist before he was the philosopher, and when philosophy began to grow ugly he turned from it without regret or qualm of conscience. Theoretically, he saw things as

Nietzsche saw them, but as an artist he could not afford to be too literal. It was true enough, perhaps, that self-sacrifice was a medieval superstition, but all the same it made effective heroes on the stage.

Nietzsche was utterly unable, throughout his life, to acknowledge anything but hypocrisy or ignorance in those who descended to such compromises. When he wrote "Richard Wagner in Bayreuth" he was already the prey of doubts, but it is probable that he still saw the "ifs" and "buts" in Wagner's individualism but dimly. He could not realize, in brief, that a composer who fought beneath the banner of truth, against custom, and convention, could ever turn aside from the battle. Wagner agreed with Nietzsche, perhaps, that European civilization and its child, the European art of the day, were founded upon lies, but he was artist enough to see that, without these lies, it would be impossible to make art understandable to the public. So in his librettos he employed all of the old fallacies — that love has the supernatural power of making a bad man good, that one man may save the soul of another, that humility is a virtue.

It is obvious from this, that the apostate was not Nietzsche, but Wagner. Nietzsche started out in life as a seeker after truth, and he sought the truth his whole life long, without regarding for an instant the risks and dangers and consequences of the quest. Wagner, so long as it remained a mere matter of philosophical disputation, was equally radical and courageous, but he saw very clearly that it was necessary to compromise with tradition in his operas. He was an atheist and a mocker of the gods, but the mystery and beauty of the Roman Catholic ritual appealed to his artistic sense, and so, instead of penning an opera in which the hero spouted aphorisms by Huxley, he wrote Parsifal. And in the same way, in his other music dramas, he made artistic use of all the ancient fallacies and devices in the lumber room of chivalry. He was, indeed, a philosopher in his hours of leisure only. When he was at work over his music paper, he saw that St. Ignatius was a far more effective and appealing figure than Herbert Spencer and that the conventional notion that marriage was a union of two immortal souls was far more picturesque than the Schopenhauer-Nietzschean idea that it was a mere symptom of the primary will to live.

In 1876 Nietzsche began to realize that he had left Wagner far behind and that thereafter he could expect no support from the composer. They had not met since 1874, but Nietzsche went to Bayreuth for the first opera season. A single conversation convinced him that his doubts were well-founded — that Wagner was a mere dionysian of the chair and had no intention of pushing the ideas they had discussed to their bitter and revolutionary conclusion. Most other men would have seen in this nothing more than an evidence of a common-sense decision to sacrifice the whole truth for half the truth, but Nietzsche was a rabid hater of compromise. To make terms with the philistines seemed to him to be even worse than joining their ranks. He saw in Wagner only a traitor who knew the truth and yet denied it.

Nietzsche was so much disgusted that he left Bayreuth and set out upon a walking tour, but before the end of the season he returned and heard some of the operas. But he was no longer a Wagnerian and the music of the "Ring" did not delight him. It was impossible, indeed, for him to separate the music from the philosophy set forth in the librettos. He believed, with Wagner, that the two were indissolubly welded, and so, after awhile, he came to condemn the whole fabric — harmonies and melodies as well as heroes and dramatic situations.

When Wagner passed out of his life Nietzsche sought to cure his loneliness by hard work and Menschliches allzu Menschliches was the result. He sent a copy of the first volume to Wagner and on the way it crossed a copy of Parsifal. In this circumstance is well exhibited the width of the breach between the two men. To Wagner Menschliches allzu Menschliches seemed impossibly and insanely radical; to Nietzsche Parsifal, with all its exaltation of ritualism, was unspeakable. Neither deigned to write to the other, but we have it from reliable testimony that Wagner was disgusted and Nietzsche's sister tells us how much the music-drama of the grail enraged him.

A German, when indignation seizes him, rises straight-way to make a loud and vociferous protest. And so, although Nietzsche retained, to the end of his life, a pleasant memory of the happy days he spent at Tribschen and almost his last words voiced his loyal love for Wagner the man, he conceived it to be his sacred duty to combat what he regarded as the treason of Wagner the philosopher. This notion was doubtlessly strengthened by his belief that he himself had done much to launch Wagner's bark. He had praised, and now it was his duty to blame. He had been enthusiastic at the first task, and he determined to be pitiless at the second.

But he hesitated for ten years, because, as has been said, he could not kill his affection for Wagner, the man. It takes courage to wound one's nearest and dearest, and Nietzsche, for all his lack of sentiment, was still no more than human. In the end, however, he brought himself to the heroic surgery that confronted him, and the result was Der Fall Wagner. In this book all friendship and pleasant memories were put aside. Wagner was his friend of old? Very well: that was a reason for him to be all the more exact and all the more unpitying.

"What does a philosopher firstly and lastly require of himself?" he asks. "To overcome his age in himself; to become timeless! With what, then, has he to fight his hardest fight? With those characteristics and ideas which most plainly stamp him as the child of his age." Herein we perceive Nietzsche's fundamental error. Deceived by Wagner's enthusiasm for Schopenhauer and his early, amateurish dabbling in philosophy, he regarded the composer as a philosopher. But Wagner, of course, was first of all an artist, and it is the function of an artist, not to reform humanity, but to depict it as he sees it, or as his age sees it — fallacies, delusions and all. George Bernard Shaw, in his famous criticism of Shakespeare, shows us how the Bard of Avon made just such a compromise with the prevailing opinion of his time. Shakespeare, he says, was too intelligent a man to regard Rosalind as a plausible woman, but the theatre-goers of his day so regarded her and he drew her to their taste. An artist who failed to make such a concession to convention would be an artist without an audience. Wagner was no Christian, but he knew that the quest of the holy grail was an idea which made a powerful appeal to nine-tenths of civilized humanity, and so he turned it into a drama. This was not conscious lack of sincerity, but merely a manifestation of the sub-conscious artistic feeling for effectiveness.

Therefore, it is plain that Nietzsche's whole case against Wagner is based upon a fallacy and that, in consequence, it is not to be taken too seriously. It is true enough that his book contains some remarkably acute and searching observations upon art, and that, granting his premises, his general conclusions would be correct, but we are by no means granting his premises. Wagner may have been a traitor to his philosophy, but if he had remained loyal to it, his art would have been impossible. And in view of the sublime beauty of that art we may well pardon him for not keeping the faith.

Der Fall Wagner caused a horde of stupid critics to maintain that Nietzsche, and not Wagner, was the apostate, and that the mad philosopher had begun to argue against himself. As an answer to that ridiculous charge, Nietzsche published a little book called Nietzsche contra Wagner. It was made up entirely of passages from his earlier books and these proved conclusively that, ever since his initial divergence from Schopenhauer's conclusions, he had hoed a straight row. He was a dionysian in Die Geburt der Tragödie and he was a dionysian still in *Also sprach Zarathustra*.

Nietzsche's Origins

An individual is never an isolated phenomenon and it is impossible to conceive any idea as existing without some cause. As Haeckel tells us, "the cell never acts; it always reacts." Therefore, it is no denial of Nietzsche to say that his philosophy could not have taken form if certain other men had not labored before him. The same thing might be said, with equal truth, of every philosophy and idea the world has ever known. As Pfleiderer has shown us, even Jesus Christ was the inevitable product of his time, just as Shakespeare, Bonaparte and Voltaire were of theirs. Without Moses there could have been no dispute in the temple and no entry into Jerusalem and no tragic journey up Calvary. Without Bacon, Comte, Schopenhauer and Darwin there could have been no Nietzsche.

It would be interesting, perhaps, to trace back to their primal sources in nascent consciousness the notions which have culminated in the monistic materialism of today, but that would require a review of the entire history of the human struggle for truth: an enterprise whose very immensity is appalling. In place of this, we must content ourselves with a rapid glance at the development of ideas since the Renaissance. The ancients evolved systems of philosophy that attained speculative heights scarcely surpassed today, but it was not until the dawn of organized disbelief in Europe that human intelligence began to arm itself with weapons capable of effectually reaching the vitals of that colossal and terrible monster, super-naturalism.

In the middle ages all experimental inquiry into natural phenomena was regarded as both futile and blasphemous — futile because God could never reveal his secrets without ceasing to be God, and blasphemous because any effort to unveil them was thus necessarily a blow at divinity. The learned men of those days contented themselves, in consequence, with interminable arguments about fanciful problems which, on their very face, were insoluble. For four hundred years, for instance, the monks of Germany debated the question whether an angel, in passing from one spot to another, had to traverse the intervening space. Any man who presumed to look into the cause of actual things was pronounced anathema. An anatomist who essayed to learn something about the human stomach by dissecting a cadaver instead of by searching for cabalistic knowledge in the scriptures, was commonly burned at the stake. A man who pointed out that the popes, despite their divine afflatus, frequently indulged in quite human offenses against decency, was regarded as a lunatic or a devil, and in either case some effort was made to kill him. The whole thought of the human race was concentrated upon the hereafter and it was considered an insult to the deity to harbor any desire to improve the conditions of existence on earth.

But in the course of time, humanity's strong inborn curiosity — the most familiar manifestation of its basic instinct to preserve life by constant adaptation to its environment — became overpowering, and brave men with the lust for knowledge raging within them defied the church and its inquisitors. Most of them were put to death, but a few managed to survive, and these taught disciples. In the end, the number of such men became so large that they were able to disregard the church openly, and the Renaissance was in full flower. The result was a wide-spread and organized inquiry into everything that promised increased knowledge. Men began to seek for facts, not in the scriptures, but in actual things. Instead of trying to puzzle out what the ancient Jewish sages thought about the heart and brain, anatomists turned to the human body and tried to learn for themselves. Instead of consulting the old law books for rules of conduct, men began to consider the actual needs and desires of their contemporaries. In Machiavelli's phrase they began to "follow the real truth of things, rather than an imaginary view of them."

This period of diligent but groping inquiry kept on for a couple of centuries and before the beginning of the French revolution a vast mass of facts had been accumulated. Bacon, Nicolas of Cusa and Machiavelli had put common-sense into ethics; the physicians had begun to know not a little about the human machine; through the efforts of Althusius, Mariana and others the old superstitions about the divine rights of kings and princes were dying out; Adam Smith was preparing to unearth the forces which made for national welfare, and a host of impious doubters were examining the current schemes of religion and showing their absurdity. The French revolution then made its blinding flash and after that the air was clear. Since the latter part of the 18th century, indeed, our whole outlook upon the universe has been changed. We have learned to judge things, not by their respectability and holiness, but by their essential truth. It is now possible, not only to approach facts with an unbiased mind, but also to make critical examinations of ideas: i.e., to consider the human mind itself as a living organism and to examine, not only its functions, but also its growth.

Comte, a Frenchman, was the first to perform this last feat with any success. He looked back over the history of the human race and found that it had progressed through three intellectual stages. During the first stage, men ascribed every act in the universe to the direct interposition of the deity. During the second, they tried to analyze this deity's motives, and so endeavored to learn why things happened: why the sun rose every morning, why one man was white and another black, one tall and another short; why everyone had to die. During the last stage, they began to realize that this inquiry was futile and that the answer would be out of their reach for all eternity. Then they turned from asking why and began to ask how. In a word, they began to accept the universe as it was and to content themselves with learning all they could about its workings and about the invariable laws which controlled these workings.

Comte called this last attitude positivism and showed that the world of his day had reached it. Out of it grew the notion that, inasmuch as man could never hope to learn anything, certainly and beyond question, about the hereafter, it behooved him to devote all of his energies to improving the conditions of life on earth. This subsidiary notion was given the name of utilitarianism and it is the impelling force in everything that we look upon as progress at present. The object of every science and industry and of every civilized scheme of government is to make life easier and humanity happier. The anarchists and the socialists are both seeking the same end, though their plans for attaining it are diametrically opposed. The biologists whose life-work is the destruction of malignant organisms, the politicians whose idea is a rich and prosperous state, the theologians whose goal is perfect peace of mind, the merchants whose life-work is the economical exchange of products, and the philosophers who are trying to determine accurately the laws which govern the universe — all are trying, as best they may, to make mankind safer and happier.

It is plain, of course, that before we may make any conscious effort to increase happiness, we must first know what happiness is. That is, we must first be sure that a certain thing will make men happier before we set about obtaining it. It is the business of metaphysicians to settle this problem. Unluckily they seldom agree about it, and so the efforts of those men, who, in a practical manner, desire to aid us is complicated by the fact that our wise men cannot come to an unanimous decision as to what we want.

This is no place to rehearse all of the ideals of happiness advanced, at different times, by the philosophers of different schools. We have time only to recall what has been set forth, in previous chapters, about the ideal evolved by Arthur Schopenhauer. His theory, as we have seen, was that the will to live was at the bottom of all human actions and that it worked by giving rise to what we call wants or desires. His final conclusion was that these wants would ever remained unsatisfied, and that, in consequence, it was best to avoid unhappiness by killing them and also the will to live at back of them. Nietzsche accepted the first part of Schopenhauer's theory, but rejected the last part. That is to say, he agreed that the will to live was the mainspring of all human action, but he denied that it was wise to seek happiness by killing it. The thing to do, he said, was to give it free rein, and to remove as far as possible, the obstacles which stood in the way of its exercise and satisfaction.

Thus Nietzsche got the groundwork of his philosophy from Schopenhauer. In much the same way, he borrowed from Comte. The latter, as we have seen, argued that the chief concern of humanity was to make life as bearable as possible here on earth, and this idea Nietzsche adopted. But Comte, going further, maintained that earthly happiness depended upon mutual help and mutual dependence, and here Nietzsche disagreed with him squarely. Thus the philosopher of the superman was a disciple of Schopenhauer and Comte and at the same time their opponent. Without their data his philosophy would have been impossible, but with their conclusions it had nothing in common. In a word, they served him merely as the farmer serves the miller: by providing grain for his mill.

Again, Nietzsche got the law of natural selection from Darwin, and with characteristic daring, gave it a universality from which Darwin shrank. In his later years he was fond of berating the English biologist, but the fact that he was a Darwinian cannot be disputed. The superman, indeed, is the crowning stone of the pyramid rising from the ultimate protoplasm, and truncated today at man. Again, from Hume, Swift, Butler, Voltaire, Montaigne, Sanchez, Kepler, Descartes and all the daring company of seekers after truth whose ranks included Lamarck, Tyndall, Humboldt, Franklin, Watt and Goethe — from these materialists he got his fine frenzy for getting at the bottom of concrete problems, without regard for the opinions, superstitions or prejudices of others. Nietzsche despised the metaphysicians, properly so-called, and heaped upon them the vials of his wrath. For Kant, whose investigation into the limitations of intelligence led him into altruistic ethical doctrines, he had boundless and unutterable contempt, and for Liebnitz and Hegel, who argued that the universe was ruled by intelligence, he had loathing. Yet he got something from all three of these men — particularly from Kant — and that something was a chronic doubt of all that passed for truth among people in general. Nietzsche came, in the end, indeed, to question at once, and as a matter of course, everything that seemed true to the average, unthinking, conventional, conservative man. "What everybody believes," he said, "is never true."

Of his immediate predecessors in the domain of philosophy, Nietzsche probably owed much to Max Stirner and not a little to Karl Marx. It may seem incongruous to seek a common idea in the prophet of the superman and the high priest of human brotherhood; yet it is nevertheless a fact that Marx's materialistic conception of history made its mark upon Nietzsche. As an American commentator(5) tells us, this conception is nothing more than the notion "that the bread and butter question is the most important question in life." That is to say, a man's whole existence is colored by the conditions which he must meet and overcome in order to survive. His method of making a living, in the broad sense, is the determining factor in the evolution of his morality and his religion. We find Nietzsche accepting this theory as something almost self-evident. It is ever his postulate in his argument that the superman's absolute fitness to meet the conditions of existence upon earth will make him careless of moral codes and independent of gods.

From Stirner he got many things, and not the least of them was the example of uncompromising and defiant courage. Stirner was the most fiery and radical of all the vast army of sham-smashers and idol-killers who fought orthodoxy during the first half of the nineteenth century. He held that the world would not be fit to live in until it had accepted complete and absolute individualism. Religion custom, morality, tradition, popular opinion — all of these things he held to be obstacles in the path of progress. Every sane man, he argued, should be permitted to do whatever he pleased, no matter what others thought of it. But though Nietzsche accepted this argument, his application of it differed vastly from Stirner's. The latter made it a justification for the most revolting sort of self-indulgence and sensuality. Nietzsche, for all his contempt for religion and law, knew very well that swinish license, instead of making the race stronger, would quickly bring it up to the dead wall of disease, weakness and sterility.

It was this very familiarity with natural laws that separated Nietzsche from all the wild mob of anarchists who raged and roared through Europe in the 1840s and 50s. He was an advocate of utter freedom, but he saw very clearly that freedom and license, instinct and emotion, were not the same. He knew, indeed, that the laws of nature stood unalterably opposed to dissoluteness. Therefore, his ideal, the superman, for all his freedom and egoism, was by no means a helpless slave to wild passions.

On the contrary, he argued that the superman would be a creature in whom all those manifestations that we call human passions, by being satisfied as quickly as they arose, would cease to trouble. In the matter of the sexual instinct, for instance, the superman would be the antithesis of a celibate, but he would be equally far from a roué. His desire, like that of a savage or an animal, would be exactly strong enough to insure the perpetuation of his race — and no stronger.

Several commentators have tried to show that Nietzsche borrowed many of his ideas from Paul Rée, some saying that he stole bodily and others that he evolved his own notions by the simple process of denying those of Rée. He himself says, in the foreword to The Genealogy of Morals that Rée's book, "The Origin of Moral Sensations," excited his violent antagonism and disgust. "Never," he says, "have I read a book to which, proposition by proposition and conclusion to conclusion, I said such an emphatic No." But it is evident that, in order to object so vigorously to an argument, a man must have already formed contrary opinions, and such, in fact, was the case with Nietzsche. His own philosophy began to take form in his mind just as soon as his mind began to function. "As a boy of 13," he says, "the problem of the origin of evil haunted me, and to it I dedicated my first literary child-play." Throughout his youth his views were being formulated, and by 1868 — when he was 22 — they had already crystallized into the idea that instinct was the only reliable guide of intelligence. It was not until 1877 that Rée's book was printed. That Rée was his friend, at least for a few years, is admitted, and that this friendship increased Nietzsche's acquaintance with the work of other investigators — particularly with that of the English materialists — and greatly amplified his store of positive knowledge, is certain, but the mad philosopher had already thought for himself and the main current of his ideas was by no means diverted from its former path. Between his work and Rée's there is no more in common than one may find in the work of any two men who seek solutions of similar problems and write in the same language and in the same age.

It is a favorite pastime of the opponents of Nietzsche to attack his claim to fame by showing that many of his ideas were voiced years ago by other men. They point out, for example, that his individualism was not unknown to the ancient Greeks, that his ethical ideas, in general, are those of Callicles, as set forth by Plato in the "Gorgias"; that his materialism comes from Lucretius and

Democritus, that his chronic skepticism recalls Xenophanes, Parmenides, Arcesilaus, Anaxagoras, Empedocles, Pyrrho and the Eleatic Zeno; that his pessimism, going beyond Schopenhauer, has its source in Hegesippus; that his distinction between master-morality and slave-morality was known to the Sophists and Epicureans and laid down by Francis Bacon, that his notions about Apollo and Dionysus and his deification of energy were prompted by William Blake, that his discovery that all morality is irksome to men of genuine force was made before him, by Machiavelli, that the Pythagoreans speculated about the doctrine of eternal recurrence thousands of years before he was born, and that his idea of sublime indifference formed the cardinal doctrine of stoicism and was voiced, besides, by certain of his contemporaries.

It may be submitted, in answer to all of this, that the same thing might be alleged against any philosopher. As we have seen, a human being is never an isolated phenomenon. His mental processes come down to him from his ancestors just as much as the shape of his nose or the number of his toes. What we understand by a philosopher is merely a man who views the ideas of his predecessors and contemporaries, points out their truth or falsity, shows how they are related, one to the other, and evolves from the mass some definite scheme of life and thought. This task Nietzsche accomplished. His scheme of things may be wrong, but the very fact that it has strongly impressed the thinking men of today, shows that it is reasonable and thinkable and workable, and that, in its essentials, it is just as much in harmony with the known facts of existence as any other effort to transmute the particular into the general — as the atomic theory, for instance, or Ehrlich's hypothesis of immunity.

Toward the end of his life Nietzsche undertook to analyze his own ideas and to show their sources in the ideas of other men, but it must be confessed that his revelations scarcely revealed. He explained, in an indefinite sort of a way, why he despised Rousseau, Seneca, Plato, Schiller, Dante, Kant, Hugo, George Sand, Carlyle, Mill, Renan, Saint-Beuve, à Kempis and Spinoza, and he voiced his admiration for Goethe, Thucydides, Sallust and Horace, and his queer half-admiration, half-contempt for Schopenhauer, Comte, Darwin and others, but his discourse was confined, in the main, to phrase-making. Reading his chapters calmly it is evident that he failed utterly to perceive his debt to many men whose work supplied him with valuable data, if not with ready-made conclusions. As he grew older, indeed, Nietzsche fell into the habit of damning utterly all who happened to disagree with his contempt for schemes of morality, of whatever sort, despite the fact that many of these men agreed with him perfectly in other things.

Nietzsche wrote with sulphuric acid upon tables of phosphorus and at times his criticisms descended to mere invective. He called Dante, "an hyena poetizing in a graveyard;" George Sand, "a milch cow with a grand manner;" Carlyle, "a pessimist whose thoughts arise from a bad stomach;" the Goncourts, "a pair of Ajaxes fighting Homer, with music by Offenbach;" Zola, "the delight to stink;" Seneca, "the toreador of virtue;" Saint-Beuve, "an anti-man with a woman's vengefulness and a woman's sensuousness;" Schopenhauer, "a king counterfeiter;" and Plato, "a coward in the presence of reality" and a "tiresome" master of "superior cheatery." There is wit upon some of these tags and a few have wisdom, too, but it is obvious that such studied striving after mere verbal brilliance, while it may produce prettiness, scarcely serves the cause of the critical art. Nietzsche learned a great deal from the masters of epigram he so much admired and they gave him his extraordinarily vivid and striking style, but he also got from them a tendency to seek the irreducible minimum just a bit too assiduously. He made phrases that sparkled like jewels, but now and again, in reading them, one longs for the slow, painstaking march of a Spencer or the illuminating prodigality of a Zola.

In his more contemplative moments Nietzsche saw very clearly that his own work was merely the natural development of the work of other men. In Morgenröte (V, § 547), and elsewhere he argued that the greatest obstacle in the path of increasing knowledge was the old notion that there was some one all-embracing secret of existence, which, on being uncovered, would answer all of humanity's questions and make all things plain. Progress, he said, was not a matter of untying a Gordian knot or of discovering a philosopher's stone: it could be thought of only as a slow, but constant accumulation of facts. It was impossible, he pointed out, for a single man, in the brief span of life allotted to human beings, to explore the whole field of knowledge. Therefore, it was necessary for every man to begin by acquiring the knowledge resulting from the explorations of those before him. Nietzsche denounced Schopenhauer and other philosophers for their insistence upon the fallacy that their schemes of thought made all things clear, and then ended by making practically the same claim for his own. The student of the mad German will find this inconsistency throughout his work. So long as he dealt with ideas his mental processes were the movements of a machine, but when he considered human beings in the concrete — and particularly when he discussed himself — his incredible intolerance, jealousy, spitefulness and egomania, and his savage lust for bitter, useless and unmerciful strife, combined to make his conclusions unreliable, and even nonsensical.

Nietzsche As A Teacher

If we would seek conclusive proof that Nietzsche has left his mark upon his time we need go no further than the ubiquitous Mr. Roosevelt and the frank and sportive Mr. George Bernard Shaw. Mr. Roosevelt is, by immense odds, the most influential man in the United States today. He is the accepted spokesman and rabbi of at least 50,000,000 human beings, and he has a quite uncanny faculty for impressing them, driving them and convincing them against their will. And among other things, he has made embryo Nietzscheans of them, for in all things fundamental the Rooseveltian philosophy and the Nietzschean philosophy are identical.

It is inconceivable that Mr. Roosevelt should have formulated his present confession of faith independently of Nietzsche. As everyone knows, he is an ardent student of German literature, and has dipped, with peculiar assiduity, into the Pierian spring of the German poets and philosophers. The motto at the head of his essay on "The Strenuous Life" — the best summary of his creed that he has yet published — is a quotation from Goethe, and in the essay itself are a multitude of thoughts borrowed boldly and bodily, though perhaps unconsciously, from none other than Friedrich Nietzsche. "The Strenuous Life," indeed, is the most eloquent and powerful statement of the dionysian philosophy ever made by anyone. "I wish to preach," it begins, "not the doctrine of ignoble ease, but the doctrine of the strenuous life, the life of toil and effort, of labor and strife: to preach the highest form of success which comes, not to the man who desires mere easy peace, but to the man who does not shrink from danger, from hardship, or from bitter toil, and who, out of these, wins the splendid ultimate triumph." How insistent sounds the voice of Zarathustra in all of this! How vividly it recalls the ancient sage's very phrases!... "I do not advise you to conclude peace, but to conquer! What is good? ye ask. To be brave is good.... Thus live your life of obedience and war!... Man is something to be surpassed!"

"When men...fear righteous war, when women fear motherhood...well it is that they should vanish from the earth." So speaks the prophet of the strenuous life. "Thus would I have man and woman: fit for warfare the one, fit for giving birth the other." So speaks Zarathustra. There is no denial of the law of natural selection in this thunderous sermon of the American dionysian — there is no meek acceptance of the Christian doctrine that self-effacement is noble. "The nation that has trained itself to a career of unwarlike and isolated ease is bound, in the end, to go down before other nations which have not lost the manly and adventurous qualities." There is no acceptance of the doctrine that all men are equal "before the Lord." On the contrary, "many of our people are utterly unfit for self-government." There is no glorifying of asceticism, sickness, death and degeneration — "the hangman's metaphysic." "Weakness is the greatest of crimes!" There is no worship of the fetish of peace and brotherly love. "The over-civilized man, who has lost the great fighting, masterful virtues" — in him there is abomination. "Thank God for the iron in the blood of our fathers!" Could there be a more direct and earnest statement of the dionysian creed? Could there be a more obvious paraphrasing of *Der Antichrist* and *Also sprach Zarathustra*? Mr. Roosevelt has a pew in a Christian church, but his whole attitude of mind is essentially and violently unchristian. If you don't believe it, compare "The Strenuous Life" and the Sermon on the Mount. Is it possible to imagine two documents which say "Nay!" to each other more riotously, vehemently and unmistakably?

And when we come to Shaw, we find the Nietzschean creed set forth with even greater earnestness and even greater fidelity to detail. Shaw, I take it, is obviously the most influential English playwright of the day. It is easy enough to profess a superior sort of contempt for him, or to dismiss him as a mere buffoon, but all the same his audience includes practically every civilized person of English speech in the world. And it is unwise, too, to call him a mere passing fashion, doomed to evanescence and nonentity. His ribald questions may still give anguish to the orthodox, but all who ponder upon the destiny of the human race ask practically the same questions and are not far from him in their answers. He is, indeed, the spokesman of that rebellion against old ideas which rages wherever English is the language of thought. The old horror of him is dying out; he has become almost decent. He is no longer a hobgoblin, but a philosopher. People now accept his ingenious propositions, not as sweetly devilish obscenities, to be whispered about and gloated over in secret, but as quite sane and even respectable ideas, to be debated openly and without shame, as one might debate some new fancy in politics, evening parties or cravats. And what is this new crusade that he preaches? Is it really new? Is it his own creation and devising? Not at all! Strip it of its braying and its hullabaloo, its hibernianism and comicalities, and you will find at bottom a most strange and amazing potpourri of borrowed dogmas, in which the notions of Schopenhauer and Karl Marx, of Bunyan and Kropotkin, of Tolstoy and Proudhon are intermingled with those of Nietzsche.

Shaw himself points out, in a dozen places, that there is more in him of the interpreter than of the pioneer. His labor, as he sees it and defines it, is not so much to think new thoughts as to seize upon and develop the thoughts of other men and translate them into symbols comprehensible to folks who dine well and feel a bit foundered afterward, and so demand that the maximum of divertisement be injected into the world problems set before them. This frank prologue to the Shaw plays has been regarded with suspicion, as if it were some sort of unusually subtle and subterranean joke, but as a matter of fact it should be accepted as a true saying. Personally, Shaw is merely "ag'in the government," which means that the existing order pains him and that he yearns to attack and overthrow it with whatever weapon or weapons seem nearest at hand. He has scarcely any preference; all he wants to do is to hit a head. And so it happens that he achieves the astounding feat of seeming to stand as sponsor, in one play and sometimes on one page, for such irreconcilable enemies as the philosopher of renunciation and the prophet of eternal defiance. It remained for Ireland, in the days of her bondage, to produce a human being who could at once subscribe to the most unpromising altruism and the most bitter and unpitying egotism. In the whole history of civilization no other man has so successfully served both the angels and the devil.

Shaw first swam into our ken as a spouter of socialistic nonsense from cart-tails, and he still poses, in a half-hearted and apologetic sort of fashion, as a Christian socialist, — whatever that may be, — but his true importance and significance lie, not in his weak variations upon stale themes by Marx, but in his thunderous bellowings of Nietzsche. Socialism was an old story before he was born and Schopenhauer's supine asceticism had long ago gone the way of all unworkable, unlivable creeds. Even Tolstoy had lost his tang and novelty and was beginning his spectacular descent from the seminaries of serious philosophers to the "home" pages of the yellow journals. But when Shaw began to absorb his emanations — unconsciously, perhaps, at the start — Nietzsche was new. Germany was beginning to grow aware of him and there is reason to believe that Ibsen and Strindberg, the Scandinavians, took home some notion of him, but in general the great world beyond Metz and Kiel knew him not. It was by Shaw's hand that the ideas for which he stands were done into the English vulgate. It was Shaw that changed his x into 1, 2 and 3. And in this benevolent enterprise the Irish dramatist borrowed many of the Prussian iconoclast's meditations bodily, and put them, with scarcely any change, into the mouths of his Jack Tanners, his Capt. Bluntschlis and his Andrew Undershafts, and into his prologues, epilogues, intermezzos and appendices. By their aid — in part, at least — he was lifted up to his present eminence as the premier scoffer and dominant heretic of the day.

Shaw devotes a page or two in his preface to "Major Barbara" to a denial of all this. His fine rage against humility, priestcraft and the slave-morality is the result, he says, of certain long-gone encounters with one Capt. Wilson, an obscure British reviler of respectability whom he met and sat under before Nietzsche's name was known beyond Basel town. There are many answers to this, but the only one necessary here lies in the fact that Shaw did not begin to write plays until Nietzsche's day had fairly dawned, and that, in practically all of the curious dramas he has sent forth since, the Nietzschean creed, in all its details — and even, in many a place, in its very phraseology — is well to the fore. Shaw, being a true dramatist, is more the artist than the preacher, and it is his object, not so much to spread new doctrines as to show, by dramatic action, the conflict between the old and the new. Against Jack Tanner, the Nietzschean, he sets Roebuck Ramsden, the godly; against the Dionysian Undershaft he sets the Salvation Army; against Bluntschli he sets romance; against the Clandons he sets Bohun. He is the father of churchmen as well as of dissenters: in his puppet show there must be all parties. But it is evident that his Nietzscheans speak his own mind. Jack Tanner, Bluntschli and Valentine go down to ignominious defeat, but it is as martyrs to the new faith. The things they think and say are said again by Shaw himself in his preludes and afterthoughts.

Consider, for instance, the leaven of Nietzsche in that most notorious and excellent of all the Shaw plays, "Mrs. Warren's Profession," a drama in which Shaw is more the serious philosopher and less the comique than in any other. This profession, as we know, is the oldest in the world and Mrs. Warren enters it knowingly and deliberately, because she sees in it her only chance to obtain decent food and lodging and her modicum of happiness. "Do you think I was such a fool," she says in after years, "as to let other people trade in my good looks, by employing me as a shop-girl, a barmaid or a waitress, when I could trade in them myself and get all the profits, instead of starvation wages?" She prospers and grows rich and there comes to her the ease and comfort for which every normal human being yearns. Also, there comes to her a daughter, who goes to Cambridge, well taught and well fed, and takes high honors. At first Mrs. Warren is proud that her outlawed trade has enabled her to do so much for her offspring — proud that, in defiance of her outlawry, she is the mother of such an uncommon child. But by and by there comes over her a fear that when the daughter discovers her means of livelihood, she will recoil in horror. The fear grows and hypocrisy comes out of it. Mrs. Warren equivocates and dissimulates. The daughter must never know.

But in the end the daughter does know, and the manner of her revolt is passing strange. She sees her mother's motive and temptation and approves her sin. "My dear mother," she says, "you are a wonderful woman — you are stronger than all England." So far mother and daughter are as one. But, in the last analysis, Mrs. Warren has failed. She has hurled her defiance at the moral code — and then sought its shelter. She has grown ashamed! And her daughter, seeing this, holds her in loathing. "If I had been you, mother," she says, "I might have done as you did; but I should not have lived one life and believed in another. You are a conventional woman at heart. That is why I am leaving you now."

Now, what are the ideas at the bottom of this play? What are the propositions its protagonist lays down? First, that every woman (like every man) has an unalienable right to seek comfort and happiness in life in the manner best calculated to procure them, and regardless of the customs and opinions of other persons. Secondly, that her methods are right and without sin so long as she accepts their consequences uncomplainingly. Third, that when she fails in this defiance and, repentant, makes complaint — when she pretends falsely to subscribe to a moral code she has cast aside and cries out when she is discovered and denounced — then she loses, at one stroke, all she has sought to gain. Such is the more obvious meaning of the drama, and thus we find the Nietzschean superman in skirts — the ya-sager in a brothel. But, as Shaw himself points out in the preface, there is beneath the action a thesis more widely applicable to the facts of existence and it is this: that any system of ethics or condition of human society which makes it necessary for a woman, in order to procure that share of happiness which instinct demands, to put to herself in dire peril of losing happiness altogether, is outrageously unfair, illogical and pernicious. "It can't be right!" wails Mrs. Warren. "I stick to that: it's wrong." Thus Shaw penned his play and pointed its moral in 1893. Nietzsche, as we have seen, put the same argument into vitriolic German a full decade before.

In greater or less measure the Nietzschean flavor will be found in all of Shaw's other dramas, mixed with and sometimes obscured or neutralized by the effluvia of other and more orthodox sages. In Major Barbara we have a hero who calls himself a dionysian and offers Nietzscheism as a substitute for

Christianity. In Man and Superman we have a hero who calls himself a nascent superman and preaches the Nietzschean doctrine of womankind. In each case there is borrowing, not only of the spirit, but also of the letter. "Dionysus," "super-man," "other-worldliness," and Undershaft's motto: "Unashamed"—in the very phrases we hear the voice of Zarathustra. "Never resist temptation," says Jack Tanner. "Prove all things: hold fast to that which is good." "What does not kill me," says Nietzsche, more epigrammatically, "strengthens me." "Vice," says Tanner, "is waste of life. Poverty, obedience and celibacy are the canonical vices." "Self-control," says Nietzsche, "destroys the nervous system as certainly and thoroughly as debauchery." "Those who minister to poverty and disease," says Tanner, "are accomplices in the two worst of all crimes." In Nietzsche appears the idea more broadly: "Sympathy is both the multiplier of misery and the conservator of misery." There is no need to pile up examples. Shaw may regard himself as a socialist, but his socialism is so overcast by the philosophy of Dionysus that its outlines are lost.

It is probable that a thousand other men, in a dozen countries, had asked themselves the questions which grew into Nietzsche's philosophy. Some of them had been debated years and years before he was born. But the world, as a world, thinks dimly and muddily, and emotion always goes before reason. It remains for some clear brain to transmute the groping half-conscious feeling of the race into a visible, understandable idea. The mind of Nietzsche had this retort-like quality. It was fed by the thought of his time, but it changed this thought from rough, gray ore into clear-running metal. Nietzsche, in brief, put into words and syllogisms the things that his contemporaries felt stirring gropingly within them, and when he spoke, there were not a few who understood.

One of these, unless I greatly err, was Henrik Ibsen, the Norwegian. He had written plays and audiences had applauded them, but as he looked back upon them they seemed to him to leave something unsaid. There were greater things in the world, he felt, than the battles of vikings. There were more imminent and important problems than those which engaged Peer Gynt. Norway, with its smug formalism, oppressed him, and he became a wanderer upon the face of the earth. He went to Germany and at Munich felt the surges of the high sea raised by Darwin. It was a time of bitter conflict in the German universities. The old order was changing and giving place to the new. Over at Basel, in Switzerland, a young professor of philology named Nietzsche was pondering the same mighty problems. He and Ibsen had much the same viewpoint and much the same habits of thought. They were outlanders and their minds were essentially cosmopolitan. The petty considerations of insularity were miles below them: on the peaks where they dwelt the air was clear and it was possible to see accurately and without distortion. By and by both came to the same general conclusion. Many of the things that men regarded as wrong, they decided, were, in reality, right; and many of the things looked upon as holy were infamous. Here we have that "translation of all values" which forms the text of the new gospel. In 1879 Ibsen put it into "A Doll's House," his first comedy of conscience, and made himself the foremost dramatist of the age. The same year Nietzsche published Menschliches allzu Menschliches.

That Ibsen remained long unacquainted with Nietzsche's writings is as unthinkable as that a Huxley could remain unaware of a Darwin. The Norwegian had brought forth his answer to the problem for himself, from the depths of his own loathing for morality as he found it, but as, one by one, the German's books came from the press, they must have heartened and influenced him profoundly. Ibsen's letters show us that he was ever more the poet than the philosopher, and that even after the world gave him ear, he still manifested a queer distrust of his own philosophy — a distrust compounded in part of modesty, and in part of that uncertainty which always marks the true agnostic. The rise of Nietzsche must have made him feel more sure of himself, for here there was a professional metaphysician whose dictata augmented and reinforced his own. His later plays demonstrated it. The onslaught upon "A Doll's House" drove him behind trenches in "Ghosts," but later on, when he came to write "Hedda Gabbler," "The Master Builder" and "When We Dead Awaken," he was sure of himself and so pounded out his ideas unheedingly and defiantly. The difference between his first audience and his last was the difference between a race not yet cured of Thomas à Kempis and a race inoculated with Nietzsche.

In the drama of today, Ibsen and Nietzsche are the dominant voices. In Germany and England, in France and America, the playmakers have gone to Ibsen for their artistry and technique and to Nietzsche for their philosophy. Ibsen taught them naturalness and truth — he showed them the absurdity of the soliloquy and the hero and the essential impossibility of Marguerite Gautier — and Nietzsche made them critics, not of kings and intrigues, but of human institutions and divine mandates. The difference between the Henry Arthur Jones of "The Silver King" and the Jones of "The Hypocrites" marks the measure of this revolution. Its leaders today are Hermann Sudermann, the German, and August Strindberg, the Swede. We who speak English know Sudermann for his Heimat, which has been rendered into our tongue as "Magda," Magda Schwartze is a Mrs. Warren with strength to face it out to the bitter end. As Nietzsche would say, she is a ya-sager — a yes-sayer — who asks nothing of the world but a chance to seek happiness in her own way. Convention — authority — respectability — stretch out their arms and would make her their own. But she has chosen for herself. "If you give us the right to hunger," she cries, — "and I have hungered!" why do you deny us the right...to happiness, as we can understand it?... I must live out my own life! That I owe to myself — to myself and mine!"

It is Dionysus speaking — that same Dionysus we find in *Der Antichrist*, and in *Also sprach Zarathustra* — that same Dionysus whose loud "Yes!" peals forth in Strindberg's Mit dem Feuer Spielen and in his war upon feminism. Strindberg, indeed, is a Nietzschean whose enthusiasm has made him a thing almost apart from humankind. In his thunderous battle against convention and delusion, he has attacked ideas which the race could not abandon today, perhaps, without risk of utter chaos. He has brought forth skeletons that had better remain in the closet; he has bored into skulls that cry aloud for burial. "He is the most remarkable creative talent," says Edmund Gosse, "started by the philosophy of Friedrich Nietzsche." But the world must learn more of Nietzsche himself before it is ready to heed his disciple. In the Teutonic countries, Strindberg finds an audience, but where the Anglo cools and conventionalizes the Saxon he is still a mere shouter of ribaldry. Of lesser Nietzscheans, however, there is a host — Fulda, Hervieu, and other continentals and the wavering disciples who write in English. It is in the dramas of these men that the thought of today is being expressed. Oratory is dead, the newspapers rattle upon the surface, and the novel has fallen from its old estate. Once more the drama gives expression to all those who have something to say. Who, since Zola, has written a novel that looms big? We have had a multitude of romances for the hammock and essays in style, but what document in covers has dealt, grandly and satisfyingly, with the eternal conflict between things as they are and things as they might be? What novel is comparable, as an event, to "The Great Divide" or "Magda" or "Lodgings for the Night?"

In all of these earnest and significant dramas you will find some trace of the Nietzschean thesis. The problem they illuminate is never, Will the brave Rudolph win the fair Angeline? but, Is this virtue really good? or, Is that sin really bad? Such things were discussed years and years ago, but until the human mind was finally freed from the bonds of theology and authority, in the latter half of the nineteenth century, these discussions were always half-hearted and vain. Let him weigh and speculate as much as he would, the philosopher and poet always came, at last, to a dead wall. He might beat upon it as much as he pleased, but he could not hope to be ranked much higher, in the human scale, than a successful hurler of muck at temple gates. Even today — such is the force of collective opinion — we think of Voltaire and Machiavelli and others of their ilk as criminals rather than as truth-tellers. The dead wall towered high. Such-and-such a rule was laid down by the laws of some king, or the commandments of some god or the dogmas of some holy man — and it was immaculate, incontrovertible and final. One might go so far — and no further. Beyond the wall lay blasphemy, lunacy and all sorts of unutterable horrors.

But the wall today is dust. We give heed, not so much to those who pretend to interpret the law as to those who presume to deny it. The typical English-speaking literary critic of the day is Gilbert K. Chesterton, a prophet of truly Nietzschean disillusion. The typical English cart-tail philosopher is Dr. Emil Reich, a bearer of the Nietzschean philosophy of defiance. Instead of accepting a given notion as right because the majority of other critics, since the dawn of civilization, have regarded it as right, Chesterton devotes his energies to examining it for himself and judging it with an open mind. For these reasons the numskulls who write reviews of his books say that he delights in what they call paradox and patronize him as a bright young man whose respect for law might be a bit stronger. Reich — a man much below Chesterton in ability — has attained the ha'penny celebrity he seems to crave in much the same manner. He is the philosophical shocker of the hour and every few days the newspapers of London print his views upon some topic of interest, just as the newspapers of New York used to print the opinions of Dr. Parkhurst and other such vaporous platitudinizers on every fresh murder, war, railroad wreck and international divorce. Reich has borrowed Nietzsche's method of "tunneling" and employs it with vast effect. Some time ago, for instance, he issued a pronunciamento upon the subject of duelling, in which he pointed out the quite obvious fact that the code duello, despite its outraging of the law, offers the sole practicable means of permitting civilized men to do what every healthy human being instinctively yearns to do — that is, slay his enemies. This quite elemental logic appalled the Londoners and as a result Reich added to his reputation as a daring heretic and profound thinker. As a matter of fact, he is a man of little more than average capacity and very frequently he entangles himself, in a most amazing manner, in banalities and fallacies. But for the nonce, he is the favorite practitioner of Nietzsche's method of teaching — which consists, as we have seen, in tracking down virtues to their primal source in expedience and in tracking down Christian sins to their primal source in the effort of the weak Jews to protect themselves against the strong Romans — and so he will serve a useful purpose until England is prepared for Nietzscheism in stronger doses, and more admirable doctors arise.

It might be interesting to attempt a roll of other conscious or unconscious retailers of the Nietzschean philosophy: George Brandes in Denmark, W. H. Hudson, Thomas Hardy, R. B. Cunninghame Graham, H. G. Wells and H. G. Carpenter in England; Maxim Gorky and the "young Russia" school, in Russia; Hugo Kaatz, Max Zerbst, Robert Schellwien, Gerhart Hauptmann and the vast "young Germany" school in Germany; Olge Hansson in Sweden; de Wysewa, Lavedan and a horde of lesser lights in France; Gabrielle D'Annunzio in Italy; Benjamin R. Tilman (who probably never heard of Nietzsche) and innumerable disciples fourth removed in America; Benjamin de Casseres in Mexico, and stray iconoclasts here and there in Norway, Austria and even Spain. The tremendous influence of Nietzsche, in truth, is admitted by even his most violent opponents. "It remains a disgrace to the German intellectual life of the present age," says Max Nordau," that in Germany a pronounced maniac should have been regarded as a philosopher and have founded a school." "Nietzsche," says the staid old Athenoeum, "for good or evil, has spoken to his age with a formidable voice. He may be fought, but he cannot be disregarded. To disregard him is like disregarding a motor-car because you prefer your carriage and pair. He is a new force, like electricity." "Nietzsche," says A. R. Orage, II is the greatest European event since Goethe... Nobody is more representative of the spirit of the age." "No modern German writer of the more earnest class," says Alois Riehl, is so, widely read." "In some ways," says Grace Neal Dolson, "Nietzsche appeals to the thought of the time.... He has had imitators and admirers in abundance." "Before long," says George Bernard Shaw, "you must be prepared to talk about Nietzsche or retire from society."

But it is vain, perhaps, to attempt to measure a philosopher's true influence by counting the noses of the disciples who copy his writings upon fresh scrolls. Such disciples bear the same relation to him that Paderewski does to Chopin or Mantell to Shakespeare or Hearst to Karl Marx. Executants are necessary because the world is large, and when the fates are propitious, they sometimes reach the estate and dignity of interpreters, but at bottom they are mere echoes. To change the figure, they are lumber sawed from a tree and not new shoots springing from its roots. But even at that, as has been said, they cut a respectable figure in the world. The best actor conceivable is of much less importance than the worst dramatist, and the most dexterous pianist seems paltry beside even the composer of the "Florodora" sextette, but we must have parrots as well as nightingales and printing presses as well as divine fire. Thus it is not well to hold in contempt those humble ones who stand below and are ready, when the great officers of the barque of life shout down an order, to repeat it respectfully, with the addition of "Aye, aye: sir!"

The ideas of Nietzsche are dominant in the German universities, and have colored the whole stream of German thought. From Leipsic and Heidelberg they journey to London and New York and bob up in the weeklies and reviews. And out of the Spectator and the Saturday, the Independent and the North American, they are translated into the vulgar tongue — with reservations and amendations — and so become leading articles in the more anarchistic and discontented section of the daily press. Thus after a long voyage and many hardships, they impinge upon the intellects of those meditative Anglo-Saxons who brave the elemental furies and the laws of political economy from their benches in City Hall Park or their inns along the Mile End Road. And that is one way in which Nietzsche reaches the great plain people of America and England. The porridge runs distressingly thin by the time it gets to them, but the flavor, though faint, is still there.

Beside this method of what may be called direct inoculation, it is evident that there is also in progress a more general and subtle infection. A philosophy, when it offers a practical solution of pressing problems or a comprehensible interpretation of contemporary phenomena, begins to saturate the air, and so influences everyone, including even those who have never heard of it directly. Human beings, in the mass, are ever the willing slaves of some prevalent suggestion. The great majority of Americans, for instance, always think much alike. One year they are unanimously outraged by Spain's crimes in Cuba; the next year they are unanimously enraged by the eccentricities of predatory wealth; another year they think deeply and indignantly about the tariff, expansion, executive usurpation, Mormonism, divorce or the negro question. As it is with concrete presentations, so it is with general ideas. At one time, in the middle ages, it was the firm opinion of practically every human being in all Europe that the most profitable way to employ time and energy was to make a pilgrimage to the Holy Land and kill as many Saracens as possible on the way. At another time, the thirst for money was uppermost and everything else was subordinated to considerations of trade. At still another time, there was an almost unanimous revolt against old ideas of government, and the French revolution was one of its symptoms. In our own time we have seen Christendom reduce Christianity to the lowly estate of a mere scheme of morality and have witnessed an unprecedented attempt to uncover the secrets of nature. Always there is some dominant trend of thought, some fashionable frame of mind, some universal idea.

Whatever the groove in which the intellect of the world happens to be working, it feels a need for some leader to give voice to its inarticulate and half-conscious longings and to serve, in some sense, as its guide. This leader is nearly always the product, rather than the cause of the movement for which he stands. Thus, at the time of the crusades, Richard Coeur de Lion neither invented the idea of slaying the Saracens nor was he particularly successful in his individual attempts at massacre, yet he visualized, in his own mind and deeds, the notion of rescuing the holy sepulchre, and so, when we think of the crusades today, we always think of Richard, too. In the same way half a dozen men are identified with the French revolution, and Roosevelt and his rough riders stand for the war with Cuba, and Bryan is accepted as the prophet of the war upon lawless millions. Again, we find ourselves unconsciously associating such purely symptomatic phenomena as Payne, Huxley and Ingersoll with the revolt against Christian supernaturalism, and Darwin with the search for knowledge and Tolstoy with the rebellion against modern systems of government.

Keeping all of this in mind, we may well call Nietzsche the prophet and embodiment of those habits of thought which are dominant among the thinking men of the world today. Humanity is questioning and making ready to reject its ancient moral ideas.(13) The masses on the surface are still law-abiding and religious, but even amongst the lowest of the slave cast there is a mute, uncertain sort of willingness to follow any iconoclast whose crusade contains aught of romance. It will be many years before the great plain people come to regard marriage as other than as a holy sacrament — just as it will be many years before they cease to regard smoking, by women, as a crime, and red plush as the acme of beauty — but already they have begun to differentiate between empty platitude and actuality. For a hundred years, for example, it had been a fundamental principle of American statesmanship that it was immoral and wrong for any state to covet the possessions of other states, no matter how much the acquirement of these possessions might benefit it. But when Schley took Cuba and Roosevelt achieved his Machiavellian coup d'état at Panama — was there a cry of outraged decency then, and a demand for restitution and repentance? Not at all. Instead, the American people suddenly awoke to conscious perception of a notion that had been growing in them for years: that the aforesaid old rule of statesmanship, despite its smug holiness, was a bit of outworn trumpery. And so the vast majority of Americans viewed the Cuban incident and the

Panama ambuscade as means fully justified by their ends, and it remained for a few peevish advocates of the discarded and outgrown morality to voice a ludicrous and ineffective protest.

In brief, the age is dionysian and the moral ideas that have come down to us in the decalogue and the beatitudes are under fire. In New York, not long ago, an old woman, incurably ill of cancer, died of poison, and it was charged that her daughter, who loved her and had nothing to gain personally by her death, had given it to her to put her out of her frightful and useless agony. It so happened that the daughter disproved this charge, but the essential thing is not this, but the fact that the great majority of New Yorkers apparently regarded it as sensible, not to say heroic, that she should do the thing she was accused of doing. A few days afterward a reputable paper in London printed a long defense of murder, as a necessary means of avenging injuries for which the law could offer no remedy, and at the same time there were in progress in the United States a dozen trials of persons accused of putting the same idea into practice, all of which resulted in practical acquittals. Since the Civil War the negro problem in the south has been hotly debated and a thousand schemes for carrying out the biblical injunction to love one another have been proposed. Recently, a clear-headed and vigorous, if slightly theatrical southerner, has courageously voiced the instinctive conviction that this injunction must be disregarded, and that the white race, to preserve itself, must pronounce upon the black race and set out to execute — as gently as possible, but still with unalterable firmness — a sentence of extermination.

It is useless to multiply examples, for every observer, I believe, has noted the tendency I have tried to describe. The civilized world has disposed of supernaturalism and is engaged in a destructive criticism of the old faith's residuum — morality. As Nietzsche himself shows us, such a campaign of criticism and revision has been in progress since the world began, but it is obvious that it was never before waged so hotly as now. A hundred years ago a man who publicly argued that the Christian ideal of sympathy and humility was degrading and outrageous would have incurred penalties almost as terrible as those that would have been meted out to an agnostic who, in the middle ages, questioned the divinity of Christ. But today a man may do both and still remain respectable. Whatever is laid down as a law, now arouses, by that very fact, criticism and examination. Whatever is called good because the patriarchs thought it good is now under fire.

Whether or not the result of this unrestrained search for ultimate truths will be a "transvaluation of all values" in the Nietzschean sense, remains to be seen. Nietzsche apparently believed that, in the course of time, the human race would substitute "thou shalt" for "thou shalt not" throughout the decalogue and that the beatitudes would eventually become a sort of roster anathema. That such a transvaluation will come during the time that human beings remain substantially as they are is beyond all possibility; that it will ever come is beyond all prophecy. But even setting this problem aside as insoluble, the fact remains that the grand assault-at-arms now in progress will result in incalculable benefit. If the race decides, in. the end, that the commandments, after all, are sound and so resolves to abide by them, it will have made an infinite advance, nevertheless, beyond the time when it accepted them unquestionably, because they were regarded as perfect by the ancient Jews. In a word, a race which looks its own problems squarely in the face and seeks solutions for them in the storehouse of its own experience, and with an eye solely to his own welfare, is a race vastly superior to one which puts an infantile trust in the wisdom of a people long lost in the struggle for existence, to whom its peculiar requirements were unknown and to whom the very world itself bore a different aspect.

Dionysus may fall short of triumph to the end of the chapter, but so long as he wages his war upon Apollo fiercely and intelligently there need be no fear of the perils of sloth, of vegetation, of bigotry, of authority, of standing still. Five hundred years ago all reasoning had its basis in authority and was necessarily ex parte. Today, the preacher who thunders from the pulpit and the statesman who howls from the rostrum must take thought of and give heed to the doubter who arises in his place and demands to know wherefore and why.

Nietzsche And His Critics

The arguments against Nietzsche, voiced in America and Europe, by a host of ingenious and industrious critics, may be reduced to five fundamental propositions, viz:

A. He was a lunatic, and in consequence, his philosophy is not worth attention.

B. His conclusions were contradictory and it is impossible to find in his writings any connected philosophical system.

C. He was ignorant of certain important facts of human existence, or purposely misstated them, and in consequence argued from erroneous data.

D. His assumption that the idea of self-sacrifice tends to make humanity less and less able to cope with the vicissitudes of existence on earth, is based upon a direct contradiction of known facts.

E. The scheme of things proposed by him is opposed by ideas inherent in all men and so is unthinkable and unworkable and if put into practice would make life impossible.

It is scarcely worth while to linger long over the first and second propositions. The first has been laid down most noisily by Max Nordau in Degeneration, a book based upon certain ideas borrowed, quite frankly, from Lombroso, an Italian quasi-scientist whose chief mission in life seems to be to furnish sensational copy for the American yellow journals. Nordau's book remains a masterpiece of erudition and rhetoric, in the highest and most honorable sense of both words; but despite its vogue a dozen years ago, it is now well nigh as archaic as a play by Bronson Howard. His definition of degeneracy is "a morbid deviation from an original type" and he lays stress upon the fact that by "morbid" he means "infirm" or "incapable of fulfilling normal functions," but straight-way he begins to regard any deviation as degenerate, despite the obvious fact that it may be quite the reverse. He says, for instance, that a man with web toes is a degenerate and entirely overlooks the fact that web toes, under easily imaginable circumstances, might be an advantage instead of a handicap, and that, under ordinary conditions of life, we are unable to determine, with any accuracy, whether they are one or the other. Dubois and other latter-day pathologists have set at rest forever this notion that every variation spells degeneracy, and today Nordau, Lombroso and the rest of that crowd, when they rise above their proper business of dispassionately recording actual phenomena, become merely ridiculous. Lombroso, for one, has unearthed a vast mass of interesting facts about criminality, but the theories which he has sought to evolve from these facts are scarcely accepted by psychiatrists. He is a skilful reporter, but a silly and extravagant philosopher.

Nordau, having started out with the knowledge that Nietzsche eventually became insane, tried to exhibit every act of his life and every idea in his philosophy as a symptom of that insanity. As a matter of fact, he failed miserably, for while he found it easy to prove that Nietzsche was a blatant egoist, that he had a fondness for repeating certain favourite arguments ad nauseum, that he hated most things that other people held sacred, and that he was intolerant, irritable, and occasionally self-contradictory, it is plain that these allegations find their effective answer in the fact that they might be urged just as truthfully against any other original thinker — Savonarola, Jenner, Malthus, Rousseau, Nordau himself, or any undoubtedly sane reformer that he might select. In a word, his symptoms of degeneracy fit everyone except the satisfied, orthodox, conventional, unoriginal, automatic bourgeois — that purely vegetable being whom Nordau seems to regard as the supreme masterpiece of the creator.

As we have seen in a previous chapter, the fact of Nietzsche's progress from mere neurasthenia, a disease which afflicts nearly all of us, to undoubted insanity, has no bearing whatever upon the essential truths of his philosophical scheme. We must judge his philosophy as we judge any other idea: by its inherent probability and its correspondence with the known facts of existence. If Nietzsche had tried to prove that cows had wings it would have been proper enough to dismiss him as a raving maniac. But when he essayed to show us that Christianity impeded human progress, he laid down a proposition which, whatever its extravagance, was not, in itself, insane. This is demonstrated, beyond a doubt, by the fact that it is possible for sane men to debate it, and to be stimulated to thought, in their consideration of it, by Nietzsche's reasoning. It is perfectly possible for a man to think clearly and yet die insane, just as it is perfectly possible for a man to attain international renown as a consumer of hot mince pies and then, in the end, to die of indigestion.

Nordau also voices the second of the objections noted at the beginning of this chapter. Nietzsche, he says, tore down without building up, and died without having formulated any definite substitute for the morality he abhorred. It is obvious, from all that has gone before, that this is nonsense. No other man, indeed, ever left a more complete system of philosophy, and if it be true that he occasionally modified details radically, it is equally true that his fundamental ideas remained unchanged from first to last. But even supposing that he had died before he had arranged his observations in any connected form, and that it had remained for his disciples to deduce and group his conclusions — even then it would have been possible to weigh his ideas and accept them for what they were worth. Nordau lays it down as an axiom that a man cannot be a reformer unless he proposes some ready-made scheme of things to take the place of the notions he seeks to overturn, and that if he does not do this he is a mere hurler of bricks and shouter of blasphemies. That this rule is an arrant absurdity is shown by the fact that every considerable reform the world has ever known has been accomplished, not by one man, but by many generations of men, working in series, and that, as a matter of actual experience, the man who first points out the need for change seldom lives long enough to evolve a complete substitute for the thing he proposes to abolish. Nordau himself furnishes a case in point, and every critic of the arts and letters is a shining example. The man who first noticed the inefficiency of sails was just as necessary to the birth of the steamboat as the man who built the pioneer steam engine.

So much for the first two arguments against Nietzsche. Both raise immaterial objections and the second makes an allegation that is not true. The other propositions are based upon better logic, and, as we shall see, afford reasonable grounds for objecting to Nietzsche's system, either wholly or in part. It would be interesting, perhaps, to give in detail the arguments supporting them, but this would necessitate a complete review of the vast mass of criticism which Nietzsche's works have brought forth in Europe and America. Instead, we must content ourselves with glancing at a few of them.

Some of these arguments, it must be admitted, are extraordinarily ingenious, but some, again, are extraordinarily absurd. One man argues, for example, that Nietzsche's criticism of the beatitudes is fallacious because, if it were not for

Christianity, there would be no asylums and refuges for the suffering, and in consequence, no concerted and effective effort to make man more efficient physically. Hence, he says, it must be admitted that Christianity's influence has been beneficial to the race. Setting aside the fact that the advantages of preserving the unfit are dubious, it is apparent that this fine syllogism is ridiculous, for, in the first place, everyone knows that the healing of the sick has been practised for ages in numerous non-Christian countries, and in the second place, a rudimentary acquaintance with history is enough to convince any sane man that the influence of Christianity has been ever hurled against that exact knowledge which alone makes our hospitals appreciably superior to those of Tibet and Bokhara.

Another sapient critic argues that Nietzsche is wrong in regarding an aversion to organization as a characteristic of the strong. A struggle, says this critic, is always a waste of strength, and power, when exerted, is weakened by the power it arouses and provokes. Darwin is summoned from his tomb to substantiate this argument, but its exponent seems to be unfamiliar with the Darwinian doctrine that strength is an effect of use, and the further Darwinian doctrine that disuse, whether produced by organized protection or in some other way, leads inevitably to degeneration. In other words, the ideal strong man of this subtle serpent of wisdom is one who seeks, with great enthusiasm, the readiest possible way of ridding himself of his strength.

Still another critic argues that Nietzsche's doctrine "of the paralyzing effect of infallibility and sanctity has been completely overthrown by the unparalleled success of the Japanese, resting upon these qualities in their Emperor." This incredibly fatuous sophist overlooks the fact that the wily Japs, whatever their ostensible belief in their Emperor's infallibility, have pushed to the front solely as the result of their quite extraordinary thirst for experiment and innovation. No other race in history has been more eager to embrace new ideas or more willing to abandon old ones. They are almost ideal dionyisians, and since accepting the learning of the western world they have explored its possibilities with a daring which has made most western nations stand aghast. In a word, their national policy is utterly skeptical and excessively individualistic, and for all their poetic pretense of accepting their sovereign's utterances as law, they are, in reality, most bitter enemies of all rigidity, ritualism and formalism in human thought. In this very contempt for authority and thirst for experiment, indeed, lies the secret of their remarkable advancement. No other race is so free from hampering conventions and doctrines; no other race is so determined to weigh an idea, not by its respectability or authority, but by its inherent truth.

Yet another critic argues that Nietzsche's plea for obedience to a willkür-gesetze (self-imposed law), and to it only, overlooks the fact that, since a man is not a companionless being in vacuo, his tastes and opinions are merely reflections of the tastes and opinions of other men, and it is therefore impossible for him to have any idea utterly and entirely his own. This seems true enough until it is recalled that, besides his ideas, which must necessarily come from without, a man also has his natural attitude of mind, which is born in him. In other words, every human being comes into the world cast in a definite mold and this mold varies so much in different individuals that it is impossible to find two men exactly alike. One man is sunny and his brother is gloomy, one is honest and another a liar, one shrewd and another a fool. One man's instincts are reliable and efficient and we see him prosper in whatever effort he makes to rise above his fellows; another is a born blunderer and we see him fail in everything. To put it more understandingly, every human being's ego is the sum of his native personality's reaction against the ideas that reach him through his consciousness. The same ideas, impinging upon two men, often produce diametrically different reactions. This is a commonplace of observation, and no Schopenhauer was needed to crystallize it into the doctrine set forth in The World as Will and Idea. If it be admitted, as it must be, it must be admitted, too, that a man's native instincts, and not his acquired ideas, constitute the determining factor in his ego. Therefore, he is most himself — and according to Nietzsche, safest and most efficient — when he most depends upon these instincts — expressed as inclinations, predispositions, predilections — for guidance. The existence of the personal equation is obvious. Nietzsche merely sought to give it a free rein.

Practically all the critics of Nietzsche agree in denying that his fundamental assumption — that self-sacrifice tends to make humanity decay — is true. Max Nordau maintains, for instance, that a race whose members have learned to help one another has really made a distinct step forward. Gregariousness, charity and co-operation are to be met with, he says, in most of the higher vertebrates, and the man-apes nurse their sick and feed their helpless just as men do. This argument, on its face, appears to be a sound one, but a bit of reflection will show that while it exhibits an undoubted fact, it is possible to draw two opposing conclusions from that fact. Admitting that the man-apes do these things, we may argue therefrom, either that they have made a step forward or that they have made a step backward. If it is true that the preservation of the unfit means progress, then the apes are advancing. But if it is true that the preservation of the unfit handicaps and retards the fit, then they are decaying. And so we get back to our original dilemma.

Setting aside those who argue in favor of self-sacrifice because they believe it to be ordained of God, its defenders may be divided into two classes: first, those who believe that, if it were not practiced, the race would become a mere herd of wild beasts, who would soon consume one another; and secondly, those who hold that despite its admitted tendency to preserve the unfit, it also tends to protect and stimulate the fit. To the first class belongs

"Vernon Lee" (Miss Violet Paget).(8) Her argument is that humility is a sort of governor placed upon human egotism to keep it from running amuck. A human being is so constituted, she says, that he necessarily looms in his own view as large as all the rest of the world put together. Now, this distortion of values is met with in the consciousness of every individual, and if there were nothing to oppose it, it would soon lead to a hopeless and deadly conflict between exaggerated egos. Humility, says Miss Paget, tempers this conflict, without wholly ending it. A man's unconscious tendency to magnify his own importance and to invite death by trying to force this unnatural view upon others, is held in check by the constant presentation of the idea that he must think, also, of the welfare of these others. In a word, humility is a corrective of the human weakness for worshipping self.

Miss Paget is a subtle metaphysician, and on the surface, this theory appears to be impeccable, but it is easy to show, all the same, that humility, as she conceives it, is nothing more than a selfish desire to avoid antagonizing others, and that, in consequence, it is a manifestation of true egotism — i.e., the instinct of the individual to preserve his life. Under present conditions the man who gave his ego free rein would soon perish at the hands of his indignant fellow men, because these fellow men would combine against him. But in Nietzsche's ideal world, there would be no such combination. Every member of the "first caste" would look after his own affairs unaided, and in consequence, his battles would be fought without allies and his opponents, too, would fight without allies. The result of this would be that the strongest would survive — the very aim and object of Nietzsche's scheme. That there is an abysmal difference between the dionysian forethought born of prudence and the Christian humility born of charity needs no demonstration. Miss Paget's picture of humility, indeed, is a very accurate picture of policy, cunning and craft.

The second argument for self-sacrifice — that it benefits the fit as much as, or more than, it benefits the unfit — is scarcely debatable in the face of the present lack of accurate data. We may maintain, for instance, that our hospitals make useful and capable citizens, every year, of thousands who would otherwise become burdens upon the fit, or perish utterly, but we cannot prove that this is entirely true. A man who has had tuberculosis, for example, and has been cured, may live to a green old age and do his full share of the world's work, but it is questionable whether the children he begets will be fully as well fitted to survive as the children of men who have never been ill at all. That is to say, we can arrest the progress of a specific case of disease, but we cannot stamp out an individual's tendency to contract that disease nor can we keep him from transmitting this tendency to his children. We may cure a man and a woman of tuberculosis in this generation, and by the same token, burden the next generation with ten potential or actual consumptives — their descendants.

It was the fashion a few years ago to pooh-pooh this idea that tendencies to disease — i.e. dispositions to perish in the struggle for existence — are inheritable, but the investigations of Sir Almroth Wright in the field of immunity have proved beyond a doubt that it is sound. The child of a consumptive, even if that consumptive be cured, is more liable to contract tuberculosis than the child of a perfectly normal person, and this liability, by Dr. Wright's opsonic method, may now be accurately gauged and even expressed in figures.(9) Now, if we can prove this of definite physical disease, we may reasonably assume it, too, of every other evidence of a subnormal capacity for surviving in the struggle for existence. In point of fact, the sociologists and criminologists have demonstrated it, in their own fields, empirically. We may induce a thief to lead a better life, we may devise corrective shoes for a club-footed man, we may cure a dipsomaniac of his craving for drink, and we may provide policemen, judges and hangmen to protect the weak from the strong, but we cannot help these unfit beings from transmitting their unfitness to their descendants. As Malthus showed more than a century ago, every pauper kept alive at the public expense becomes the ancestor of a hundred other paupers. Inasmuch as the time will come, soon or late, when some of these descendants will have to starve, would it not be wiser to let their solitary progenitor himself starve, and so confine the attendant suffering to one individual instead of spreading it among many?

As Nietzsche points out, this notion that the unfit should be preserved artificially leads to another danger. It makes sympathy a virtue, and thus gives us a sneaking liking — a sort of unconscious gratitude — for those who inspire it in us. That this is true is demonstrated by the alacrity and zest with which the charitably-inclined pounce upon any new object of charity. Modern Christianity, indeed, has translated "Blessed are the poor in spirit" into "Blessed are the poor." But it is obvious, on a moment's reflection, that there is nothing honorable in poverty, considered in itself, and that, on the contrary, it is invariably a symptom of actual dishonor — of neglect, license, ignorance and inefficiency — if not in the individual, at least in his family. "Whenever you see a woman struggling for a livelihood in the world," said a recent philosopher,(10) "you see proof that some man has neglected his duty." In the same way, whenever you see a poor man or a sick man, you see a proof that some one — perhaps the man himself and perhaps his grandfather — has swallowed too much whiskey, basked too much in the sun, breathed bad air, shirked work and got too little nourishing food, or dreamed futile dreams.

It would be easy to pile up examples showing that a reverence for the unfit causes nations as well as individuals to perish. The Southern Confederacy furnishes a case in point. The ideals of the South, before the war, were essentially Christian. Women were protected entirely from the struggle for existence and so lost efficiency in mind and body. The courtesy of the period crucified self. Even the dionysian institution of slavery was transformed — in theory, at least — into a scheme for protecting and maintaining a weaker race. The net result was that the culture of the South came to be based upon an admiration of inefficiency, and the shock of the civil war left the whole country below the Potomac in chaos. It was not that the southerners were craven warriors, but that they were unfitted to meet the vicissitudes of a harsh existence in times of peace. Not until an infusion of northern blood gave them back their old Anglo-Saxon efficiency — which commonly expresses itself in a desire to obtain power by accumulating wealth, i.e., in a "business-like" outlook upon life and a liking for sharp trading — did they rise out of their slough of despond. Those ancient southerners who have clung to their antebellum ideals remain useless, miserable and poverty-stricken today. It is only those who have abandoned the old Southern culture for the ideals of the Yankee that have shown a fitness to survive.

Nietzsche points out that, in considering the part co-operation has played in the advancement of the human race, the historian is apt to make two grievous errors. In the first place, he is easily led into assuming that it is invariably efficacious, which is not true, and in the second place he is prone to assume that it is always based upon an altruistic impulse to self-sacrifice, which is untrue also. As a matter of fact progress is nearly always the work of individuals rather than of associations, and, in the only forms of co-operation which really work for advancement, self-interest, rather than self-sacrifice, is the ruling motive. Men commonly combine because each man in the combination sees in it a possible advantage to himself — i.e. a possible means of widening the gap which separates him from the hewers of wood and drawers of waters — and not because he harbors a yearning to sacrifice himself for his fellow men. When Isabella of Spain pawned her jewels and so enabled Columbus to cross the western ocean, her motive was not a saintly desire to make the poor man happy or an impulse to save the Indians' souls, but a quite lowly yearning to invest her money in a venture which promised a large profit in glory and cash. Such co-operation is entitled to no little respect, because it raises all the parties to it, to some measurable extent, above the herd, and so makes them, to that extent, pioneers of progress. But that form of co-operation by which the strong give of their strength to the weak, without hope of profit, is of dubious value, because it depletes the vanguard of progress to swell the horde of camp-followers. Had Isabella, for example, used her money to support a colony of lepers and so enabled them to live at ease and beget their kind, it is plain that her investment, without tending to her personal benefit in the slightest degree, would have outrageously burdened and handicapped posterity.

Whenever co-operation is thus tainted with the notion of self-sacrifice, the weak are benefited at the expense of the race as a whole. All those forms of universal co-operation which men accept as inherently righteous and beneficial because they seem necessary to the maintenance of the church or state are costly to the strong and vigorous man — the only man who is capable, in any sense, of increasing the knowledge and relative importance of the human race. As one very keen observer puts it, "the weakest have fared best by our legislation." That is to say, any co-operative scheme which forces all the members of a race, a nation or a community to become parties to it, with the idea of elevating all en masse, is grounded upon a fallacy, and this fallacy is the notion that one man may gain without making some other man lose. When two men combine against the herd — as in business, for example — the herd, having less intelligence, usually loses, and so the distance between these men and the common level is increased and their potential value, as heralds of progress, is increased, too. But when the whole body politic enters into a scheme of co-operation — when the strong permit the assumption that the weak are their equals, "before God" or "in the eyes of the law" — then this assumed equality tends to become an actual equality, and the strong lose as the weak gain.

This means progress, true enough, at the bottom, but it also means retrogression at the top and it is evident that the only progress worth while is that which takes place at the top. It would be pleasant, perhaps, if the masses could be made to understand that it is dangerous to introduce the tetanus bacillus into wounds, but it was of infinitely more importance to the race when certain learned pathologists discovered it, and so invented the art of aseptic surgery and made it possible to save the lives of many very important and valuable men, who might have died, otherwise, of wound infections. The death of a hundred ploughmen is regrettable, but not costly because there are always plenty of ploughmen, but the death of one Pasteur was a calamity, because there was only one of him.

Civilization expends its main energy in combating the law of natural selection, by artificially preserving the weak and so increasing the quantity of men at the expense of their quality, but in the long run this great law gets its revenge. We may battle against it, conceal it and deny it, but we cannot suspend its operation. We may preserve the lives of sickly babies and permit them to grow up into men and women, but the death rate among these men and women will be greater than the death rate among those who were born healthy. We may send grain ships to the starving Russians today, but ten years hence their sterile fields, their dry skies and their racial incompetence will combine to weed out their weakest once more — and the number of possible victims will grow larger every year. "We may compare civilized man," says Prof. Lankester, "to a successful rebel against nature, who by every step forward, renders himself liable to greater and greater penalties." The self-sacrifice of today, indeed, is but the forerunner of a race-sacrifice tomorrow.

Let us now look into the allegation that Nietzsche's scheme of things, as a whole, is opposed to ideas and impulses inherent in the nature of man, and that, in consequence, it is unworkable and impossible. Taking the latter part of this allegation first, let us consider the claim that, if our present conception of morality were abandoned and each individual of the Nietzschean first caste were permitted to seek his own welfare in obedience to his own impulses and without considering the desires and "rights" of his fellows — that if we were to cease living in accordance with the will of the majority and to cease trying to glorify this majority by raising its weakest members up and so putting all mankind, as far as possible, upon a common level — that if we were to put these enterprises behind us forever, the race would slip back to the state it exhibited in the days of the cave-men and all progress would be turned to decay.

It is big with soothing and eloquent phrases — this argument for brotherhood, for humility and for a love unlimited and unspeakable — but isn't it true, nevertheless, that despite our poetry and our platitudes, our rhetorical psalming of ideal Christianity and our efforts, now and then, to gain halo and harp by immolation and flagellation — isn't it true, all the while, that we really put self above the Golden Rule in our working scheme of daily life? Isn't it true, in a word, that we are utterly unchristian at bottom, that we are well aware of it, and that this spirit of unchristianity is to be credited with all our advancement and "success" — that it is, indeed, the moving spirit of our progress? Miss Paget attempts to prove, in the essay I have quoted, that self-sacrifice is of benefit to those who practice it by asserting that, in the struggle for existence, many genera of plants and animals save themselves by dwindling, which action relieves them of hopeless competition with stronger species. But isn't it obvious that dwindling, no matter what its temporary efficacy, is essentially degeneration, and that, if it is persisted in, it will inevitably lead to death? Isn't it plain, indeed, that this very argument constitutes a powerful indictment of the slave-morality which Nietzsche denounced? A species which dwindles thereby confesses its unfitness to survive. It accepts death as its goal. It acquiesces in its own decay. Not even the most ardent advocate of humility will admit, I take it, that it is mankind's end and aim thus to degenerate and perish. If we accept death as a goal we must regard life as an infliction. And despite the effort of slave-morality to make us so regard it, our primary life instinct roars a deafening "Nay!" Every thinkable scheme of human living — every deed worth doing and every thought worth thinking — tends, first of all, to perpetuate the race. To love and hate, to hope and dream — we must first live. Unless we hold that it is pleasant to be alive and that death is something to be dreaded and put afar — unless we take this as our fundamental axiom, all existence becomes a mockery and all thought a torture.

We try hard to live up to our code of slave-morality, but, for the life of us, we cannot. We say that humility means bliss eternal, and try thereby to forget that it also means decay on earth, but the hard facts of existence make the truth ever imminent and ever plain. Isn't it obvious to all sane men that when European civilization put its weapons into the hands of the Japanese, instead of destroying or enslaving them with those weapons before they were capable of making effective resistance — isn't it evident that this action resulted in the creation of a new enemy, whose power has been demonstrated already? Isn't it plain that when we set a burglar free and give him "another chance," instead of enslaving him forever or killing him at once, we merely increase our risk of being robbed? Isn't it plain that, in the long run, it is wiser to shoot savages or poison them with whiskey than to educate them — and thus make formidable rivals of them? Isn't it plain that if the unfit survivors of the American civil war had been permitted to perish in the struggle for existence instead of being preserved artificially at the expense of the whole population — isn't it plain that, in such an event, this whole population would have been fated to live under conditions more favorable than those which confront it to-day? In England, it is said, one fiftieth of all the inhabitants are in receipt of daily assistance from the rest. This means that every normal man has to give up one-fiftieth of his earnings, roughly speaking, [depending on the wages earned and the size of the dole payment], to the unfit. Isn't it plain that this scheme of things handicaps the fit and so tends to increase the number of unfit, and that, if the whole body of unfit were permitted to perish tomorrow, the surviving fit would have their fitness increased by one-fiftieth?

Isn't it patent, therefore, that self-sacrifice is costly to all security, health, power and efficiency? We deny it, and try to make ourselves believe that it is not so, and even enter upon disastrous experiments to prove its error, and yet, at the same time, a multitude of familiar facts show that we feel instinctively that it is true. We preach the doctrine of brotherly love in our synagogues, and send out missionaries to convey it to the heathen, and yet all the while, we maintain vast navies and huge armies, whose sole purpose it is to force our will upon other peoples, including these same heathen.

We preach humility and self-effacement — the cardinal virtues of ideal Christianity — and applaud and practise the very reverse. Consider, for example, the matter of marriage. It is the law of our largest and most consistent sect and the theory of all of the others, that marriages are made in heaven and that what God hath joined together no man shall put asunder. But isn't it a fact that our native common-sense teaches us that this is nonsense? There was no need for "A Doll's House" and "Ghosts" to show us that the actual and unmistakable needs of the individual are more reliable guides than the theoretical or purely imaginary needs of others. Therefore, while we still talk of indissoluble marriages in our churches, we know very well that, in real, every-day life, we must take account of the individual's powerful instinct to live under the most favorable conditions possible, and that unions which make life intolerable must and should be dissolved.

Again, we hold to the theoretical proposition that vengeance is the Lord's and that the casting of the first stone should be left to him who is without sin — and yet, all the while, we build penitentiaries for the confinement of those who combat our instinctive desire to live long and happily, and kill those whose opposition is violently strong. Again, we hold in theoretical abhorrence the man who commits the sin of Dives, and yet, when his offense grows so aggravated that it brings him an unusually rich profit, we envy him, honor him and show by our every action that we see in him dionysian qualities which we would like to possess ourselves. I am not going to multiply examples. In a previous chapter I have cited many more — racial as well as individual. Taken together, they prove, I think, that, despite the naked ugliness of the proposition, Nietzsche was not far wrong when he maintained that we subscribe to the doctrine of humility and self-sacrifice by the mouth only, and that our primary life instinct warns us against putting it into actual and unqualified practice. We write the law upon our scrolls, but we are dionysians at heart, and we are becoming more and more aware of it and more and more disposed to admit it.

Now for the final argument: that the impulse to self-sacrifice, for all its costliness, is native to the soul of man, and that, no matter how much we strive to destroy it, we must ever harbor it in our bosoms. Herein we perceive a thesis that has provided ammunition for theologians and metaphysicians since the dawn of civilization, and is accepted today, as an irrefutable axiom, by all who pound pulpits and wave their arms and call upon their fellow men to repent. It has clogged all philosophy for ten thousand years; it has been a premise in a million moral syllogisms; it has survived the assaults of all the iconoclasts that ever lived. It is taught in our schools and lies at the bottom of all our laws, prophecies and revelations. And what is this king of all axioms and emperor of all fallacies? Simply the idea that there are rules of "natural morality" engraven upon the heart of man — that all men, at all times and everywhere, have agreed, do now agree, and will agree forever, unanimously and without reservation, that certain things are right and certain other things are wrong.

In every treatise upon ethics and "moral philosophy" these rules of "natural morality" are given in the first chapter. One of them is the rule that murder is a crime. Another is the rule that the liar is an abomination. Another is the rule that the thief is an outcast. To them the moralists of Christendom have added another. It is the rule that every normal man loves his brother — that the soul of the Samaritan is in all of us. Ages ago some primeval soothsayer made the rough draft of this catalogue, and ever since then each successive moralist has adopted it and expanded it. It is now the Cabala and Magna Charta of all who discourse upon evil and describe the face and qualities of sin. And yet, despite this vast sound and glitter of authority, the fallacy of assuming that these are "natural" laws is demonstrated by all history and human experience. Nothing is right to all men and nothing is wrong. There has never existed an idea that someone did not combat. There has never been a virtue that someone did not denounce as a sin. There has never been a sin that someone did not exalt as a virtue. There is today, and ever has been, but one universal impulse in all healthy human beings — and that one, as everyone knows, is the impulse to remain alive — the life instinct — the will to power.

Nietzsche spent his best years proving this, and we have seen how he set about the task — how he showed that the "good" of one race and of one age was the "bad" of some other race and some other age. All history bears him out. Mankind is ever revising and abandoning its "inherent" ideas. We say that the human mind "instinctively revolts" against cruel and excessive punishments, and yet a moment's reflection recalls the fact that the world is, and always has been, peopled with millions to whom cruelty seems and seemed natural and agreeable. We say that man has an "inherent" impulse to be fair and just, and yet it is a commonplace of observation that multitudes of men, in the midst of our most civilized societies, are the very reverse. Therefore we may set aside the argument that a "natural" instinct for humility and self-sacrifice stands as an impassable barrier in the path of Nietzsche's dionysian philosophy. There is no such barrier. There is no such instinct. It is an idea merely — an idea powerful and persistent, but still mutable and mortal. Some day, perhaps, we shall abandon it.

It is not pleasant thus to use the knife upon our souls. It is not pleasant to smash the axioms of ages and cast them out forever. What pain is greater than that of dis-illusion? But it is only by facing pain unafraid that men move on to higher things.

"Every step toward the truth has had to be fought for at the expense of all that human hearts and human love hold dear."

Herein we find the cornerstone of Nietzsche's philosophy, and herein, perhaps, we discern the germ of that future philosophy which will rise beyond it. Today we cling to our illusions and guard them from sacrilegious hands, because we know that their death brings us exquisite anguish. But some day — who knows? — there may arise a race of men to whom disillusion will mean, not sorrow, but joy — a race in whom the yearning for the truth will transcend the yearning for a rock and a refuge. And when that time comes — will there remain any color of extravagance in the dream of a superman?

Perhaps, after all, the time has come already. Perhaps, if we studied history aright, we would not find that the world has always had its sect of disillusionists. In the ages of faith these men faced, not only the stake, but also doubts and damnation. A human being is the child alike of his forebears and of his environment. If the men about him and the men who have gone before him, believe and believed in hell, purgatory, grace, salvation and divine intercession, he must believe in these things, too, to some slight extent — in the face of all his intelligence and his reason. And so he will suffer. But, in the end, these doubts will turn upon themselves and give him renewed confidence. The more he is opposed and tortured, the more he will stand by his guns. And in this fact lies the value of all organized opposition to free and clean thinking. Looking back over the history of Christianity we are prone to see only the blood and the flames — the great and good men of the race tortured and butchered; Galileo on his knees; Bruno in his flames; pyres of books; the ruin of nations — one long, sickening orgy of murder, robbery, persecution, brutality, dishonesty, tyranny, corruption and ignorance. But we forget that the higher man yearns for a life that is hard — that, had he been made a bishop, Galileo's retraction might have been sincere — that, had the church been clean and Christianity beneficent, men might still believe, with St. Augustine, that "it is impossible that there should be inhabitants on the opposite side of the earth... for, on the day of judgment, these men could not see the Lord descending through the air." All of this Nietzsche seems to have overlooked. Forgetting his own words, he took no account, toward the end, of the fact that stimulation comes only by opposition — that, without enemies, there can be no heroes — that without abuses, there can be no reforms. He forgot, in a word, that morality has served the race by giving the strong man something to wield his sword upon — to fight, to wound, to hate. He forgot that every effect must have a cause. He forgot his own maxims and so thundered against himself. And this, then, is the one ineradicable fault in his philosophy: he showed the strong man's need for an enemy and yet argued that all enemies should be enchained. There is no way to rid the Nietzschean system of this paradox.

www.ingramcontent.com/pod-product-compliance
Lightning Source LLC
Chambersburg PA
CBHW030528100426
42813CB00001B/181